Study Guide

to Accompany

West's Legal Environment
of Business
Text & Cases—Ethical, Regulatory,
and International Issues
Second Edition

Study Guide

to Accompany

West's Legal Environment of Business
Text & Cases—Ethical, Regulatory, and International Issues
Second Edition

FRANK B. CROSS
MSIS Department
and
Associate Director, Center for Legal
  and Regulatory Studies
University of Texas at Austin

ROGER LeROY MILLER
School of Law
University of Miami

Prepared by

Roger LeRoy Miller
School of Law
University of Miami

William Eric Hollowell
Member of
Minnesota State Bar
Florida State Bar

West Publishing Company
Minneapolis/St. Paul•New York•Los Angeles•San Francisco

WEST'S COMMITMENT TO THE ENVIRONMENT

In 1906, West Publishing Company began recycling materials left over from the production of books. This began a tradition of efficient and responsible use of resources. Today, up to 95% of our legal books and 70% of our college texts and school texts are printed on recycled, acid-free stock. West also recycles nearly 22 million pounds of scrap paper annually—the equivalent of 181,717 trees. Since the 1960s, West has devised ways to capture and recycle waste inks, solvents, oils, and vapors created in the printing process. We also recycle plastics of all kinds, wood, glass, corrugated cardboard, and batteries, and have eliminated the use of Styrofoam book packaging. We at West are proud of the longevity and the scope of our commitment to the environment.

Production, Prepress, Printing and Binding by West Publishing Company.

Table of Contents

List of Supplements vi
Preface vii

UNIT ONE: The Foundations

1 Business and Its Global Legal Environment 1
2 Business Ethics 9
3 The Court System 16
4 Alternative Dispute Resolution 24

UNIT TWO: The Public and International Environment

5 Constitutional Law 31
6 Administrative Law 39
7 Comparative Law 47
8 International Law 56

UNIT THREE: The Private Environment

9 Contracts: Part I 63
10 Contracts: Part II 72
11 Sales 79
12 Torts and Strict Liability 88
13 Torts and Crimes Related to Business 99
14 Product Liability 106
15 Intellectual Property and Computer Law 114
16 Creditor-Debtor Relations and Bankruptcy 125
17 Business Organizations 134
18 Rights and Duties within the Corporation 142

UNIT FOUR: The Employment Environment

19 Agency 148
20 Employment Relationships 156
21 Employment Discrimination 163
22 Labor Law 171

UNIT FIVE: The Regulatory Environment

23 Consumer Protection 179
24 Environmental Law 187
25 Land-Use Control and Real Property 195
26 Antitrust and Monopoly 203
27 Antitrust and Restraints of Trade 210
28 Securities Regulation 217

Appendix A: Answers A-1

West's Legal Environment of Business,
Second Edition

Additional Student Supplements

Printed Materials

West's Advanced Topics and Contemporary Issues:
  Expanded Coverage, Second Edition
An Introduction to Critical Thinking and Writing in the Legal
Environment
Handbook of Selected Statutes
Student User's Guide to LEGAL CLERK
Student User's Manual to LEGAL REVIEW
Citation-At-A-Glance

Software

Microguide—Study Guide
LEGAL CLERK Research Software System
LEGAL REVIEW Tutorial
Interactive Software—Contracts
Interactive Software—Sales
You Be the Judge

Videos and videodiscs

West's Legal Environment Laserdisc
Drama of the Law Video Series
Drama of the Law II Video Series
PBS Ethics in America Series
The Making of a Case

A Supreme Court Case
Anatomy of a Trial—Contracts
A Product's Liability Trial
Law and Literature

Preface

To the Student

This *Study Guide* is designed to help you read and understand *West's Legal Environment of Business*, **Second Edition.**

How *Study Guide to Accompany West's Legal Environment of Business*, Second Edition Can Help You

This study guide can help you maximize your learning, subject to the constraints and the amount of time you can allot to this course. There are at least six specific ways in which you can benefit from using this guide.

1. *Study Guide to Accompany West's Legal Environment of Business*, **Second Edition** can help you decide which topics are the most important. Because there are so many topics analyzed in each chapter (and in *all* textbooks) many students become confused about what is essential and what is not. You cannot, of course, learn everything; this study guide can help you concentrate on the crucial topics in each chapter.

2. If you are forced to miss a class, you can use this study guide to help you learn the material discussed in your absence.

3. There is a possibility that the questions that you are required to answer in this study guide are representative of the types of questions that you will be asked during examinations.

4. You can use this study guide to help you review for examinations.

5. This study guide can help you decide whether you really understand the material. Don't wait until examination time to find out!

6. Finally, the questions in this study guide will help you develop critical thinking skills that you can use in other classes and throughout your career.

The Contents of *Study Guide to Accompany West's Legal Environment of Business*, Second Edition

Business law sometimes is considered a difficult subject because it uses a specialized vocabulary and also takes most people much time and effort to learn. Those who work with and teach business law believe that the subject matter is exciting and definitely worthy of your efforts. Your text, **West's Legal Environment of Business, Second Edition**, and this student learning guide have been written for the precise purpose of helping you learn the most important aspects of business law. We always try to keep you, the student, in mind.

Every chapter includes the following sections:

1. Key Points: From five to ten "check points" are presented to you. By the time you finish studying each chapter you should be able to "pass" each checkpoint.

2. Introduction: You are introduced to the main subject matter of each chapter in this section titled: What this Chapter Is About.

3. Chapter Outline: Using an outline and paragraph format, the salient points in each chapter are presented.

4. Study Tips: In clearly identified boxes, numerous study tips are presented throughout this learning guide.

5. True-False Questions: True-false questions are included for each chapter. Generally, these questions test knowledge of terminology and principles. The answers are given at the back of the book. Whenever an answer is false, the reasons why it is false are presented at the back of the book also.

6. Fill-in Questions: Here you are asked to choose between two alternatives for each space that needs to be filled in. Answers are included at the back of the book.

7. Multiple-Choice Questions: Multiple-choice questions are given for each chapter. The answers, along with an explanation, are included at the back of this book.

8. Short Essay Questions: Two essay questions are presented for each chapter.

9. Issue Spotters: These questions alert you to the certain principles within the chapter. Brief answers to these questions are included at the end of this text.

How to Use This Study Guide

What follows is a recommended strategy for improving your grade in your business law class. It may seem like a lot of work, but the payoffs will be high. Try the entire program for the first three or four chapters. If you then feel you can skip some steps safely, try doing so and see what happens.

For each chapter we recommend you follow the sequence of steps below:

1. Read the Key Points, introduction, Chapter Outline, and Issue Spotters.

2. Read about half the textbook chapter (unless it is very long), being sure to underline only the most important topics (which you should be able to recognize after having read no more than two chapter outlines in this study guide). Put a check mark by the material that you do not understand.

3. If you find the textbook's chapter easy to understand, you might want to finish reading it. Otherwise, rest for a sufficient period before you read the second half of the chapter. Again, be sure to underline only the most important points and to put a check mark by the material you find difficult to understand.

4. After you have completed the entire textbook chapter, take a break. Then read only what you have underlined throughout the entire chapter.

5. Now concentrate on the difficult material, for which you have left check marks. Reread this material and *think about it*; you will find that it is very exciting to figure out difficult material on your own.

6. Now reread the Issue Spotters. Answer them in the book and compare your answers with those at the back of this book. Next, do the True-False Questions, Fill-In Questions, and Multiple-Choice Questions. Compare your answers with those at the back of this book. Make a note of the questions you have missed and find the pages in your textbook upon which these questions are based. If you still don't understand, ask your instructor.

Now reread the Key Points and see if you have mastered all of the points.

7. If you still have time, do one or both of the essay questions.

8. Before your examination, study your class notes. Then review the chapter outline in the text and write out your answers to the Issue Spotters in the study guide again. Reread the Key Points and Chapter Outline in this study guide, then redo all of the questions within each chapter. Compare your answers with the answers at the back of this study guide. Identify your problem areas and reread the relevant pages in *West's Legal Environment of Business*, **Second Edition**. Think through the answers on your own.

If you have followed the strategy outlined above, you should feel sufficiently confident and be relaxed enough to do well on your exam.

Study Skills for *West's Legal Environment of Business*, Second Edition

Every student has a different way to study. We give several study hints below that we think will help any student to master better the textbook *West's Legal Environment of Business*, **Second Edition**. These skills involve outlining, marking, taking notes, and summarizing. You may not need to use all these skills. Nonetheless, if you do improve your ability to use them, you will be able to understand more easily the information in *West's Legal Environment of Business*, **Second Edition**.

MAKING AN OUTLINE

An outline is simply a method for organizing information. The reason an outline can be helpful is that it shows how concepts relate to each other. Outlining can be done as part of your reading or at the end of your reading, or as a rereading of each section within a chapter before you go on to the next section. Even if you do not believe that you need to outline, our experience has been that the act of *physically* writing an outline for a chapter helps most students to improve greatly their ability to retain the material in *West's Legal Environment of Business*, **Second Edition** and master it, thereby obtaining a higher grade in the class, with less effort.

To make an effective outline you have to be selective. Outlines that contain all the information in the text are not very useful. Your objective in outlining is to identify main concepts and to subordinate details to those main concepts. Therefore, your first goal is to *identify the main concepts in each section*. Often the large first-level headings within your textbook are sufficient as identifiers of the major concepts within each section. You may decide, however, that you want to phrase an identifier in a way that is more meaningful to you. In any event, your outline should consist of several levels written in a standard outline format. The most important concepts are assigned a roman numeral; the second most important a capital letter; the third most important, numbers; and the fourth most important, lower-case letters. Even if you make an outline that is no more than the headings in the text, you will be studying more efficiently than you would be otherwise. As we stated above, the process of physically writing the words will help you master the material.

MARKING A TEXT

From kindergarten through high school you typically did not own your own textbooks. They were made available by the school system. You were told not to mark in them. Now that you own your own text for a course, your learning can be greatly improved by marking your text. There is a trade-off here. The more you mark up your textbook, the less you will receive from your bookstore when you sell it back at the end of the semester. The benefit is a better understanding of the subject matter, and the cost is the reduction in the price you receive for the resale of the text. Additionally, if you want a text that you can mark with your own notations, you necessarily have to buy a new one or a used one that has no markings. Both carry a higher price tag than a used textbook with markings. Again there is a trade-off.

Different Ways of Marking   The most commonly used form of marking is to underline important points. The second most commonly used method is to use a felt-tipped highlighter, or marker, in yellow or some other transparent color. Marking also includes circling, numbering, using arrows, brief notes, or any other method that allows you to remember things when you go back to skim the pages in your textbook prior to an exam.

Why Marking is Important   Marking is important for the same reason that outlining is—it helps you to organize better the information in the text. It allows you to become an *active* participant in the mastery of the material. Researchers have shown that the physical act of marking, just like the physical act of outlining, helps you better retain the material. The better the material is organized in your mind, the more you will remember. There are two types of readers—passive and active. The active reader outlines and/or marks. Active readers typically do better on exams. Perhaps one of the reasons that active readers retain more is because the physical act of outlining and/or marking requires greater concentration. It is through greater concentration that more is remembered.

Points to Remember When Marking

1. Read one section at a time before you do any extensive marking. You can't mark a section until you know what is important and you can't know what is important until you read the whole section.

2. Don't over mark. Just as an outline cannot contain everything that is in a text (or in a lecture), marking can't be of the whole book. Don't fool yourself into thinking you've done a good job just because each page is filled up with arrows, asterisks, circles, and underlines. When you go back to review the material you won't remember what was important. The key is *selective* activity. Mark each page in a way that allows you to see the most important points at a glance. You can follow up your marking by writing out more in your subject outline.

SUMMARIZING THE MATERIAL

Even if each chapter has a chapter summary, it is still worthwhile for you to make your own summary points. The reason is that the more active you are as a reader, the better you will understand the material.

Summarization helps you in your reading comprehension. It is the final step in reviewing the book. There is probably nothing else you can do that works as well to help you remember what your textbook has to say.

The importance of summarization is that the notes you make are in your own words, not in the words of the author. Writing down a summary in your own words is the most effective use of your time. This allows you to process the information into your own memory by being required to think about it. You also have to make it part of your vocabulary. Whenever you cannot state important legal concepts in your own words, you probably haven't understood the concepts necessary to master the material. Indeed, summary notes are a good way to determine whether you have actually understood something. Don't simply make a mechanical listing of quotes taken right out of the textbook. Rather, you should make summary notes using complete sentences with correct grammar. This forces you to develop your ideas logically and clearly. Also, summary notes written in this matter can be more easily remembered.

Be Brief. Your notes should condense the information in the text into statements that summarize the concepts. It is when you force yourself to make the statements brief that you best learn the material. By making only brief summary notes, you have to think about the essence of each concept and present it in a form that is compact enough to remember. You should typically have no more than a one-paragraph summary for each important topic in the chapter.

What Format to Use? The authors find that using 5" x 8" cards is the best way to take summary notes. Don't fill up each note card. You need to leave room to make additional notes later on when you are reviewing for the final exam. That is to say, leave margins for further notes and study markings. Additionally, if you leave enough room, you can integrate the notes that you take during lectures on to these summary note cards.

Another reason to place your summary notes on 5" x 8" cards is because in so doing you have a set of flash cards that you can use in studying for a final exam.

HOW TO STUDY AND TAKE EXAMS

There is basically one reason why you have purchased *Study Guide to Accompany West's Legal Environment of Business,* **Second Edition**—to improve your exam grade. By using this study guide assiduously, you will have the confidence to take your mid-terms and final examinations and to do well. The study guide, however, should not just be used a day before each exam. Rather, the guide is most helpful if you use it at the time that you read the chapter. That is to say, after you read a chapter in *West's Legal Environment of Business,* **Second Edition** you should directly go to the appropriate chapter in the study guide. This systematic review technique is the most effective study technique you can use.

Besides learning the concepts in each chapter as well as possible, there are additional strategies for taking exams. You need to know in advance what type of exam you are going to take—essay or objective or both. You need to know which reading materials and lectures will be covered. For both objective and essay exams (but more importantly for the former) you need to know if there is a penalty for guessing incorrectly. If there is, your strategy will be different: you will usually only mark what you are certain of. Finally, you need to know how much time will be allowed for the exam.

FOLLOWING DIRECTIONS

Students are often in a hurry to start an exam so they take little time to read the instructions. The instructions can be critical, however. In a multiple-choice exam, for example, if there is no indication that there is a penalty for guessing, then you should never leave a question unanswered. Even if there only remains a few minutes at the end of the exam, you should guess for those questions about which you are uncertain.

Additionally, you need to know the weight given to each section of an exam. In a typical multiple-choice exam, all questions have equal weight. In some exams, particularly those involving essay questions, different parts of the exam carry different weights. You should use these weights to apportion your time accordingly. If an essay part of an exam accounts for only 20 percent of the total points on the exam, you should not spend 60 percent of your time on the essay.

You need to make sure you are answering the question correctly. Some exams require a No. 2 lead pencil to fill in the dots on a machine-graded answer sheet. Other exams require underlining or circling. In short, you have to look at the instructions carefully.

Lastly, check to make sure that you have all the pages of the examination. If you are uncertain, ask the instructor or the exam proctor. It is hard to justify not having done your exam correctly because you failed to answer all the questions. Simply stating that you did not have them will pose a problem for both you and your instructor. Don't take a chance. Double check to make sure.

TAKING OBJECTIVE EXAMINATIONS

The most important point to discover initially with any objective test is if there is a penalty for guessing. If there is none, you have nothing to lose by guessing. In contrast, if a half-point is subtracted for each incorrect answer, then you probably should not answer any question for which you are purely guessing.

Students usually commit one of two errors when they read objective-exam questions: (1) they read into the questions things that don't exist, or (2) they skip over words or phrases.

Most test questions include key words such as:

- all
- always
- never
- only

If you miss these key words you will be missing the "trick" part of the question. Also, you must look for questions that are only *partly* correct, particularly if you are answering true/false questions.

Never answer a question without reading all of the alternatives. More than one of them may be correct. If more than one of them seems correct, make sure you select the answer that seems the most correct.

Whenever the answer to an objective question is not obvious, start with the process of elimination. Throw out the answers that are clearly incorrect. Even with objective exams in which there is a penalty for guessing, if you can throw out several obviously incorrect answers, then you may wish to guess among the remaining ones because your probability of choosing the correct answer is high.

Typically, the easiest way to eliminate incorrect answers is to look for those that are meaningless, illogical, or inconsistent. Often test authors put in choices that make perfect sense and are indeed true, but they are not the answer to the question under study.

WRITING ESSAY EXAMS

To write an essay exam, you should be prepared. One way of being prepared is to practice writing timed essays. In other words, find out in advance how much time you will have for each essay question, say 15 minutes, and then practice writing an answer to a sample essay question during a 15-minute time period. This is the only way you will develop the skills needed to pace yourself for an essay exam. Do your timed essay practice without using the book, since most essay exams are closed book.

Usually you can anticipate certain essay exam questions. You do this by going over the major concept headings, either in your lecture notes or in your text; search for the themes that tie the materials together and then think about questions that your instructor might ask you. You might even list possible essay questions as a review device; then write a short outline for each of those most likely questions.

As with objective exams, you need to read the directions to the essay questions carefully. It's best to write out a brief outline *before* you start writing. The outline should present your conclusion in one or two sentences, then your supporting argument. It is important to stay on the subject. We can tell you from first hand experience that no instructor likes to read answers to unasked questions.

Finally, make a strong attempt to write legibly. Again speaking from experience, we can tell you that it's easier to be favorably inclined to a student's essay if we don't have to reread it five times to decipher the handwriting.

Acknowledgments

We wish to thank Suzanne Jasin of K & M Enterprises for her expert design and composition of this guide.

We welcome comments and criticisms to help us make this guide even more useful. All errors are our sole responsibility.

Roger LeRoy Miller
Eric Hollowell

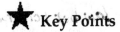 **Key Points**

The **key points** in this chapter include:

1. The answer to the question, "What is law?"

2. The common law sources and traditions of American law, including the doctrine of *stare decisis*.

3. Other sources of American law.

4. The difference between remedies at law and remedies in equity.

5. The explanation of how to read and analyze case citations and court opinions.

Chapter 1: Business and Its Global Legal Environment

WHAT THIS CHAPTER IS ABOUT

The first chapters in Unit 1 provide the background for the entire course. Chapter 1 sets the stage.

To be successful in this course, you must understand that (1) the law is a set of general rules, (2) in applying these general rules, a judge cannot fit a case to suit a rule, but must fit (or find) a rule to suit the case, and (3) in fitting (or finding) a rule, a judge must also supply reasons for the decision.

CHAPTER OUTLINE

I. WHAT IS LAW?

A. WHAT LAW CONSISTS OF AND WHAT LAW DOES
Law consists of enforceable rules governing relationships among individuals and between individuals and society. Its primary function is to simultaneously maintain stability and permit change. The law does this by providing for dispute resolution, the preservation of political, economic, and social institutions, and the protection of property.

B. SCHOOLS OF JURISPRUDENTIAL THOUGHT

1. Natural Law School
Adherents of this school believe that government and the legal system should reflect universal moral and ethical principles that are inherent in the nature of human life. The basis is the belief that all persons have natural rights.

2. **Positivist School** *there is no higher law but l created by society*
   Followers of this school believe that there can be no higher law than a nation's positive law (the law created by a particular society at a particular point in time). Rights are not "natural;" they are only acquired through the law.

3. **Legal Realists**
   This school believes that judges are influenced by the beliefs and attitudes unique to their individual personalities, that the application of precedent should be tempered by each case's specific circumstances, and that extra-legal sources should be considered in making decisions.

II. SOURCES OF AMERICAN LAW

A. CASES

1. **Common Law and *Stare Decisis***
   The American legal system, based on the decisions judges make in cases, is a common law system, which involves the application of principles applied in earlier cases with similar facts. This use of **precedent** is the doctrine of *stare decisis*. *Stare decisis* makes the legal system more efficient, just, uniform, stable, and predictable.

2. **Legal Reasoning**
   A judge may decide that a precedent is incorrect if there have been changes in technology, business practices, or society's attitudes. In applying an old precedent or establishing a new one, judges use many forms of reasoning—**deductive reasoning**, reasoning by **analogy**, and others— to harmonize theirs decisions with earlier cases.

3. **Legal and Extra-Legal Sources**
   When determining which rules and policies to apply, and applying them, a judge may examine: prior case law; the principles, policies, and historical settings behind the decisions; statutes and the policies behind them; society's values and customs; and data and principles from other disciplines (economics, sociology).

B. CONSTITUTIONS

The U.S. Constitution distributes power among the branches of government. It is the supreme law of the land. Any law that conflicts with it is invalid. The states also have constitutions, but the federal constitution prevails if their provisions conflict.

C. STATUTES

Statutes and ordinances are enacted by Congress, and state and local legislative bodies. Uniform laws (such as the Uniform Commercial Code) and model codes are created by panels of experts and scholars and adopted at the option of each state's legislature.

D. ADMINISTRATIVE RULES AND REGULATIONS

Administrative law consists of the rules and regulations issued by administrative agencies, which derive their authority from the legislative and executive branches of government.

III. IMPORTANT DISTINCTIONS IN THE LAW

A. CLASSIFICATIONS OF LAW

1. Substantive and Procedural Law
Substantive law includes laws that define, describe, regulate, and create rights and duties. *Procedural law* includes the rules for enforcing substantive rights.

2. Public and Private Law
Public law concerns the relationship between government and individuals. *Private law* involves relationships between individuals.

3. Criminal and Civil Law
Criminal law regulates relationships between individuals and society. *Civil law* regulates relationships between individuals.

B. REMEDIES AT LAW AND REMEDIES IN EQUITY

1. Remedies at Law
Remedies at law include awards of land, money, and items of value. A jury trial is available only in an action at law.

2. Remedies in Equity
Remedies in equity include decrees of specific performance, injunctions, and rescission. Decisions to award equitable remedies are guided by equitable maxims (for example, "equity aids the vigilant, not those who rest on their rights").

IV. HOW TO FIND THE LAW

A. CASE LAW

1. Publication of Court Opinions
State appellate court opinions are often published by the state in consecutively numbered volumes. They may also be published in units of the *National Reporter System,* by West Publishing Company. Federal court opinions appear in other West publications.

2. Finding a Court Opinion in a Publication
After a decision is published, it is usually referred to by the name of the case and the volume, name, and page number of one or more reporters (which are often, but not always, West reporters). This information is called the **citation.**

B. STATUTES

1. Publication of Statutes
Federal statutes are arranged by date of enactment in *United States Statutes at Large.* State statutes are collected in similar state publications. Statutes are also published in codified form (the form in which they appear in the federal and state codes) in other publications.

2. Finding a Statute in a Publication
Statutes are usually referred to in their codified form. In the codes, laws are compiled by subject. For example, the *United States Code* (U.S.C.) arranges by subject most federal laws. Each subject is assigned a title number and each statute a section number within a title.

C. ADMINISTRATIVE RULES AND REGULATIONS

1. Publication of Rules and Regulations
Rules and regulations adopted by federal administrative agencies are published initially in the *Federal Register*. They are also compiled by subject in the *Code of Federal Regulations* (C.F.R.).

2. Finding a Rule or Regulation in a Publication
In the C.F.R., rules and regulations are arranged by subject. Each subject is assigned a title number and each rule or regulation a section number within a title.

V.   HOW TO ANALYZE CASE LAW

A. THE PARTIES

1. Plaintiff v. Defendant
In the title of a case (*Adams v. Jones*), the *v.* means versus (against). Adams is the plaintiff (the person who filed the suit) and Jones the defendant. Some appellate courts place the name of the party appealing a decision first, so that this case on appeal may be called *Jones v. Adams*.

2. Appellant v. Appellee
The appellant is the party who appeals a case to another court or jurisdiction from the one in which the case was originally brought. An appellant may be referred to as a **petitioner**. The appellee is the party against whom an appeal is taken. An appellee may be referred to as a **respondent**.

B. THE COURT'S OPINION
The opinion contains the court's reasons for its decision, the rules of law that apply, and the judgment.

1. Unanimous Opinion
When more than one judge (or justice) decides a case, and they all agree, a unanimous opinion is written for the whole court.

2. Majority Opinion
If a decision is not unanimous, a majority opinion outlines the views of the majority.

3. Concurring Opinion
A concurring opinion is one in which a judge emphasizes a point that was not emphasized in the unanimous or majority opinion.

4. Dissenting Opinion
A dissenting opinion may be written by a judge who does not agree with the majority. A dissent may form the basis of arguments used years later in overruling the majority opinion.

STUDY TIP 👉 <u>The Facts in a Case</u>

The facts in a case should be accepted as they are given. For example, under some circumstances, an oral contract may be enforceable. If there is a statement in a case about the existence of an oral contract, it should be accepted that there was an oral contract. Arguing with the statement ("How could you prove that there was an oral contract?") will only undercut your learning. Once you have learned the principle for which the case is presented, then you can ask, "What if the facts were different?"

TRUE-FALSE QUESTIONS (Answers at the Back of the Book)

____ 1. Law consists of enforceable rules governing relationships between individuals and society and among individuals.

____ 2. Jurisprudence is the study of law. The positivist school of jurisprudence adheres to the belief that law should reflect universal moral and ethical principles that are part of human nature.

____ 3. The practice of deciding new cases with reference to previous decisions forms the doctrine of *stare decisis*.

____ 4. Common law is a term that normally refers to the body of law that consists of rules of law announced in court decisions.

____ 5. In a civil law system, a statutory code is the primary source of law, and judges are not bound by case precedent.

____ 6. Each state's constitution, whether or not it conflicts with the U.S. Constitution, is supreme within each state's borders.

____ 7. The Uniform Commercial Code, which was designed to facilitate commercial transactions, was enacted by Congress for adoption by the states.

____ 8. In a civil case, one party tries to make another party comply with a duty or pay for damage caused by the failure to comply.

____ 9. In most states, the same courts can exercise both legal and equitable powers.

____ 10. Opinions of the United States Supreme Court are published officially by the federal government in the *United States Reports*.

____ 11. A reference to "26 U.S.C. Section 2627" means that the statute may be found in Section 2627 in Volume 26 of the *United States Code*.

____ 12. When more than one judge or justice decides a case, and the decision is not unanimous, a majority opinion is written, outlining the views of the majority of the judges or justices, and the others do not express their views.

FILL-IN QUESTIONS (Answers at the Back of the Book)

The common law system, on which the American legal system is based, involves the application of principles applied in earlier cases _____ _____(with similar facts/ whether or not the facts are similar). This use of previous case law, or _____ (precedent/ pre-eminent), known as the doctrine of *stare decisis*, _____ _____ (emphasizes a flexible/ permits a predictable) resolution of cases.

MULTIPLE-CHOICE QUESTIONS (Answers at the Back of the Book)

____   1. Which of the following is FALSE?

  a. The natural law school of jurisprudence adheres to the belief that law should reflect universal moral and ethical principles that are part of human nature.
  b. The positivist law school of jurisprudence adheres to the belief that there can be no higher law that a nation's positive law (the law created by a particular society at a particular point in time).
  c. The legal realist school of jurisprudence adheres to the belief that the law should not reflect human realities (specific circumstances surrounding each case).
  d. All legal philosophers agree that logic, ideals, history, and custom influence the development of the law.

____   2. The doctrine of *stare decisis* performs many useful functions. These do NOT include

  a. efficiency.
  b. uniformity.
  c. stability.
  d. retroactivity.

____   3. Legal reasoning means that a judge must harmonize his or her decision with decisions that have been made before. When determining which rules and policies to apply in a given case, and in applying them, a judge may consider

  a. previous case law, and the legal principles and policies behind the decisions, as well as their historical setting.
  b. statutes and the policies underlying the legislature's decision to enact a particular statute.
  c. social values and custom.
  d. all of the above.

____   4. In addition to case law, when making decisions, courts may have to consider other sources of law, which do NOT include

  a. the U.S. Constitution.
  b. state constitutions.
  c. uniform codes proposed but not yet adopted.
  d. administrative agency rules and regulations.

____   5. Laws can be classified in various ways—public and private, substantive and procedural, civil and criminal. Which of the following is FALSE?

    a. Public law addresses the relationship between persons and their government. Private law concerns relationships among individuals.

    b. Substantive law includes all laws that define, describe, regulate, and create legal rights and obligations. Procedural law establishes the methods of enforcing the rights established by substantive law.

    c. Civil law concerns the duties that exist between persons or between citizens and their governments, excluding tort duties. Criminal law is concerned with wrongs, including torts, committed against the public as a whole.

    d. None of the above

____   6. Which of the following is the CORRECT statement regarding the distinction between law and equity?

    a. Equity involves different remedies from those available at law.

    b. A jury in an action at law serves only in an advisory capacity.

    c. Most states maintain separate courts of law and equity.

    d. Damages may be awarded only in actions in equity.

____   7. State appellate court opinions may appear in

    a. consecutively numbered volumes titled *Reports*.

    b. regional units of West Publishing Company's *National Reporter System*.

    c. both a and b.

    d. neither a nor b.

____   8. A reference to "132 N.E.2d 580" is a reference to

    a. page 580 in volume 132 of the *North Eastern Reporter, Second Series*.

    b. page 580 of volume 132 of the *New England Reporter, Second Series*.

    c. section 580 of Title 132 of the *North Eastern Reporter, Second Series*.

    d. section 580 of Title 132 of the *New England Reporter, Second Series*.

____   9. In the title of a case (*Abel v. Cain*, for example)

    a. the names are always in alphabetical order.

    b. the name on the left is always the name of the party who brought the suit.

    c. the names are in no particular order.

    d. none of the above.

____   10. When a case is decided by more than one judge or justice, a dissenting opinion may be written by

    a. a judge or justice who does not agree with the majority's decision.

    b. a judge or justice who agrees with the majority's decision but for different reasons.

    c. the party who loses the case.

    d. the party who wins the case.

____   11. The most common form of legal reasoning consists of

    a. reasoning in the form of syllogism.

    b. deductive reasoning.

    c. a major premise, a minor premise, and a conclusion.

    d. all of the above.

____ 12. To reason by analogy, a judge compares the facts in one case to

a. the facts in another case.
b. the plaintiff's hypothetical.
c. the defendant's arguments.
d. none of the above.

SHORT ESSAY QUESTIONS

1. Discuss the primary function of law.

2. Define *stare decisis* and discuss its importance.

ISSUE SPOTTERS (Answers at the Back of the Book)

1. Adam and Eve are involved in a lawsuit. Adam argues that for fifty years, in cases that involved circumstances similar to those in this case, judges have ruled in a way that requires the judge in this case to rule in Adam's favor. Eve argues that times have changed, and it is time to change the law. Can the judge rule in Eve's favor?

2. The U.S. Constitution provides protection for the free exercise of religion. A state legislature enacts a law that outlaws all religions that do not derive from the Judeo-Christian tradition. Is this state law valid?

3. Where would you find the case that is referred to as "*Hoffman v. Red Owl Stores, Inc.*, 26 Wis.2d 683, 133 N.W.2d 267 (1965)"?

4. In the title of a case (*Jones v. Smith*, for example), is the name on the left (Jones) always the name of the party who brought the suit?

5. In a case argued before more than one judge or justice, what happens if all the judges or justices do not unanimously agree on a resolution of the issues or on the reasons for the decision?

 **Key Points**

The **key points** in this chapter include:

1. The difference between ethical decision making in business and ethical decision making in other contexts.

2. The connection between law and ethics.

3. The nature of tradeoffs in the ethical decision making process.

4. Ethical issues that arise in a business context.

5. The impact of change on ethical concerns.

Chapter 2: **Business Ethics**

WHAT THIS CHAPTER IS ABOUT

The concepts set out in this chapter include the nature of business ethics and the relationship between ethics and the law. Ultimately, the goal of this chapter is to provide you with basic tools for analyzing ethical issues in a business context.

CHAPTER OUTLINE

I.   NATURE OF BUSINESS ETHICS

A.   ETHICS, BUSINESS ETHICS, AND RATIONAL DECISION-MAKING

1. **Ethics**
   Ethics is the branch of philosophy that focuses on morality (right and wrong behavior) and the way in which moral principles are applied to daily life.

2. **Business Ethics**
   Business ethics focuses on what constitutes right or wrong behavior in business and on how moral principles are applied to situations that arise in a business context. Business ethics is *not* a separate kind of ethics.

3. **Rational Decision-Making**
   As a businessperson, you must be prepared to justify—to superiors, co-workers, employees, shareholders, or a court—whatever decision you make. You will need to explain the rational basis for the decision.

B. TRADE-OFFS

1. Ethical Dilemmas
Ethical dilemmas arise when two or more ethical goals come into conflict. Often, a trade-off must be made between arguably equally "good" alternatives. For example, if a certain product benefits many people but harms a few, should it be pulled from the market?

2. Type I and Type II Errors
A product's undesirable side effect is a sin of commission—a Type I error. Type II errors are sins of *omission*, such as benefits that would have accrued if a product had been sold but do not exist if the product is not marketed.

II.   SOURCES OF BUSINESS ETHICS

A. LAW

1. The Relation Between Law and Ethics
The law reflects social customs and values and reinforces principles of behavior that society deems right and just. In a way, law consists of particular applications of general ethical precepts expressed through statutes and court decisions.

2. Law Is a Limited Ethical Standard
Because the law reflects society's ethical values, many ethical decisions are made for us. But when the law has limits, ethical standards must guide the decision-making process.

B. RELIGION AND PHILOSOPHY

1. Religious Standards
Religious standards provide that when an act is prohibited by religious teachings, it is unethical and should not be undertaken, regardless of the consequences. Religious standards also involve compassion (the Golden Rule—"Do unto others as you would have them do unto you").

2. Philosophical Standards

a. Duty-Based Ethics
Immanual Kant believed that because people are qualitatively different from other physical objects, they should be respected. Individuals should evaluate their actions in light of what would happen if everyone acted the same way. This **categorical imperative** can be applied to any action.

b. Utilitarian Ethics
Utilitarianism is a belief that an action is ethical if it produces the greatest good for the greatest number. This approach is often criticized, because it tends to reduce the welfare of people to plus and minus signs on a cost-benefit worksheet.

III.   OBSTACLES TO ETHICAL BUSINESS BEHAVIOR

A. RATIONALIZING

It is easy to rationalize unethical behavior by arguing that nobody will ever know or that it is ethical if it harms no one.

B. CORPORATE STRUCTURE

The corporate structure seems to shield corporate actors from personal responsibility or protect them from the consequences of their decisions (they do not witness or deal directly with the harm or injuries generated by their decisions).

C. UNCLEAR STANDARDS

A firm's policies may not be communicated clearly to employees. Management may indicate (by condoning or rewarding unethical conduct, or by setting unrealistic goals) that ethical considerations take second place.

D. SITUATIONS THAT SEEM TO REQUIRE UNETHICAL CONDUCT

Employees asked to commit unethical or illegal acts face a difficult ethical dilemma—a duty of loyalty to their employer against a duty of loyalty to his or her conscience (and his or her spouse, children, or both).

IV. ETHICAL ISSUES IN BUSINESS

A. EMPLOYMENT-RELATED ISSUES

1. **Reverse Discrimination**

Employers are prohibited from discriminating on the basis of race, color, national origin, sex, pregnancy, religion, age, or disability. Affirmative action policies sometimes cause "reverse discrimination" (discrimination against members of the majority). Is this fair?

2. **Loyalty to Long-Term Employees v. the Bottom Line**

Does an employer have an ethical duty to loyal, long-term employees not to replace them with workers who will accept lower pay? Should this duty take precedence over a duty to maintain or increase the profitability of the firm?

3. **Potential Lawsuits**

Under some state laws and employment agreements, employers are prohibited from firing employees without "just cause." An employee's illegal conduct may or may not constitute just cause.

B. CONSUMER-RELATED ISSUES

1. **Marketing Unhealthy Products**

Marketing a legal product could be unethical under some circumstances (for example, selling a type of baby food that babies like and mothers buy but that is not nutritional).

2. **Misuse of Products by Consumers**

If a consumer is harmed by a product because he or she misused the product, who should bear the responsibility, the consumer or the manufacturer?

V. THE CHANGING ETHICAL LANDSCAPE

Our sense of what is ethical—what is fair or just or right in a given situation—changes over time. Conduct that was considered ethical ten years ago might be considered unethical today (for example, the bribery of foreign government officials).

STUDY TIP ☞ <u>Learning to Think Analytically</u>

Learning to "think like a lawyer"—that is, to think analytically—can have applications in fields of study and work outside the law. Thinking analytically is a method that may be applied when considering and deciding ethical issues, for example.

TRUE-FALSE QUESTIONS (Answers at the Back of the Book)

____   1.   Ethics is the study of what constitutes right and wrong behavior.

____   2.   Compliance with the law always equates with ethical behavior.

____   3.   According to duty-based ethics, telling a lie is ethical if it helps someone.

____   4.   According to utilitarianism, the consequences of an act are irrelevant in determining how ethical the act is.

____   5.   In making business decisions, a socially responsible firm considers an act's profitability, its legality, and whether it is ethically justifiable.

____   6.   Ethical trade-offs normally faced by businesspersons are clear-cut trade-offs between good and bad alternatives.

____   7.   Not marketing a product that is beneficial to most but harmful to some would be a Type II error.

____   8.   A manufacturer is absolutely liable for harm caused by its products.

____   9.   In doing business internationally, a company must take into consideration that what is prohibited in one country may be legal in another.

____   10. Conduct that would have been considered acceptable twenty years ago is acceptable today.

FILL-IN QUESTIONS (Answers at the Back of the Book)

A law is what society deems _____ (proper behavior/ a static concept). An ethical value is also an expression of what is considered _____ (appropriate conduct/ a concrete concept). When people wish to enforce or change an ethical value, they often politicize the issue, urging politicians to

_____ (create or amend a law/ enforce or change their own ethical values). When the law changes, it _____ (may coincidentally reflect/ more effectively represents) the ethic that served as impetus for its change.

MULTIPLE-CHOICE QUESTIONS (Answers at the Back of the Book)

____   1.   Business ethics focuses on

    a.   the application of moral principles in a business context.
    b.   the application of different philosophies of business to business activities.
    c.   the impact of business decisions on social values.
    d.   only ethical policy guidelines and codes of conduct issued by business firms.

____   2.   Which ethical standards derive from religious sources?

    a.   Duty-based ethics
    b.   Utilitarianism
    c.   Libertarianism
    d.   Rationalism

____   3.   Religious ethical standards are absolute, but also involve an element of

    a.   Selfishness
    b.   Discretion
    c.   Compassion
    d.   Calvinism

____   4.   Which ethics is premised on acting so as to do the greatest good for the greatest number of people?

    a.   Duty-based ethics
    b.   Utilitarianism
    c.   Libertarianism
    d.   Rationalism

____   5.   Which of the following is a criticism of utilitarianism?

    a.   It requires choosing among conflicting ethical principles.
    b.   It tends to reduce the welfare of people to plus and minus signs on a cost-benefit worksheet.
    c.   It is overly concerned with ideals of perfection.
    d.   It is an outdated philosophy.

____   6.   A firm has developed a new medication that is effective in the treatment of high blood pressure, but the firm estimates that one person in a million using the product may have a reaction resulting in death. Marketing the drug would be

    a.   a Type I error.
    b.   a Type II error.
    c.   both a Type I and a Type II error.
    d.   neither a Type I nor a Type II error.

___ 7. A corporate employer who responds to what the employer sees as a moral obligation to correct for past discrimination by adjusting pay differences raises an ethical conflict between which parties?

    a. Employees
    b. Employer and employee
    c. Corporation and shareholder
    d. Both b and c

___ 8. Employees who work for Chemco, a subsidiary of Mega Corporation, must work with hazardous chemicals. Mega Corporation adopted a policy to protect pregnant women and their fetuses by prohibiting them from working for Chemco. Mega Corporation's policy provided a safe workplace, but did it also violate an ethical and legal duty to provide equal employment opportunity?

    a. Yes. Equal employment opportunity is a "higher good" than a safe workplace.
    b. Yes. Distinctions based on sex must relate to the ability to perform a job, and pregnant women can perform as well as anyone else.
    c. No. Distinctions based on sex must relate to the ability to perform a job, and pregnant women cannot perform as well as men or non-pregnant women.
    d. No. There is no "higher good" than protecting unborn children.

___ 9. When one ethical duty conflicts with another, a decision has to be made as to which duty is more fundamental. Ethical trade-offs

    a. do not normally have clear-cut answers.
    b. involve choices between equally good and bad alternatives.
    c. both a and b.
    d. none of the above.

___ 10. Ethical dilemmas in a business context require determining

    a. how much consideration to give to making a profit.
    b. obeying the law.
    c. adhering to certain ethics.
    d. all of the above.

___ 11. To ensure that an action is simultaneously profitable, legal, and ethical

    a. some profitability or ethical consideration must be traded off.
    b. the religious implications must be considered.
    c. the welfare of the people involved must be reduced to plus and minus signs on a cost-benefit worksheet.
    d. none of the above.

SHORT ESSAY QUESTION

Discuss the difference between legal and ethical standards.

ISSUE SPOTTERS (Answers at the Back of the Book)

1. If, like Robin Hood, a person robs the rich to pay the poor, does his or her benevolent intent make his or her actions ethical?

2. When a manufacturer has to decide whether to close a plant, the costs of doing so may be weighed against the benefits. If the benefits are greater than the costs, can closing the plant be ethically justified, considering the effect on the employees who will be laid off?

3. When a corporate executive has to decide whether to market a product that would be beneficial to most consumers but that might have undesirable side effects for a small percentage of users, what is the trade-off?

4. Acme Corporation decides to respond to what Acme sees as a moral obligation to correct for past discrimination by adjusting pay differences among its employees. Does this raise an ethical conflict between Acme's employees? Between Acme and its employees? Between Acme and its shareholders?

5. Does a manufacturer owe an ethical duty to remove from the market a product that is capable of seriously injuring consumers, even if the injuries result from misuse?

★ Key Points

The **key points** in this chapter include:

1. The procedural steps leading up to a civil trial.

2. The pretrial, trial, and posttrial motions that a party may file.

3. The events that can occur at a trial.

4. The types of jurisdiction and the differences between jurisdiction and venue.

5. The concept of judicial review.

6. The requirements for federal jurisdiction.

Chapter 3:
The Court System

WHAT THIS CHAPTER IS ABOUT

This chapter explains which courts have power to hear what disputes and when. This chapter also outlines what happens before, during, and after a civil trial.

CHAPTER OUTLINE

I. WHAT IS REQUIRED FOR A COURT TO HEAR A DISPUTE

A. WHAT A PLAINTIFF MUST HAVE—STANDING
Standing is the interest (injury or threat) that a plaintiff has in a case.

B. WHAT THE COURT MUST HAVE—JURISDICTION AND VENUE

1. Jurisdiction
To hear a case, a court must have jurisdiction over (1) the defendant or the property involved and (2) the subject matter.

a. Jurisdiction over Persons or Property

1) *In Personam* **Jurisdiction**
A court can exercise personal jurisdiction over state residents and those who can be served with a summons within the state.

2) *In Rem* **Jurisdiction**
A court can exercise *in rem* jurisdiction ("jurisdiction over the thing") over property located within its borders.

3) *Quasi In Rem* **Jurisdiction**
Quasi in rem jurisdiction is based on a person's interest in property within a court's jurisdiction, but the action is brought against the party personally.

4) **Long Arm Statutes**
Permit a court to exercise jurisdiction over a nonresident who has *minimum contacts* with the state.

b. **Subject Matter Jurisdiction**

1) **General Jurisdiction**
A *court of general jurisdiction* can decide virtually any type of case, including some that involve federal law.

2) **Limited Jurisdiction**
Jurisdiction may be limited by the subject of a lawsuit, the amount of money in controversy, whether a case is civil or criminal, or whether a proceeding is a trial or an appeal.

3) **Exclusive and Conclusive Jurisdiction**
When cases can be tried only in federal courts or only in state courts, exclusive jurisdiction exists. When both federal and state courts can hear a case, concurrent jurisdiction exists.

2. **Venue**
Venue is concerned with the most appropriate location for a trial.

II.   STATE COURT SYSTEMS

A. **TRIAL COURTS**
Trial courts are courts in which trials are held and testimony is taken.

B. **APPELLATE COURTS**
Appellate courts hear appeals from the trial courts.

1. **What an Appellate Court Looks At**
Questions of law (what law should govern a dispute) but not *questions of fact* (what happened in regard to the dispute being tried), unless a trial court's finding of fact is clearly contrary to the evidence.

2. **Options of an Appellate Court**
(1) Affirmance: enforcement of the lower courts' orders; (2) reversal: if an error was committed during the trial; or (3) remand: sent back to the court that originally heard the case for a new trial.

III. THE FEDERAL COURT SYSTEM

A. **JURISDICTION OF THE FEDERAL COURTS**

1. **Federal Questions**
Any suit involving a federal question can originate in a federal court.

2. **Diversity of Citizenship**
Federal jurisdiction extends to cases involving (1) citizens of different states, (2) a foreign government and citizens of a state or of different states, or (3) citizens of a state and citizens or subjects of a foreign government. The amount in controversy must be more than $50,000.

B. DISTRICT COURTS

The federal equivalent of a state trial court of general jurisdiction. There is at least one federal district court in every state. Other federal trial courts include the U.S. Tax Court and the U.S. Bankruptcy Court.

C. COURTS OF APPEALS

The U.S. (circuit) courts of appeals for twelve of the circuits hear appeals from the federal district courts located within their respective circuits. The court of appeals for the thirteenth circuit (the federal circuit) has national jurisdiction over certain cases.

D. THE UNITED STATES SUPREME COURT

The highest level of the federal court system. The Supreme Court can review any case decided by any of the federal courts of appeals, and it has authority over some cases decided in state courts. To appeal a case to the Supreme Court, a party asks for a writ of *certiorari*. Whether the Court issues the writ is within its discretion.

IV. JUDICIAL REVIEW

Any court may refuse to enforce any statute or executive act that violates the Constitution. Federal courts may rule on provisions of state constitutions.

V. PRETRIAL PROCEDURES

A. THE PLEADINGS

1. Complaint

Filed by the plaintiff with the clerk of the trial court. Contains (1) a statement alleging the facts for the court to take jurisdiction, (2) a short statement of the facts necessary to show that the plaintiff is entitled to a remedy, and (3) a statement of the remedy the plaintiff is seeking.

2. Summons

Served on the defendant, with the complaint. Notifies the defendant to answer the complaint (usually within twenty to thirty days).

3. Defendant's Choices after Receipt of the Complaint and Summons

a. Motion to Dismiss

If the court denies the motion, and the defendant does not file a further pleading, a judgment will be entered for the plaintiff. If the court grants the motion, the defendant is not required to answer the complaint. If the plaintiff does not file an amended complaint, a judgment will be entered for the defendant.

b. Answer

An answer admits the allegations in the complaint or denies them and sets out any defenses. May include a **counterclaim** against the plaintiff, who will have to answer it with a **reply**.

c. No Response

Results in a default judgment for the plaintiff.

B. DISMISSALS AND JUDGMENTS BEFORE TRIAL

1. Motion to Dismiss

(See above.)

2. **Motion for Judgment on the Pleadings**

    Any party can file this motion (after the complaint, answer, and any counterclaim and reply have been filed), when no facts are disputed and only questions of law are at issue. A court may consider only those facts stated in the pleadings.

3. **Motion for Summary Judgment**

    Any party can file this motion, if there is no disagreement about the facts and the only question is which laws apply. A court can consider evidence outside the pleadings.

C. DISCOVERY

The process of obtaining information from the opposing party or from witnesses. Privileged material is safeguarded and only relevant matters are discoverable. Discovery may include depositions; interrogatories; request for admissions; requests for documents, objects, and entry on land; and requests for physical or mental examinations.

VI. THE TRIAL

A. OPENING STATEMENTS

Each side sets out briefly his or her version of the facts and outlines the evidence that will be presented. The plaintiff goes first.

B. EXAMINATION OF WITNESSES

1. **Plaintiff's Side of the Case**

    The plaintiff questions the first witness (direct examination); the defendant questions the witness (cross-examination); the plaintiff questions the witness again (redirect); the defendant follows (recross). The plaintiff's other witnesses are called.

2. **Defendant's Side of the Case**

    a. **Motion for a Directed Verdict**

    After the plaintiff's case, the defendant can ask the judge to direct a verdict on the ground that the plaintiff presented no evidence that would justify granting the plaintiff relief. The judge grants the motion if there is insufficient evidence to raise an issue of fact.

    b. **Defendant's Witnesses**

    If the motion is denied, the defendant calls his or her witnesses (and there is direct, cross-, redirect, and recross-examination). At the end, either side can move for a directed verdict.

3. **The Plaintiff Can Present a Rebuttal**

4. **The Defendant Can Refute the Rebuttal in a Rejoinder**

C. CLOSING ARGUMENTS

Each side summarizes briefly his or her version of the facts, outlines the evidence that supports his or her case, and reveals the shortcomings of the points made by the other party. The plaintiff goes first.

D. JURY VERDICT

In a jury trial, the jury specifies the factual findings and the amount of damages to be paid by the losing party. This is the verdict.

VII. POSTTRIAL MOTIONS

A. MOTION FOR A NEW TRIAL
This motion is granted if the judge believes that the jury erred but that it is not appropriate to grant a judgment for the other side.

B. MOTION FOR JUDGMENT *N.O.V.*
The defendant can file this motion, if he or she previously moved for a directed verdict. The standards for granting this motion are the same as those for granting a motion to dismiss or a motion for a directed verdict.

VIII. APPEALS

A. PAPERS TO BE FILED AND ORAL ARGUMENTS
The appellant files a notice of appeal with the clerk of the trial court, and the record on appeal, an abstract, and a brief with the reviewing court. The appellee files an answering brief. The parties can present oral arguments.

B. DECISION
Appellate courts do not usually reverse findings of fact unless the findings are contradicted by the evidence presented at the trial in the lower court.

C. FURTHER APPEALS
If the reviewing court is an intermediate appellate court, the case may be appealed to the state supreme court. If a federal question is involved, the case may be appealed to the United States Supreme Court.

STUDY TIP 👉 Study Schedules

All students have different requirements in regards to the amount of study time that they need to prepare for a class or an exam. The same temptation is faced by all of us: putting off until tomor - row what should be done today. The best remedy for this tempta - tion is not to give into it but to be disciplined. You should set up a study schedule and make every effort to stick to it. This way you will achieve your best results.

TRUE-FALSE QUESTIONS (Answers at the Back of the Book)

____ 1. In a civil case, the pleadings inform each party of the other's claims and specify the issues. The pleadings consist of a complaint, an answer, and a motion to dismiss.

____ 2. In ruling on a motion for summary judgment, a court cannot consider evidence outside the pleadings.

____   **3.**   At a pretrial conference, the parties and the judge consider the issues and may attempt to simplify them.

____   **4.**   If a party who has been served with a complaint and a summons does not deny the truth of the complaint, he or she will be held in default.

____   **5.**   To obtain documents and other materials in the hands of an opposing party, in anticipation of a trial a party utilizes the appeals process.

____   **6.**   In a jury trial, the parties (or their attorneys) have a right to conduct *voir dire*.

____   **7.**   In a civil case, a plaintiff must establish his or her case beyond a reasonable doubt.

FILL-IN QUESTIONS (Answers at the Back of the Book)

A motion _____ (to dismiss/for summary judgment) alleges that even if the facts in the complaint are true, their legal consequences are such that there is no reason to go on with the suit and no need for the defendant to present an answer. A motion _____ (to dismiss/for judgment on the pleadings) is properly filed after the complaint, answer, and any counterclaim and reply have been filed, when no facts are disputed, and only if questions of law are at issue. A motion for _____ (summary judgment/ a new trial) is proper if there is no disagreement about the facts and the only question is which laws apply to those facts.

MULTIPLE-CHOICE QUESTIONS (Answers at the Back of the Book)

____   **1.**   The first step in a lawsuit is the filing of pleadings, and the first pleading filed is the complaint. The complaint contains

a. a statement alleging jurisdictional facts.
b. a statement of facts entitling the complainant to relief.
c. a statement asking for a specific remedy.
d. all of the above.

____   **2.**   A motion to dismiss for failure to state a claim on which relief can be granted alleges that according to the law, even if the facts in the complaint are true

a. the court lacks subject matter or personal jurisdiction.
b. the defendant is not liable.
c. venue is improper.
d. none of the above.

____   **3.**   After the pleadings are filed, the next step is discovery. The purposes of discovery include

a. saving time by preserving evidence.
b. narrowing the issues.
c. preventing surprises at trial.
d. all of the above.

____ 4. After discovery and a pretrial hearing, if the right to a jury trial has been requested, the jury is selected. Once a jury is chosen, the trial proceeds in the following order

  a. each party's opening statement, each party's case, each party's rebuttal, each party's closing argument, the verdict.

  b. each party's opening statement, the plaintiff's case, the defendant's rebuttal, the plaintiff's closing argument, the verdict.

  c. the plaintiff's opening statement, case, and rebuttal; the defendant's opening statement, case, and rebuttal; each party's closing argument; the verdict.

  d. the defendant's opening statement, case, and rebuttal; the plaintiff's opening statement, case, and rebuttal; each party's closing argument; the verdict.

____ 5. After the verdict, the losing party can file a motion

  a. for a directed verdict.

  b. for summary judgment.

  c. for a new trial or for a judgment notwithstanding the verdict.

  d. for judgment on the pleadings.

____ 6. In deciding whether to sue, a person should consider all of the following EXCEPT

  a. the cost of going to court.

  b. the patience to follow a case through the judicial system.

  c. alternatives to settling the dispute without going to court.

  d. refusing to settle for less than you think you are owed.

Questions 7 through 9 involve the following situation: Todd and Denny are involved in an automobile accident. Wendy is a passenger in Denny's car.

____ 7. After Todd serves a complaint on Denny, Denny files a motion to dismiss. Denny will also need to file an answer to the complaint if

  a. the motion to dismiss is granted.

  b. the motion to dismiss is denied.

  c. Todd files a motion for judgment on the pleadings.

  d. Todd files a reply.

____ 8. Todd wants to ask Wendy, as a witness, some questions concerning the accident. Wendy's answers to the questions are given in

  a. a deposition.

  b. response to interrogatories.

  c. response to a request for admissions.

  d. response to a judge's request at a pretrial conference.

____ 9. The case goes to trial. After the opening statements, Todd calls and questions Wendy. What happens next?

  a. Denny questions Wendy.

  b. Todd questions Wendy again.

  c. Todd calls his second witness.

  d. Denny calls his first witness.

SHORT ESSAY QUESTIONS

1. Define jurisdiction.

2. Discuss discovery, what it is, what devices it uses, and what its advantage is.

ISSUE SPOTTERS (Answers at the Back of the Book)

Jan contracted with Dean to deliver a quantity of CDs to Jan's Music Galore Store. In a dispute over the amount, the delivery date, the price, and the quality of the CDs, they are unable to resolve their differences.

1. Jan wants to sue Dean. What are the first steps Jan must take?

2. As Jan prepares her suit against Dean, Jan wants to see copies of Dean's paperwork relating to the deal—Dean's copy of the original order, any notes of later telephone conversations, and so on. Jan also wants Dean to answer some questions relating to their dispute. What means should Jan use to see the papers and get Dean's answers?

3. At the trial, after Jan calls her witnesses, offers her evidence, and otherwise presents her side of the case, Dean has at least two choices between courses of actions. Dean can call his first witness. What else might Dean do?

4. After the trial, the judge issues a judgment that includes a grant of relief for Jan, but the relief is not as much as Jan wanted. Neither Jan nor Dean are satisfied with this result. Can either party—or both—appeal to a higher court?

5. The appellate court upholds the lower court's judgment and rules against Dean, who decides not to appeal further. How can Jan enforce the judgment?

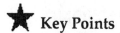 **Key Points**

The **key points** in this chapter include:

1. The processes of negotiation and mediation.

2. Steps in the arbitration process.

3. Court-annexed arbitration.

4. Summary jury trials and mini-trials.

Chapter 4:
Alternative Dispute Resolution

WHAT THIS CHAPTER IS ABOUT

This chapter outlines alternatives to judicial resolution of legal controversies. These alternatives include negotiation, conciliation, mediation, and arbitration.

CHAPTER OUTLINE

I. THE PROBLEMS OF COST AND COMPLEXITY

Reasons for methods of alternative dispute resolution (ADR) include: the complexity of litigation (complex rules, complicated facts) and its expense in time and money.

II. THE SEARCH FOR ALTERNATIVES TO LITIGATION

ADR is any procedure or device for resolving disputes other than the traditional judicial process. Besides the solutions outlined elsewhere in this chapter, proposals include—

A. CAPS ON DAMAGE AWARDS

For pain and suffering, to deter some potential litigants from suing.

B. PENALIZING THOSE WHO BRING FRIVOLOUS LAWSUITS

Rule 11 of the Federal Rules of Civil Procedure allows for sanctions against lawyers and litigants who bring frivolous lawsuits in federal courts.

C. CASE-MANAGEMENT PLANS

Require courts to place cases on different tracks, to hear simple cases sooner.

III.   NEGOTIATION AND MEDIATION
Nonadversarial in nature—the goal is to find grounds for agreement.

A.   NEGOTIATION
Parties come together informally, with or without attorneys, to try to settle or resolve their differences without involving independent third parties.

B.   MEDIATION
Parties come together informally with a mediator, who may propose solutions for the parties to consider. A mediator is often an expert in a particular field and charges a fee.

1.   Advantages of Mediation
Few procedural rules; proceedings can be made to fit the parties' needs; the parties reach agreement by consent; the parties select a mediator.

2.   Disadvantages of Mediation
The mediator can only help the parties reach a decision, not make a decision for them; no deadline; no threat of sanctions if a party fails to negotiate in good faith.

IV.   ARBITRATION
An arbitrator—the third party hearing the dispute—decides the dispute. The decision may (or may not) be legally binding. Disputes are often arbitrated because of an arbitration clause in a contract entered into before the dispute.

A.   THE FEDERAL ARBITRATION ACT (FAA) OF 1925
Provides means for enforcing whatever arbitration procedure the parties agree on. Under the FAA, the parties can ask a federal district court to—

1.   Compel Arbitration
The FAA enforces any arbitration clause in a contract that involves interstate commerce (which may include business activities only slightly connected to the flow of commerce) [Section 4].

2.   Confirm the Arbitrator's Decision
One party obtains a court order directing another party to comply with the terms of the arbitrator's decision [Section 9].

3.   Set Aside the Arbitrator's Decision
Grounds are limited to misconduct, fraud, corruption, or abuse of power in the arbitration process; a court will not review the merits of the dispute or the arbitrator's judgment [Section 10]. (See below.)

B.   STATE ARBITRATION STATUTES
The states follow the federal approach to enforce voluntary agreements to arbitrate disputes between private parties. Most states require that (1) an agreement to submit a dispute to arbitration be in writing and (2) the submission be within a certain time of the dispute (generally six months).

C.   THE ARBITRATION PROCESS
Unless a statute provides otherwise, the rights and duties of the parties are set by their agreement. (For example, by including a choice-of-law clause, they may have the law of a specific state govern their agreement.)

1. **Submission**
   Typically includes the identities of the parties, the nature of the dispute, the monetary amounts involved, the place at which arbitration is to occur, and a statement that the parties intend to be bound by the arbitrator's award.

2. **Hearing**
   The parties must decide on the issues and the arbitrator's powers. They may stipulate rules of procedure or have the arbitrator set rules. Typically, the parties present opening arguments and evidence, call and examine witnesses, and present closing arguments.

3. **Award**
   The final decision of the arbitrator. Under most statutes, an arbitrator must render an award within thirty days of the close of a hearing. In most states, the award must be in writing but does not need to state findings of fact or conclusions of law.

D. **ENFORCEMENT AND APPEAL**

1. **Enforcement of Agreements to Submit to Arbitration**
   A court can decide whether or not the parties agreed to submit a particular matter to arbitration (without ruling on the issue in dispute).

2. **Setting Aside an Arbitration Award**
   A losing party may appeal the arbitrator's award to a court.

   a. **Fact Findings and Legal Conclusions**
      The arbitrator's fact findings and legal conclusions are normally conclusive. Whether the arbitrator erred is no basis for setting aside an award. A court will not look at the merits of a dispute, the sufficiency of the evidence, or the arbitrator's reasoning.

   b. **Public Policy and Illegality**
      No award will be enforced if compliance would result in the commission of a crime, or conflict with or undermine public policy.

   c. **Defects in the Arbitration Process**
      An award may be set aside if—

      1) The award was the result of corruption, fraud, or other "undue means" (such as a bribe or *ex parte* communications).
      2) The arbitrator exhibited bias or corruption.
      3) The arbitrator refused to postpone the hearing despite sufficient cause, refused to hear material evidence, or otherwise acted to substantially prejudice the rights of a party.
      4) The arbitrator exceeded his or her powers or failed to use them to make a mutual, final, and definite award.

   d. **Waiver**
      A party may forfeit the right to challenge an award by failing to object to a defect in a timely manner.

V.   INTEGRATION OF ADR AND COURT PROCEDURES

A. COURT-ANNEXED ARBITRATION

Many, if not most, federal courts require parties to attempt to settle their differences through some form of ADR before proceeding to trial. Some states compel the arbitration of certain types of disputes. Many states refer certain types of cases for mediation or arbitration.

1. Differences Between Court-annexed and Voluntary Arbitration
In court-annexed arbitration—

a . Certain Disputes Are Not Arbitrable
Disputes involving title to real estate or a court's equity powers.

b. No Discovery Without Court Approval
After a hearing commences, a party seeking discovery must usually secure approval from the court that mandated the arbitration.

c. Rules of Evidence May Be Different
Most states impose the same rules on arbitration hearings and trials. Others allow all relevant evidence whether or not it would be admissible at trial. Some leave it to the arbitrator to decide.

d. A Court Can Review an Arbitrated Dispute *De Novo*
Either party may reject an award for any reason; the case proceeds to trial, and the court considers all the evidence and legal questions as though no arbitration had occurred.

e. Court Costs and Fees May Be Imposed
Many statutes impose such expenses on a party who rejects an award but does not improve his or her position by going to trial.

2. Role of the Arbitrator
Essentially the same in court-annexed and voluntary proceedings.

B. SUMMARY JURY TRIAL
A jury renders a non-binding verdict. Mandatory negotiations follow. If no settlement is reached, either side can seek a full trial.

VI.   ADR FORUMS AND SERVICES
Services facilitating dispute resolution outside the courtroom are provided by government agencies and private organizations, including programs in the insurance, automobile, and securities industries.

A. MINI-TRIAL
A private proceeding in which attorneys briefly argue each party's case. If the parties fail to reach an agreement, a third party renders an opinion as to how a court would likely decide the issue.

B. FOR-PROFIT ALTERNATIVES (RENT-A-JUDGE)
Litigants have their cases heard before former judges. Jurors can be selected from public jury rolls; verdicts can be appealed to a state appellate court.

VII.   ALTERNATIVES TO ADR
It may be possible to combine the advantages of litigation and ADR. In some states, in certain cases, a court may limit discovery, schedule a more immediate

hearing, and otherwise expedite proceedings. In most cases, parties can agree on many techniques to simplify the resolution of a dispute in a judicial context.

STUDY TIP ☞ Organization

Organization is important to efficiently preparing for your class. You may find it helpful to develop an overall strategy at the beginning of your study, whether your technique involves underlining or highlighting your text, taking notes, preparing notecards or flash cards, reviewing this outline, or doing any other activities. You can adapt your approach as you learn what is most effective for you.

TRUE-FALSE QUESTIONS (Answers at the Back of the Book)

_____ 1. The major difference between negotiation and mediation is that mediation involves fewer procedural rules.

_____ 2. No dispute can be arbitrated unless the parties agree in writing, before the dispute arises, to submit any dispute to arbitration.

_____ 3. The Federal Arbitration Act requires courts to defer to all voluntary arbitration agreements in cases governed by federal law.

_____ 4. Most states require that a dispute must be submitted to arbitration within a certain time, usually six months from the date that it arises.

_____ 5. The basic difference between voluntary and court-annexed arbitration is that in court-annexed arbitration an award is final and non-reviewable.

_____ 6. A summary jury trial is a mock trial in which evidence is presented in an abbreviated form, but in which the jury nevertheless reaches a verdict.

FILL-IN QUESTIONS (Answers at the Back of the Book)

_____ (Arbitration/ Mediation/ Negotiation) is the settling of a dispute by parties meeting informally, with or without attorneys, to discuss and resolve their differences without the involvement of independent third parties. _____ (Arbitration/ Mediation/ Negotiation) is the settling of a dispute by parties meeting informally with a third party, _____ (an arbitrator/ a mediator/ a negotiator), who assists the parties in reaching an agreement. _____ (Arbitration/ Mediation/ Negotiation) is the settling of a dispute by an impartial third party, _____ (an arbitrator/ a mediator/ a negotiator), who does more than assist the parties in resolving their dispute—he or she renders a decision that may be legally binding.

MULTIPLE-CHOICE QUESTIONS (Answers at the Back of the Book)

____   **1.**   Sommer Shoes, Inc., agrees to sell to Lifland Sporting Goods 1,000 pairs of Nikes. Lifland picks up the shoes, but does not pay for them, claiming that they are in defective condition. To resolve the dispute, Sommer and Lifland enter into mediation. Lifland fails to negotiate in good faith. On Sommer's request, the mediator can

    a.   impose any sanction that could be imposed by a court.
    b.   impose no sanctions that Sommer and Lifland did not agree to initially.
    c.   issue an immediate decision in Sommer's favor.
    d.   issue a decision in Sommer's favor if the parties do not resolve the dispute before deadline expires.

____   **2.**   Arbitration is an alternative to judicial resolution of disputes. Arbitration is the settling of

    a.   a dispute by an impartial third party who renders a legally binding decision.
    b.   a dispute that involves less than a certain amount of money.
    c.   a dispute that arises from an agreement in writing.
    d.   all of the above.

____   **3.**   Assembly Workers of America (AWA) is a union that represents the employees of Flick Company. When AWA and Flick cannot agree on a new contract, they submit their dispute to arbitration. Flick disagrees with the arbitrator's decision and refuses to comply with it. If AWA sues to compel Flick's compliance, the court will

    a.   look at the merits of the dispute.
    b.   consider the reasoning that the arbitrator used to arrive at a decision.
    c.   determine whether there is a valid award with which Flick can be made to comply.
    d.   all of the above.

____   **4.**   Under the Federal Arbitration Act, an arbitrator's award may be set aside if the arbitrator

    a.   failed to make a final and definite award.
    b.   failed to use "undue means" to resolve a complex dispute.
    c.   exhibited bias toward no party to the dispute.
    d.   postponed the hearing of the dispute, regardless of the reason.

____   **5.**   In most states, court-annexed arbitration is available only

    a.   when a party demands a jury trial.
    b.   when a dispute involves title to real estate.
    c.   when a court's equity powers are not involved.
    d.   at the appellate level.

____   **6.** A traditional trial is public and the verdict is legally binding. Regarding summary jury trials and mini-trials, which of the following is TRUE?

   a. A summary jury trial is private and the verdict is legally binding.
   b. A summary jury trial is public and the verdict is advisory.
   c. A mini-trial is private and the verdict is legally binding.
   d. A mini-trial is public and the verdict is advisory.

SHORT ESSAY QUESTIONS

1. Discuss the principal advantages and disadvantages of using the mediation process to resolve disputes.

2. Discuss the difference between voluntary arbitration and court-annexed arbitration.

ISSUE SPOTTERS (Answers at the Back of the Book)

1. Why can't society rely exclusively on the courts to resolve disputes?

2. Beth rents an apartment from Prentice. Beth and Prentice disagree over $200 in back rent. Beth and Prentice get together, discuss the matter, and compromise to resolve the dispute with a payment of $100. This informal resolution of a dispute is known as negotiation. What is the basic difference between negotiation and litigation?

3. Federal policy favors arbitration of disputes. That is, it is the policy of the federal government—as expressed in federal law—to favor the settling of a dispute by an impartial third party who, following a proceeding involving less formality than a court trial, renders a legally binding decision. Most states follow the federal approach. If federal and state arbitration law conflict, however, which takes precedence?

4. Werder Hybrids, Inc., agrees to supply Newman Farms with specific agricultural hybrids. In using the hybrids, problems develop. Newman claims that the hybrids are genetically inferior. Werder claims that they are not. Werder and Newman submit their dispute to Amelia, an arbitrator who is an expert in genetic engineering. Werder and Newman give Amelia the power to set the rules to govern the arbitration. Why are these rules likely to be less restrictive than rules governing a court proceeding?

5. Some states require that certain disputes—usually those involving less than a specific amount of money—be submitted to mediation or nonbinding arbitration. If the dispute is not resolved, or if a party disagrees with the decision of the mediator or arbitrator, will a court hear the case?

 Key Points

The **key points** in this chapter include:

1. The relationship between the federal government and the state govern-ments.

2. Protections against government interference that are embodied in the Bill of Rights.

3. The impact of the commerce clause and the supremacy clause.

4. The application of the Bill of Rights' guarantees in a business context.

5. The application of the Constitution's due process and equal protection guarantees.

Chapter 5:
Constitutional Law

WHAT THIS CHAPTER IS ABOUT

This chapter emphasizes that the Constitution is the supreme law in this country. Neither Congress nor any state may pass a law that conflicts with the Constitution. To sustain a federal law or action, a specific federal power must be found in the Constitution. A state has inherent power (to enact laws that have a reasonable relationship to the welfare of its citizens). The power of the federal government was delegated to it by the states, which retain all other powers. The Constitution limits the states' exercise of powers not delegated to the federal government.

CHAPTER OUTLINE

I.   THE CONSTITUTIONAL POWERS OF GOVERNMENT

    A. FEDERALISM
    The basis for the structure of the government of the United States. A federal form of government is one in which the states form a union and sovereign power is divided between a central authority and the states.

    B. SEPARATION OF POWERS
    The Constitution (Articles I, II, III) provides for three branches of government: the legislative branch makes the laws; the executive branch enforces the laws; and the judicial branch interprets the laws. Each branch has some power to limit the actions of the other two, thereby establishing a system of checks and balances.

C. COMMERCE CLAUSE
The Constitution (Article I, Section 8) gives Congress the power to regulate commerce among the states.

1. **Regulatory Power of the National Government**
The national government can regulate every commercial enterprise in the United States. This power means that Congress can legislate in areas in which it has no explicit grant of power.

2. **Regulatory Power of the States**
States possess police powers (the right to regulate private activities to protect or promote the public order, health, safety, morals, and general welfare). Statutes covering almost every aspect of life have been enacted under the police powers.

3. **When State Laws Impinge on Interstate Commerce**
Courts balance the state's interest in the merit and purpose of the law against the burden on interstate commerce. State laws that *substantially* interfere with interstate commerce violate the commerce clause.

D. SUPREMACY CLAUSE
The Constitution (Article IV) provides that the Constitution, laws, and treaties of the United States are the supreme law of the land.

1. **When Federal and State Laws Are in Direct Conflict**
The state law is rendered invalid.

2. **Federal Preemption**
If Congress chooses to act exclusively in an area in which states have concurrent power, Congress preempts the area (the federal law takes precedence over a state law on the same subject).

E. THE TAXING POWER
The Constitution (Article I, Section 8) gives Congress the power to levy taxes, but Congress may not tax some states and exempt others. Any tax that is a valid revenue-raising measure will be upheld.

F. THE SPENDING POWER
The Constitution (Article I, Section 8) gives Congress the power to spend the money it raises with its taxing power. This involves policy choices, with which taxpayers may disagree. Congress can spend funds to promote any objective, so long as it does not violate the Bill of Rights.

II. THE BILL OF RIGHTS AND BUSINESS ISSUES

The first ten amendments to the Constitution protect individuals and business entities against some types of interference by the federal government. Under the due process clause of the Fourteenth Amendment (and the doctrine of selective incorporation), most of the amendments also apply to the states.

A. FIRST AMENDMENT—FREEDOM OF SPEECH
The First Amendment guarantee of freedom of speech applies to both the federal and state governments.

1. **Protected Speech**
Includes symbolic speech—nonverbal expressions, such as gestures, articles of clothing, some acts (flag burning, for example) and so on. Governments can regulate the time, place, and manner of speech.

2. **Unprotected Speech**

   a. **Defamatory Speech**
   Speech that harms the good reputation of another. Such speech can take the form of libel (if it is in writing) or slander (if it is oral).

   b. **Lewd and Obscene Speech**
   The Supreme Court has upheld state laws banning the sale and possession of child pornography. At least one court has banned lewd speech and pornographic pinups in the workplace (to protect women against sexual harassment).

   c. **"Fighting Words"**
   Words that are likely to incite others to violence.

3. **Speech with Limited Protection**

   a. **Commercial Speech**
   A state restriction on commercial speech (advertising) is valid as long as it (1) seeks to implement a substantial government interest, (2) directly advances that interest, and (3) goes no further than necessary to accomplish its objective.

   b. **Political Speech**
   States can prohibit corporations from using corporate funds for independent expressions of opinion about political candidates.

B. **FIRST AMENDMENT—FREEDOM OF RELIGION**
The government may not establish a religion nor prohibit the free exercise of religion (under the establishment clause and the free exercise clause).

1. **"Sunday Closing Laws"**
   Restrictions on commercial acts on Sunday have been upheld on the ground it is a legitimate government function to provide a day of rest.

2. **Government Accommodation**
   This amendment mandates government accommodation of all religions and forbids hostility toward any.

3. **Business Accommodation**
   Statutes prohibit employers and unions from discriminating against persons because of their religion. Employers must "reasonably accommodate" the religious practices of their employees, unless it would cause undue hardship to the employer's business.

C. **FOURTH AMENDMENT—SEARCHES AND SEIZURES**
Government officers cannot conduct unreasonable searches or seizures.

1. **Search Warrant**
   A law enforcement officer must obtain a search warrant before searching or seizing private property. The warrant must describe what is to be searched or seized.

   a. **Probable Cause**
   To obtain a warrant, the officer must convince a judge that there is probable cause (evidence that would convince a reasonable person a search or seizure is justified).

b. **"General and Neutral Enforcement Plan"**
To obtain a warrant to inspect business premises, government inspectors must have probable cause, but the standard is different: a "general and neutral enforcement plan" is enough.

2. **No Search Warrant**
No warrant is required for seizures of spoiled or contaminated food or searches of businesses in highly regulated industries. General manufacturing is not considered a highly regulated industry.

D. **FIFTH AMENDMENT—PRIVILEGE AGAINST SELF-INCRIMINATION**
No person can be compelled to give testimony that might subject him or her to a criminal prosecution.

1. **Sole Proprietors**
Individuals who own their own businesses and have not incorporated cannot be compelled to produce their business records.

2. **Partnerships and Corporations**
Partnerships and corporations *can* be compelled to produce their business records, even if the records incriminate the persons who constitute the business entity.

E. **RIGHT TO PRIVACY**
There is no specific guarantee of this right, but it is derived from guarantees in the First, Third, Fourth, Fifth, and Ninth Amendments.

III. OTHER CONSTITUTIONAL PROTECTIONS

A. **PRIVILEGES AND IMMUNITIES**

1. **State Citizens**
The Constitution (Article IV, Section 2) requires each state to provide the citizens of other states with the same privileges and immunities it provides its own citizens. A state cannot treat nonresidents engaged in basic, essential activities differently without substantial justification.

2. **U.S. Citizens**
The Fourteenth Amendment prohibits a state from infringing on the privileges or immunities (such as the right to travel) of U.S. citizens.

B. **DUE PROCESS**
Both the Fifth and the Fourteenth Amendments provide that no person shall be deprived "of life, liberty, or property, without due process of law."

1. **Substantive Due Process**
Substantive due process focuses on the content (substance) of legislation.

a. **Rational Basis Test**
Restrictions on business activities must relate rationally to a legitimate government purpose. Most business regulations qualify.

b. **Compelling Interest Test**
A statute can restrict an individual's fundamental right (such as all First Amendment rights) only if the statute promotes a compelling or overriding governmental interest (speed limits, for example, protect public safety).

2. Procedural Due Process
Procedural due process requires that any government decision to take away the life, liberty, or property of an individual be accompanied by procedural safeguards to ensure fairness.

C. EQUAL PROTECTION

The Fourteenth Amendment prohibits a state from denying any person "the equal protection of the laws." The due process clause of the Fifth Amendment applies the equal protection clause to the federal government.

1. What Equal Protection Means

Equal protection means that the government must treat similarly situated individuals in a similar manner. If a law distinguishes among individuals the basis for the distinction (classification) is examined.

a. Rational Basis Test
In matters of economic or social welfare, the classification will be considered valid if there is any conceivable rational basis on which it might relate to any legitimate government interest.

b. Compelling Interest Test

1) Fundamental Rights
A law that inhibits some persons' exercise of a fundamental right must be necessary to promote a compelling state interest.

2) Suspect Traits
A classification based on a suspect trait must be necessary to promote a compelling interest.

c. Substantial Relation Test
Laws using classifications based on gender or legitimacy must be substantially related to important government objectives.

2. The Difference Between Substantive Due Process and Equal Protection
A law that limits the liberty of *all* persons to do something may violate substantive due process. A law that limits the liberty of only *some* persons may violate equal protection.

STUDY TIP ☞ Remember Judicial Review

Constitutional law is concerned primarily with the exercise of judicial review (see Chapter 3). The emphasis is on the way that courts in general, and the United States Supreme Court in particular, interpret provisions of the U.S. Constitution. *Stare decisis* (see Chapter 1) does not have as much impact in constitutional law as in other areas of the law. In this area, courts are not reluctant to overrule statutes, regulations, precedential case law, or other law.

TRUE-FALSE QUESTIONS (Answers at the Back of the Book)

____ 1. The federal government is superior to the state governments.

____ 2. The rights secured by the Bill of Rights are absolute.

____ 3. Under the constitutional system of checks and balances, the executive, legislative, and judicial branches of government may not exercise each other's authority, but each has some power to limit the actions of the others.

____ 4. The commerce clause has been interpreted to permit the federal government to legislate in areas in which there is no express grant of power to Congress.

____ 5. When there is a direct conflict between a federal law and a state law, the state law is valid, if concurrent federal and state powers are involved.

____ 6. If a tax law reasonably relates to revenue production, it is generally held to be within the federal taxing power.

____ 7. Under the First Amendment, governments may regulate the time, place, and manner of speech so long as they do not favor some ideas over others.

____ 8. Government inspectors do not have the right to enter business premises without a warrant, and the standard of probable cause to obtain the warrant is the same as in nonbusiness contexts.

____ 9. Both the Fifth and the Fourteenth Amendments include due process clauses.

FILL-IN QUESTIONS (Answers at the Back of the Book)

Police power is possessed by the _____ (federal government/ states). Police power refers to the right of the _____ (federal government/ states) to regulate private activities to protect or promote the public order, health, safety, morals, and general welfare. Building codes, licensing requirements, and many other _____ (federal/ state) statutes have been enacted under the police power. It is difficult to predict the outcome in a particular case, but _____ (federal/ state) laws enacted pursuant to police powers carry a strong presumption of _____ (validity/ invalidity).

MULTIPLE-CHOICE QUESTIONS (Answers at the Back of the Book)

____ 1. When conflicts arise concerning which government—federal or state—should be exercising power in a certain area, the United States Supreme Court resolves them by

   a. deciding in favor of the federal government.
   b. deciding in favor of the state governments.
   c. dividing power between federal and state governments as if they were partners.
   d. deciding which government is empowered to act under the Constitution.

____   **2.** The Bill of Rights embodies protections against various types of interference by the federal government. Most of these guarantees

a. apply to state governments, through the Civil Rights Act of 1964.
b. apply to state governments, through the Fourteenth Amendment.
c. do not apply to state governments, except as individual states apply them.
d. do not apply to state governments, through the Fourteenth Amendment.

____   **3.** Congress determines the jurisdiction of the federal courts

a. but the president can veto congressional legislation.
b. but the United States Supreme Court can hold acts of Congress unconstitutional.
c. both a and b.
d. neither a nor b.

____   **4.** As part of a tax audit, the Internal Revenue Service asks to see the business records of Investment Corporation. If Investment challenges the request to produce the records, Investment will

a. win, because the Fourth Amendment prohibits unreasonable searches and seizures.
b. win, because the Fifth Amendment guarantees that no person can be compelled to testify against himself or herself.
c. lose, because business records are an exception to the warrant requirement.
d. lose, because the Fifth Amendment privilege against self-incrimination is available only to natural persons, and a corporation is not a natural person.

____   **5.** A state statute prohibited the advertising of prices of prescription drugs by pharmacists as unprofessional. In a suit by a pharmacist challenging the statute, the pharmacist will

a. win, because commercial speech is protected under the First Amendment unless it concerns an unlawful activity or is misleading.
b. win, because commercial speech is protected under the First Amendment to the same extent as noncommercial speech.
c. lose, because the statute is a reasonable exercise of the state's police power.
d. lose, because commercial speech is not protected under the First Amendment.

____   **6.** The First Amendment, which requires that the government not establish any religion nor prohibit the free exercise of religious practices, means that

a. a law that does not promote or significantly burden a religion is constitutional.
b. a government must generally accommodate all religions.
c. a government must maintain neutrality toward religion.
d. all of the above.

____   **7.** If the content, or substance, of a law or other action limits the liberty of *all* persons in a way that is not compatible with the Constitution, it may be said to be a violation of

a. substantive due process.
b. procedural due process.
c. equal protection.
d. none of the above.

_____   8.   If the content, or substance, of a law or other action limits the liberty of *some* persons in a way that is not compatible with the Constitution, it may be said to be a violation of

    a.   substantive due process.
    b.   procedural due process.
    c.   equal protection.
    d.   none of the above.

SHORT ESSAY QUESTIONS

1.   Discuss the effect of the supremacy clause.

2.   Discuss the significance of the commerce clause.

ISSUE SPOTTERS (Answers at the Back of the Book)

1.   If a farmer grows wheat wholly for consumption by her family on her farm, which is a local operation, can Congress regulate that activity?

2.   Can a state, in the interest of energy conservation, ban all promotional advertising by electric utilities?

3.   There is a state statute disqualifying, for unemployment compensation, employees who are discharged for work-connected misconduct. Under this statute, would it violate the First Amendment to deny unemployment compensation to an employee who is discharged for using drugs for "sacramental purposes" during a religious ceremony?

4.   Would a state law imposing a fifteen-year term of imprisonment without allowing a trial on all businesspersons who appear in their own television commercials be constitutional?

5.   Can a state impose a higher tax on out-of-state companies doing business in the state than it imposes on in-state companies if the only reason for the tax is to protect the local firms from out-of-state competition?

 Key Points

The **key points** in this chapter include:

1. The basic functions of agencies—rulemaking, investigation and prosecution, and adjudication.

2. How agency authority is held in check.

3. Laws that make agencies more accountable through public scrutiny..

Chapter 6:
Administrative Law

WHAT THIS CHAPTER IS ABOUT

Federal, state, and local administrative agencies regulate virtually every aspect of a business's operation. Agencies' rules, orders, and decisions make up the body of administrative law. How agencies function is the subject of this chapter.

CHAPTER OUTLINE

I. **AGENCY CREATION AND POWERS**

To create an agency, Congress passes enabling legislation, which specifies the powers of the agency. Agency powers include functions associated with the legislature (rulemaking), the executive branch (investigation and prosecution), and the courts (adjudication).

II. **RULEMAKING**

The power an agency has to make rules is conferred in its enabling legislation. Generally, agencies have substantial control over their rulemaking agendas.

A. TYPES OF RULES

1. **Interpretative Rules**
Statements and opinions issued by an agency explaining how the agency interprets and intends to apply the statutes it enforces. They do not have the force of rules of law.

2. **Procedural Rules**
Describe an agency's methods of operation and establish procedures for dealings with the agency in and through hearings, negotiations, settlements, presentation of evidence, and other activities.

3. **Legislative Rules**
Carry the same weight as congressionally enacted statutes. The rule-making requirements discussed below apply only to these rules.

B. **TYPES OF RULEMAKING PROCEDURES**
The Administrative Procedure Act (APA) of 1946 imposes procedural requirements that agencies must follow.

1. **Informal Rulemaking**

   a. **Notice of Proposed Rulemaking**
   Agencies begin by publishing this notice in the *Federal Register*.

      1) **What the APA Requires the Notice to State**
      Time and place in which proceedings on a proposed rule will be held, the proposed rule or a description of its substance, nature of the proceedings, legal authority for the proceedings (usually the agency's enabling legislation) [APA 553(b)].

      2) **What Courts Require the Notice to State**
      Research data and methods on which the agency relied in establishing the rule.

   b. **Comment Period**
   Interested parties can express their views. The agency must respond to significant comments by modifying the final rule or explaining, in the statement accompanying the final rule, why it did not.

   c. **The Final Rule**
   The agency publishes the final rule in the *Federal Register*. The date of publication must precede the rule's effective date by at least thirty days. The final rule will have binding legal effect unless overturned by judicial review.

      1) **If a Final Rule Varies Too Substantially from a Proposed Rule**
      A court may order the agency to undertake another notice-and-comment proceeding.

      2) **The Rulemaking Record**
      Generally, an agency may adopt only a rule that has support in the rulemaking record (notice of proposed rulemaking, comments filed by the public, final rule, and relevant documents prepared by the agency). The agency cannot rely exclusively on *ex parte* communications.

2. **Formal Rulemaking**
Begins with publication of a notice of proposed rulemaking in the *Federal Register*. A public hearing is held. Proponents (including the agency) and opponents of the rule present evidence and question witnesses. After the hearing, the agency prepares a formal written statement of its findings.

3. **Hybrid Rulemaking**
Incorporates advantages of both formal and informal procedures. As with formal rulemaking, there is an opportunity for direct participation through a public hearing, but the right of interested parties to cross-examine witnesses is much more restricted.

4. **Negotiated Rulemaking**
The agency publishes in the *Federal Register* the subject and scope of the rule to be developed, the parties who will be significantly affected, and other information. Interested parties apply to be members of the committee that will negotiate the final rule. A neutral third party presides. Once the committee agrees on the rule, notice of it is published in the *Federal Register*, followed by a comment period.

III. ENFORCEMENT

Agency enforcement powers have two aspects: investigation and prosecution.

A. INVESTIGATION

Agencies must have knowledge of facts and circumstances pertinent to proposed rules. Agencies must also obtain information and investigate conduct to ascertain whether its rules are being violated.

1. **Investigative Tools**
With subpoenas, agencies compel witnesses to testify and compel individuals or organizations to hand over specified books, papers, records, or documents. Through on-site inspections and testing, agencies also gather information.

2. **Limitations on Investigative Powers**

   a. **Fourth Amendment**
   Protects against unreasonable searches and seizures by requiring that in most instances a physical search must be conducted under the authority of a search warrant.

   b. **Fifth Amendment**
   The privilege against self-incrimination is limited in this context—available only to the person asserting it; cannot be asserted on behalf of another individual or an organization.

   c. **APA 555(c)**
   Provides that an agency can exercise only such powers as have been delegated to it by Congress.

   d. **Information Must Be Relevant and Demands Must Be Specific**
   Information sought must be relevant to a legitimate purpose, and demands must be specific (in relation to the nature, purposes, and scope of the agency's inquiry) and not unreasonably burdensome.

B. PROSECUTION

An agency's decision to prosecute a violation of its rules may be prompted by its own investigation or by private individuals or interest groups. The agency may issue a formal complaint, to which the person or entity charged responds by filing an answer. At any stage, settlement negotiations may be held. Most complaints are resolved through settlement.

IV. ADJUDICATION

Involves the resolution of disputes through a hearing conducted by the agency.

A. HEARING PROCEDURES

A formal hearing resembles a trial (see Chapter 3), but more items and testimony are admissible in an administrative hearing than at a trial.

1. **Agency Discretion**

   Procedures vary widely from agency to agency. Agencies exercise substantial discretion over the type of procedures used.

2. **Administrative Law Judge (ALJ)**

   Presides over the hearing. An ALJ is a member of the agency prosecuting the case, but is separated from the investigative and prosecutorial staff. *Ex parte* communications between the ALJ and anyone who is party to an agency proceeding are prohibited.

B. AGENCY ORDERS

After a hearing, the ALJ issues an initial order (to pay damages; to cease and desist). Either side may appeal to a federal appeals court (some intermediate decisions are appealed to a federal district court). The commission that governs the agency may review the case. If there is no appeal or review, the initial order becomes final.

V. CONTROL OVER ADMINISTRATIVE AGENCIES

A. JUDICIAL REVIEW

In most cases, a court defers to the facts as found in an agency proceeding. A court will conduct a *de novo* review if (1) it is required by statute, (2) the agency used inadequate fact-finding proceedings, or (3) new facts are raised in a proceeding to enforce a nonadjudicatory action.

1. **Requirements for Judicial Review**

   (1) The action must be reviewable (under the APA, agency actions are presumed reviewable); (2) the challenger must have standing (see Chapter 3); (3) the challenger must have exhausted all administrative remedies; and (4) an actual controversy must be at issue (ripeness).

2. **Scope of Review**

   A court will review whether an agency has (1) exceeded its authority under its enabling legislation; (2) properly interpreted laws applicable to the action under review; (3) violated any constitutional provisions; (4) acted in accord with procedural requirements; (5) taken actions that are arbitrary, capricious, or an abuse of discretion; and (6) reached conclusions that are not supported by substantial evidence.

3. **Standards of Review**

   The APA provides for two standards of review—

   a. **Substantial Evidence Test**

      Applied in review of formal agency actions, such as hearings. Only findings not supported by substantial evidence are overturned.

   b. **Arbitrary and Capricious Test**

      Applied in review of informal agency actions. A court avoids substituting its judgment for that of the agency (which has more technical expertise), if the agency had an adequate factual basis.

B. EXECUTIVE CONTROLS

Most agencies are part of the executive branch (independent regulatory agencies are outside the major executive departments). The president may veto enabling legislation or subsequent modifications to agency authority that Congress seeks to enact. The president appoints and removes many federal officers, including those in charge of agencies.

C. **LEGISLATIVE CONTROLS**
Congress can give power to an agency, take it away, reduce or increase agency finances, or abolish the agency.

1. **Legislation**
Congress can require an agency to (1) make rules governing a certain area within a certain time or (2) engage in formal rulemaking. Under the APA, agencies must consider petitions promptly. If an agency denies a petitioner's request, it must give a reasonable explanation [APA 553(e)].

2. **Congressional Investigations and Casework**
Congress can investigate the implementation of its laws and the agencies that it creates. It may also affect policy through individual legislators' attempts to help their constituents deal with agencies.

VI.   PUBLIC ACCOUNTABILITY

A. **FREEDOM OF INFORMATION ACT (FOIA) OF 1966**
The federal government must disclose certain "records" to "any person" on request. A failure to comply may be challenged in federal district court.

B. **GOVERNMENT-IN-THE-SUNSHINE ACT OF 1976**
Requires (1) that "every portion of every meeting of an agency" that is headed by a "collegial body" is open to "public observation" and (2) procedures to ensure that the public is provided with adequate advance notice of meetings and agendas (with exceptions).

C. **REGULATORY FLEXIBILITY ACT OF 1980**
Whenever a new regulation will have a "significant impact upon a substantial number of small entities," the agency must conduct a regulatory flexibility analysis. The analysis must measure the cost imposed by the rule on small businesses and must consider less burdensome alternatives.

VII.   STATE ADMINISTRATIVE AGENCIES

A state agency often parallels a federal agency, providing similar services on a localized basis. The supremacy clause requires that the federal agency's operation prevail over an inconsistent state agency's action.

STUDY TIP 👉   <u>In the News</u>

Many legal principles, including much of the material in this chapter, are diffi cult to grasp in the abstract. Basic factual information is easier to understand. Basic fact situations can also make abstract principles easier to understand and remember, when the facts illustrate the principles. For this reason, you may find the material in this chapter more understandable by paying attention to current affairs and tracking their effects on the law. For example, watch for news articles about current business-related problems being dealt with by agencies.

TRUE-FALSE QUESTIONS (Answers at the Back of the Book)

_____ 1. To create an agency, Congress passes enabling legislation, which specifies the name, composition, and powers of the agency being created.

_____ 2. After an investigation, an agency, private citizen, or an organization may prosecute an administrative action against an individual or organization.

_____ 3. All four types of agency rulemaking procedures can result in binding rules, but only one procedure offers the public an opportunity to object to a proposed rule.

_____ 4. After an agency adjudication, and the ALJ issues an initial order, the order must be appealed to become final.

_____ 5. Because there must be congressional authorization for appropriation of funds to an agency, Congress's taxing and spending powers give it power to influence agency policy.

_____ 6. It is a defense to an agency action that a party believes an action to be unlawful.

_____ 7. Under the Regulatory Flexibility Act, when a new regulation will have a "significant impact" on a substantial number of small entities, an analysis must be conducted to measure the cost imposed by the rule on small businesses.

FILL-IN QUESTIONS (Answers at the Back of the Book)

Under the APA, _____ (formal/ informal) rulemaking, requires notice, opportunity for comment, and a _____ (formal, written statement describing its findings/ general statement of basis and purpose). The process begins with publication in the _____ (_Congressional Record/ Federal Register_) of a Notice of Proposed Rulemaking. A comment period allows private parties to comment _____ (in writing/ orally) before the agency drafts a final version. The final version _____ (must/ need not) be reproposed if it is considerably different from the original. The final version is published in the _____ (_Congressional Record/ Federal Register_), but is not binding for at least _____ (ten/ thirty) days unless there is good cause for its becoming effective sooner.

MULTIPLE-CHOICE QUESTIONS (Answers at the Back of the Book)

_____ 1. The Bureau of Indian Affairs (BIA) wants to close a series of its meetings to the public, fearing that expert witnesses will not testify candidly if the public attends. Susette, a member of the public, wants to attend the meetings. If Susette sues the BIA, under what law could the BIA be enjoined from closing the meetings?

    a. Freedom of Information Act
    b. Government-in-the-Sunshine Act
    c. Regulatory Flexibility Act
    d. Administrative Procedure Act

_____ 2. Agencies must obtain information concerning activities and organizations that they oversee. Which of the following is one of the ways that an agency obtains its information?

a. Compel disclosure through a subpoena or a search and seizure
b. Compel disclosure through coercive actions of local police
c. Receive information from public interest groups, disgruntled competitors, or dissatisfied consumers
d. Both a and c

_____ 3. In making rules, an agency must follow certain procedures. Concerning those procedures, which of the following is TRUE?

a. Informal rulemaking includes notice, opportunity for comment, and a general statement of basis and purpose.
b. Formal rulemaking applies only in special circumstances such as military matters or foreign affairs.
c. Negotiated rulemaking incorporates parts of formal and informal procedures—there is an opportunity for participation through a public hearing, for instance, but the right to cross-examine witnesses is more restricted.
d. Hybrid rulemaking includes notice, a public hearing conducted in the manner of a trial, and a formal, written statement in which the agency describes its findings.

_____ 4. The National Oceanic and Atmospheric Administration (NOAA) takes actions with which the president does not agree. Congress supports NOAA. Which of the following is the president authorized to do to check the authority of NOAA?

a. The president can abolish NOAA.
b. The president can take away NOAA's power.
c. The president can veto legislative modifications to NOAA's authority.
d. The president can refuse to appropriate funds to NOAA.

_____ 5. After a hearing, the United States Fish and Wildlife Service (USFWS) orders Gil to stop using a certain type of fishing net from Gil's fishing boat. Gil is angry, because he believes that the USFWS is trying to undercut his livelihood. Before a court will hear Gil's appeal of the order, Gil

a. must show the order to be reviewable, because the APA presumes otherwise.
b. must exhaust all other means of resolving the controversy with the USFWS.
c. need not show that he has standing to sue, because it is presumed that he does.
d. must show that the dispute constitutes an actual case or controversy, or that it is suitable for the court to issue an advisory opinion.

_____ 6. Through its basic functions, an administrative agency has flexibility and considerable power. Which of the following are those functions?

a. Rulemaking
b. Adjudication
c. Enforcement
d. All of the above

SHORT ESSAY QUESTIONS

1.   Discuss what is at the heart of much of the controversy surrounding the regulatory process.

2.   Describe general restraints on the arbitrariness of agency power.

ISSUE SPOTTERS (Answers at the Back of the Book)

1.   The Securities and Exchange Commission (SEC) makes rules regarding what disclosures must be made in a stock prospectus, prosecutes and adjudicates alleged violations, and prescribes punishment. This would seem to concentrate considerable power in the SEC's hands. What checks exist against this power?

2.   Administrative agencies—like the Securities and Exchange Commission, the Federal Trade Commission, and the Food and Drug Administration—make rules. There are three types of rules: legislative rules, which carry the same weight as statutes, and interpretative and procedural rules, which do not. To be valid, what must a legislative rule NOT do?

3.   Administrative agencies prosecute alleged offenders of agency rules in trial-like proceedings. An administrative law judge (ALJ) is a member of the agency that prosecutes the cases the ALJ hears. What safeguards promote an ALJ's fairness?

4.   Because an agency is believed to have expertise in its field, and because those to whom evidence is presented firsthand are believed more suited to judge its value, a court will defer to an agency's findings of fact, in most cases. Under what circumstances will a court make an independent finding of fact?

5.   Itex Corporation would like to know what information federal agencies have about Itex's business operations, so that Itex will know what its competitors may be able to learn about Itex. Under what federal law can Itex require the agencies to disclose whatever information they may have concerning Itex?

 **Key Points**

The **key points** in this chapter include:

1. Cultural differences among nations that can complicate efforts to do business abroad.

2. Differences between the common law and civil law legal systems.

3. Selected laws that highlight the legal environments in different nations.

4. The government of the European Union.

Chapter 7: Comparative Law

WHAT THIS CHAPTER IS ABOUT

This chapter compares the cultures and legal systems of various nations, as well as specific legal concepts and principles relating to contracts, torts, employment relationships, and other areas of the law. To conduct business successfully in a foreign nation requires a knowledge of that nation's culture and how that nation's laws will affect business activities.

CHAPTER OUTLINE

I. CULTURAL DIFFERENCES

A. COMMUNICATION
Language differences and different understandings of body movements, gestures, facial expressions, colors, and numbers can confound efforts to do business abroad. For example, advertising slogans translated word-for-word may be nonsense in other languages.

B. MANAGEMENT STYLE
American managers employ a direct, pragmatic, competitive style. Latin American managers are more humanistic and indirect. Asian managers also use techniques that are indirect and designed to avoid confrontation. Managers in Mediterranean nations deemphasize competition and are more family oriented than in the United States.

C. ETHICS

1. **Gift Giving and Bribery**

   In many countries, gift giving is common among companies or between companies and government. U.S. firms are prohibited from offering payments to foreign officials to secure favorable contracts (see Chapter 8). Payments to minor officials to, for example, facilitate paperwork are not prohibited.

2. **Women in Business**

   Some countries reject any role for women professionals. Others impose cultural restrictions. Because of these restrictions, many U.S. companies are reluctant to assign women to work overseas. Equal employment opportunity is a fundamental policy in the United States, however (see Chapter 21).

II.   COMPARATIVE LEGAL SYSTEMS

A. CONSTITUTIONAL FOUNDATIONS

The foundation of a country's legal system is its constitution. (The United Kingdom has no single document but refers to its constitution as a series of fundamental documents, including the Magna Carta and others.)

1. **Branches of Government**

   Most nations have several branches of government to exercise legislative, executive, and judicial powers.

2. **Division of Power**

   Some nations have federal systems, in which powers are divided between national and provincial governments. Others have centralized governments (unitary systems), with no independent local governments.

3. **Judicial Review**

   In the United States and in India, the courts can declare a law illegal if it violates their constitution (see Chapter 3). British courts do not have this power. In France, a special constitutional council can invalidate laws. In Germany, only a special court has this power.

4. **Commercial Law Courts**

   Some nations (France, United Kingdom) have specialized commercial law courts to deal with business disputes.

B. COMMON LAW AND CIVIL LAW SYSTEMS

Legal systems are generally divided into common law and civil law systems.

1. **Common Law Systems**

   Based on case law. Common law systems exist in countries that were once a part of the British Empire (such as Australia, India, the United States). The judges of different common law nations have produced differing common law principles. For example, the principles governing contracts differ in the United States and India.

2. **Civil Law Systems**

   Civil law systems are based on codified law (statutes). Courts interpret the code and apply the rules without developing their own laws.

> ### a. Places with Civil Law Systems
> Most European nations, as well as the Latin American, African, and Asian countries that were colonies of those nations; Japan; South Africa; Muslim countries; the state of Louisiana; Puerto Rico; Quebec; and Scotland.
>
> ### b. Differences Among Civil Law Systems
> The French code sets out general principles of law; the German code is more specific. In some Middle Eastern countries, the code is grounded in religious, Islamic directives, known as *shari'a*. This makes it difficult to change.

3. Similarities Between Common and Civil Law Systems
Much of the law in a common law system is statutory. In a civil law system, judges must develop some law because codes cannot address every issue.

C. JUDGES AND PROCEDURES
In all countries, the primary function of judges is the resolution of litigation.

1. Differences Among Judges
In the United States, a judge normally does not actively participate in a trial, but in many countries, judges are involved, such as by questioning witnesses. In the United States, a federal judge is less likely to be influenced by politics (he or she serves for life and cannot be removed by impeachment except in extreme cases). In India, judges ruling contrary to the prime minister have been transferred or demoted.

2. Differences Among Procedures
The procedures employed in resolving cases varies from country to country. For example, in Saudi Arabia, a defendant can "demand the oath"—swear before God that he did not do what he is charged with doing—and be released.

D. LAWYERS AND LITIGATION

1. Differences Regarding Lawyers

> ### a. Role of a Lawyer
> In the United States, an attorney is required by law to advocate his or her client's interests. In the People's Republic of China, lawyers must first further the interests of the government.
>
> ### b. Attitudes Towards Lawyers
> In some countries, the presence of lawyers and accountants on a businessperson's negotiating team implies deception.
>
> ### c. Numbers of Lawyers
> The United States may have more lawyers (as a percentage of the population) than any other country in the world (except Iceland), but comparisons are difficult, because there is no global definition of *lawyer*.

2. Differences Regarding Litigation
In some nations, such as Japan, citizens and businesses are less disposed to go to court than they are in the United States.

III.   COMPARATIVE LAWS

A.   CONTRACT LAW

1. **United Nations Convention for the International Sale of Goods (CISG)**
   Some contract law has been internationalized through the Convention for the International Sale of Goods, but parties can agree to apply other law to their contract disputes.

2. **Offer and Acceptance**
   In Germany, a written offer must be held open for a reasonable time, unless the offer states otherwise. Oral offers must be accepted immediately or they expire. In Mexico, if a time for acceptance is not stated in an offer, the offer is deemed to be held open for three days (plus whatever time is necessary for the mails).

3. **Consideration**
   In Germany, consideration is not required for a contract to be binding—agreements to make gifts may thus be enforceable by the recipient. In India, some contracts are lawful in the absence of consideration, such as promises in exchange for a past act.

4. **Unenforceable Contracts**
   In Saudi Arabia, contracts for goods forbidden in the Koran (alcohol, pork products) are unenforceable. In India, contracts may be invalidated if they are considered immoral or contrary to public policy. In China, some contracts require formal approval by the government; failure to obtain it will void the contract.

B.   TORT LAW

1. **Application of Tort Principles**
   In Germany, a person is normally not liable for failing to rescue someone in distress. Some nations provide explicit liability for negligent omissions.

2. **Damages**
   Swiss and Turkish courts reduce damages if an award of full damages would cause undue hardship to a party who was found negligent. In some nations of northern Africa, different amounts of damages are awarded depending on the type of tort.

3. **Statutes of Limitations**
   In Italy, a plaintiff must sue within five years of a tort's commission. The general French limitations period is ten years.

4. **Burden of Proof**
   In the United States, the burden of proof is on the plaintiff. In Russia, the defendant has the burden of proving that he or she was not at fault.

C.   EMPLOYMENT LAW

Under the employment-at-will doctrine (see Chapter 20), employers are free to hire and fire employees "at will"—that is, for any reason or no reason at all.

1. Reasons for Discharging Employees

Employers may fire employees without notice only for causes such as violence, imprisonment, excessive absenteeism, or lying on a job application (Taiwan), or if the worker commits a criminal offense, loses a license or other employment qualification, or seriously breaches his or her duties (Poland).

2. Discharge Procedures

In some countries, to discharge an employee for cause, an employer must first submit the proposed discharge to mediators (France) or a committee (Egypt).

D. INTELLECTUAL PROPERTY

Business depends on local protection of copyrights, patents, trademarks, and trade secrets.

1. Strong Protection

Japan and Brazil provide strong formal protection for patents, trademarks, and other forms of intellectual property. But the Japanese Patent Office is slow, and Brazil has little patent protection for chemical compounds or pharmaceuticals.

2. Moderate Protection

In Mexico, patent protection extends for twenty years but can be lost by lack of lack of use or by failure to pay annual fees. Trademark registration is denied if the mark has already been used in any country by another person.

3. Weak Protection

The Gulf Cooperation Council (formed in 1981 by Saudi Arabia, Kuwait, Bahrain, Qatar, the United Arab Emirates, and Oman) offers little intellectual property protection.

4. "Moral Rights"

Some European nations recognize "moral rights" in creative products. (Even if an artist has sold his or her copyright to a company, moral rights prevent the company from modifying the work, such as through colorization of a black-and-white film.)

E. CORPORATE LAW

1. Doing Business in a Foreign Country

A company cannot operate in Nigeria without incorporating there. In Argentina, a company may conduct business as an incorporated entity (a *sociedad anonima*, or S.A.), a partnership, a sole proprietorship, or a branch of a foreign corporation.

2. Limited-Liability Enterprises

The Nigerian Enterprises Promotion Act of 1977 provides for several classes of limited-liability enterprises. In Korea, the most common form of business firm is a large limited-liability company known as a *Chusik Hoesa*. A *Chusik Hoesa* must hire an auditor to examine its operations and to report to the shareholders.

F. GOVERNMENT REGULATION

1. **Price Controls**

Taiwan controls prices that can be charged for some basic goods. India regulates the prices of necessary goods, raw materials, and some intermediate products. In Mexico, the president can impose price controls, or place restraints on products to correct for surpluses or shortages.

2. **Antitrust Laws**

Taiwan's Fair Trade Law prevents harmful monopolies. India regulates any firm that has a market share in excess of 25 percent. Germany may block the acquisition or merger of a company with more than 20 percent of a major market segment.

3. **Environmental Laws**

German regulations are strict. Egypt has strict controls on herbicides and may impose severe penalties (such as plant closures) for violations.

4. **Consumer Protection**

German laws against unfair competition render legally ineffective any "fine print" in consumer contracts. In Egypt, private firms are generally not subject to consumer protection laws.

IV. **THE EUROPEAN UNION (EU)**

The EU consists of Belgium, France, Germany, Italy, the Netherlands, Luxembourg, Spain, the United Kingdom, Denmark, Greece, Ireland, and Portugal. Eastern European nations are applying for membership.

A. GOVERNING AUTHORITIES

The Council of Ministers coordinates economic policies. A commission proposes regulations to the Council and an elected assembly oversees the commission. The European Court of Justice can review each nation's court decisions and is the ultimate authority on EU law.

B. DIRECTIVES

The council and the commission issue regulations or directives that define EU law and are binding on member states. EU directives govern such issues as environmental law, antitrust law, corporate structure, and securities law.

STUDY TIP ☞ __Self-Discipline Is the Key__

To maximize efficiency when reviewing the material in this and the other chapters in this book, it is best to study—not merely read—the material. To study effectively, it is important to formulate a study program and to carry it through. A quick read can result in a familiarity with the general outline of the information, but there is no substitute for a good study program. Implementing a study program can produce a grasp and knowledge of the material that should result in a successful completion of this course. Self-discipline is key.

TRUE-FALSE QUESTIONS (Answers at the Back of the Book)

____ 1. U.S. firms are prohibited from offering payments to foreign officials to secure favorable contracts.

____ 2. U.S. companies doing business in countries that reject any role for women professionals can also reject any such role for women in the United States.

____ 3. The foundation of a country's legal system is its constitution.

____ 4. Legal systems are generally divided into criminal law and civil law systems.

____ 5. In all countries, the primary function of judges is the resolution of litigation.

____ 6. Because all contract law has been internationalized through the CISG, the parties to an international contract are subject to that law regardless of any desire to the contrary.

____ 7. Under the employment-at-will doctrine, employees are guaranteed employment for life.

____ 8. Businesses depend on international legal protection of copyrights, patents, trademarks, and trade secrets.

____ 9. In some countries, a firm cannot do business unless it is incorporated in that country.

FILL-IN QUESTIONS (Answers at the Back of the Book)

The European Community (EC) consists of Belgium, France, Germany, Italy, the Netherlands, Luxembourg, Spain, the United Kingdom, Denmark, Greece, Ireland, and Portugal. The _____ (Ghent Organization/Council of Ministers) coordinates economic policies. _____ (A commission/an elected assembly) proposes regulations to the _____ (Organization/Council). This _____ (commission/elected assembly) is overseen by _____ (a commission/an elected assembly). Regulations or directives issued by the _____ (Organization/Council) and _____ (commission/elected assembly) that define EC law and are _____ (binding/nonbinding) on member states. The _____ (Council of Ministers/European Court of Justice) can review each nation's court decisions and is the ultimate authority on EC law.

MULTIPLE-CHOICE QUESTIONS (Answers at the Back of the Book)

____ 1. In doing business internationally, a company should

a. ignore foreign political issues.
b. be sensitive to the economic and cultural differences between nations.
c. consider itself a representative of its home country.
d. do business no different than it would do business domestically.

____ 2. A nation that divides its governmental power between a national government and provincial governments has a system of government that is generally classified as

a. federal.
b. centralized.
c. unitary.
d. none of the above.

____ 3. In the United States and in India, courts have the power of judicial review. This means that the courts can

a. declare a law illegal if it violates their constitution.
b. review a law but cannot declare it illegal even if it violates their constitution.
c. recommend the invalidation of a law to a special constitutional council.
d. recommend the invalidation of a law to a special court.

____ 4. Common law systems

a. are based on codified law.
b. are based on case law.
c. have produced differing common law principles in different countries.
d. both b and c.

____ 5. Civil law systems

a. are based on codified law.
b. are based on case law.
c. require that courts apply the rules without developing their own laws.
d. both a and c.

____ 6. In the United States, a judge

a. normally actively participates in a trial.
b. normally does not actively participate in a trial.
c. is likely to be influenced by politics.
d. can be impeached, except in extreme cases.

____ 7. In the area of contract law

a. there are so few differences among nations that the law is for all practical purposes uniform.
b. some of the basic principles are similar among nations but some are very different.
c. there is an international law enforced by the United Nations that applies to all international contracts.
d. there are no basic principles that any two nations share.

____ 8. In the area of tort law, some countries

a. provide explicit liability for negligent omissions.
b. reduce damages if an award of full damages would cause undue hardship to a party who was found negligent.
c. provide a five-year statute of limitations.
d. all of the above.

SHORT ESSAY QUESTIONS

1. Discuss the efforts of the member countries of the European Union to become the "United States of Europe."

2. Discuss the most significant developments of the last decade that have created opportunities for businesses to expand internationally.

ISSUE SPOTTERS (Answers at the Back of the Book)

1. In a country in which gift giving is common among companies and between companies and the government, how much can an American firm "give" to secure a favorable contract without violating any U.S. laws?

2. How can language and nonverbal differences among cultures cause problems when doing business abroad? What are other cultural differences that could cause difficulties in doing business in another country?

3. France is one of the member nations of the European Union (EU). France has its own national law, but the EU also issues directives and regulations covering such matters as environmental law that apply to all of the EU members. Can a French court issue a decision on an EU regulation? If so, and a party disagrees with the ruling, can he or she appeal the case further?

4. If you were to do business outside the United States, what sort of government regulation in the area of price controls might you confront?

5. Under the employment-at-will doctrine, employers are free to hire and fire employees for any reason or no reason at all. What sort of restrictions are there on this doctrine in countries other than the United States?

Chapter 8:
International Law

WHAT THIS CHAPTER IS ABOUT

This chapter notes sources of international law, some of the ways in which U.S. businesspersons do business in foreign countries, and how that business is regulated.

CHAPTER OUTLINE

I. SOURCES OF INTERNATIONAL LAW

A. INTERNATIONAL CUSTOMS
Customs that have evolved among nations in their relations with one another. "[E]vidence of a general practice accepted as law" [Article 38(1) of the Statute of the International Court of Justice].

B. TREATIES AND INTERNATIONAL AGREEMENTS
A treaty is an agreement or contract between two or more nations that must be authorized and ratified by the supreme power of each nation. A bilateral agreement occurs when only two nations form an agreement; multilateral agreements are those formed by several nations.

C. INTERNATIONAL ORGANIZATIONS AND CONFERENCES
Composed mainly of nations; usually established by treaty; such entities adopt resolutions that require particular behavior of nations.

II. LEGAL PRINCIPLES AND DOCTRINES

A. PRINCIPLE OF COMITY
One nation defers and gives effect to the laws and judicial decrees of another country, so long as those laws and judicial decrees are consistent with the law and public policy of the accommodating nation.

B. ACT OF STATE DOCTRINE

A judicially created doctrine under which the judicial branch of one country will not examine the validity of public acts committed by a recognized foreign government within its own territory.

C. DOCTRINE OF SOVEREIGN IMMUNITY

Exempts foreign nations from the jurisdiction of the domestic courts. In the United States, the Foreign Sovereign Immunities Act (FSIA) of 1976 exclusively governs the circumstances in which an action may be brought against a foreign nation.

1. **When Is a Foreign State Subject to U.S. Jurisdiction?**

When the state has (1) waived its immunity expressly or impliedly, or (2) engaged in actions that are taken "in connection with a commercial activity carried on in the United States by the foreign state" that have "a direct effect in the United States" [Section 1605].

2. **What Entities Fall Within the Category of Foreign State?**

A political subdivision and an instrumentality (an agency or entity acting for the state) [Section 1603].

3. **What Are Commercial Activities?**

Courts decide whether an activity is governmental or commercial.

III. REGULATION OF SPECIFIC BUSINESS ACTIVITIES

A. INVESTING

When property is confiscated by a government without just compensation, few remedies are available. Many countries guarantee compensation to foreign investors in their constitutions, statutes, or treaties. Some countries provide insurance for their citizens' investments abroad.

B. EXPORT CONTROL

1. **Restricting Exports**

The U.S. Congress cannot tax exports, but may set export quotas. Under the Export Administration Act of 1979, restrictions can be imposed on the flow of technologically advanced products and technical data.

2. **Stimulating Exports**

Devices to stimulate exports include export incentives and subsidies.

C. IMPORT CONTROL

1. **Prohibitions and Quotas**

Laws prohibit, for example, the importation of illegal drugs, books that urge insurrection against the United States, and agricultural products that pose dangers to domestic crops or animals. Quotas limit the amounts of goods that can be imported.

2. **Tariffs**

Taxes on imports (usually a percentage of the value of the import, but can be a flat rate per unit). For example, a tariff may be assessed on imports to prevent dumping (the sale of imported goods at "less than fair value," usually determined by prices in the exporting country).

D. **GENERAL AGREEMENT ON TARIFFS AND TRADE (GATT)**
The principal instrument for regulating international trade (most of the world's leading trade nations are signatories). Each member country agrees to grant most-favored-nation status to other member countries (that is, to give them the most favorable treatment with regard to imports or exports).

E. **EUROPEAN UNION (EU)**
A regional trade association that minimizes trade barriers by eliminating financial, technical, and physical barriers that restrain trade between the sixteen member nations.

F. **NORTH AMERICAN FREE TRADE AGREEMENT (NAFTA)**
Created a regional trading unit consisting of Mexico, the United States, and Canada. The primary goal is to eliminate tariffs among those countries on substantially all goods over a period of fifteen to twenty years, while retaining tariffs on goods imported from other countries.

IV.   SELECTED U.S. LAWS IN A GLOBAL CONTEXT

A. **U.S. ANTITRUST LAWS**
For U.S. courts to exercise jurisdiction over a foreign entity under U.S. antitrust laws, a violation must (1) have a "direct, substantial, and reasonably foreseeable effect" effect on U.S. commerce or (2) constitute a *per se* violation (see Chapters 26 and 27). Foreign governments and persons can also sue U.S. firms and persons for antitrust violations.

B. **PATENT LAWS**
U.S. patent laws (see Chapter 15) provide no direct protection overseas. To be protected in another country, an invention must be patented under the laws of that country. Internationally, the Paris Convention guarantees nondiscriminatory treatment under the laws of other nations, but it does not provide independent international patent protection.

C. **DISCRIMINATION LAWS**
U.S. employers must abide by U.S. employment discrimination laws (see Chapter 21) unless to do so would violate the laws of the country in which their workplace is located.

V.   RESOLVING INTERNATIONAL CONTRACT DISPUTES

A. **ARBITRATION**
Arbitration clauses (see Chapter 4) are often in international contracts.

1. **The Arbitrator**
May be a neutral entity, a panel of individuals representing both parties' interests, or another group.

2. **Enforcement of Arbitration Clauses**
The United Nations Convention on the Recognition and Enforcement of Foreign Arbitral Awards assists in the enforcement of arbitration clauses, as do provisions in specific treaties between nations.

B. **LITIGATION**
Litigation may be subject to forum-selection and choice-of-law clauses. If no forum and law are specified, litigation may be complex and uncertain (held simultaneously in two countries, for example, without regard of one for the other; a judgment may not be enforced).

VI. BRIBING FOREIGN OFFICIALS

The Foreign Corrupt Practices Act (FCPA) of 1977 applies to—

A. U.S. COMPANIES

Including their directors, officers, shareholders, employees, and agents.

1. What Is Prohibited

Bribery of most foreign government officials if the purpose is to get an official to act in his or her official capacity to provide business opportunities.

2. What Is Permitted

Payments to (1) minor officials whose duties are ministerial, (2) foreign officials if such payments are lawful within the foreign country, or (3) private foreign companies or other third parties unless the U.S. firm knows that the payments will be passed on to a foreign government.

B. ACCOUNTANTS

1. What Is Required

All companies must (1) keep detailed records that "accurately and fairly" reflect the company's financial activities and (2) have an accounting system that provides "reasonable assurance" that all transactions entered into by the company are accounted for and legal.

2. What Is Prohibited

Making false statements to accountants or false entries in any record or account.

C. PENALTIES

Firms may be fined up to $2 million. Officers or directors may be fined up to $100,000 (the fine cannot be paid by the company) and be imprisoned for up to five years.

STUDY TIP 👉 <u>Checking Your Knowledge</u>

A good way to determine if you are prepared to be tested on the material that you are going to be held responsible for is to orally explain each topic to a friend or a classmate. If you can put into words what you are supposed to know, you can most likely respond to your professor's questions to the professor's satisfaction. Another good way to check your knowledge is to write a short essay on the topic.

TRUE-FALSE QUESTIONS (Answers at the Back of the Book)

____   1. To facilitate international trade and commerce, sovereign nations can voluntarily agree to be governed in certain respects by international law.

____   2. The act of state doctrine and the doctrine of sovereign immunity tend to subject foreign nations to the jurisdiction of U.S. courts.

____   3. The Foreign Sovereign Immunities Act sets forth the major exceptions to the jurisdictional immunity of the United States.

____   4. Each member of the General Agreement on Tariffs and Trade must treat every other member as well as it treats a country that receives its most favorable treatment with regard to imports or exports.

____   5. Under the Foreign Corrupt Practices Act, accountants who make false entries in any record or account may be fined up to $10,000.

____   6. When unfair methods are involved in U.S. export trade with foreign countries, the Sherman Act may not apply.

FILL-IN QUESTIONS (Answers at the Back of the Book)

_____ (A confiscation/ An expropriation) occurs when a national government seizes a privately owned business or privately owned goods for a proper public purpose. _____ (A confiscation/ An expropriation) occurs when the taking is made for an illegal purpose. When _____ (a confiscation/ an expropriation) occurs, the government pays just compensation. When _____ (a confiscation/ an expropriation) occurs, the government does not pay just compensation.

MULTIPLE-CHOICE QUESTIONS (Answers at the Back of the Book)

____   1. A cartel of foreign manufacturers organize to control the price for portable compact disk players, hand-held video cameras, and similar compact electronic products in the United States. Liberty Company, a U.S. firm, joins the cartel. If the cartel has a substantial restraining effect on U.S. commerce, which of the parties may be sued for violation of U.S. antitrust laws?

a. Only the foreign manufacturers
b. Both the foreign manufacturers and Liberty
c. Only Liberty
d. Neither the foreign manufacturers nor Liberty

____   2. The Foreign Corrupt Practices Act prohibits bribery

a. to all foreigners.
b. to foreign officials to influence official acts.
c. by corporations only.
d. by foreign officials to U.S. corporations.

____   3.   Fairweather, a country near the Canary Islands, issues bonds to finance the construction of an international airport. Fairweather sells some of the bonds in the United States to Beryl. When a local terrorist group destroys the airport, Fairweather refuses to pay interest or principal on the bonds. Beryl files suit in a U.S court. The court will hear the suit, if

a.   Fairweather falls within the definition of a foreign state and selling bonds is a commercial activity under the Foreign Sovereign Immunities Act.

b.   Fairweather in effect confiscated Beryl's funds by refusing to pay interest or principal on the bonds.

c.   Fairweather in effect expropriated Beryl's funds by refusing to pay interest or principal on the bonds.

d.   the principle of international commercial relations requires that the court hear the suit.

____   4.   The petroleum industry of the country of Erebus is government-run. To install a communications system, Erebus accepts bids from U.S. firms, including Guiterrez & Sons, Inc., and Clapper Corporation. When Erebus grants the contract to Guiterrez, Clapper objects, on grounds that the sole shareholder of Guiterrez is the brother of the wife of Erebus's minister of commerce. If Clapper sues Guiterrez in a U.S. court, Clapper will

a.   win, because the principle of international commercial relations requires that a U.S. court declare the contract illegal.

b.   win, because the act of state doctrine requires that a U.S. court declare the contract illegal.

c.   lose, because the act of state doctrine prevents a U.S. court from declaring the contract illegal.

d.   lose, because the principle of international commercial relations prevents a U.S. court from declaring the contract illegal.

____   5.   Sources of international law include

a.   international corporate charters, articles of incorporation, and bylaws.

b.   international religious organizations' interpretations of religious doctrine.

c.   international customs that have evolved among nations.

d.   all of the above.

____   6.   Read, Inc., employs U.S. citizens in positions in foreign countries. In Islamic countries, religious and social customs sometimes undermine American women's effectiveness in doing their jobs. Nicole, an American woman, works for Read in Zena, an Islamic country. She believes that Zena's "customs" to which she is subjected on the job by male Zena citizens who are employed by Read constitute harassment under Title VII of the U.S. Civil Rights Act. If Nicole sues Read under Title VII, Nicole will

a.   win, because Title VII applies extraterritorially.

b.   win, because, although Title VII does not apply extraterritorially, Title VII applies to Read, because Read is not an foreign corporation.

c.   lose, because, although Title VII applies extraterritorially, Zena's customs do not constitute a violation.

d.   lose, because Title VII does not apply extraterritorially.

SHORT ESSAY QUESTIONS

1. What are the sources of international law?

2. Discuss how Congress has tried to reduce the practice of bribing foreign officials.

ISSUE SPOTTERS (Answers at the Back of the Book)

1. South Newland, a country near North Newland, agrees to abide by tariff reductions negotiated under the international General Agreement on Tariffs and Trade (GATT). Later, South Newland decides to increase its tariffs beyond what it agreed to do under the GATT. What can other countries do to enforce the GATT against South Newland?

2. Treaties and other explicit agreements between or among foreign nations represent an important source of international law. A treaty is an agreement or contract between two or more nations that must be authorized and ratified by each nation. Who in the United States has the power to make treaties?

3. Cordillera Roja, Ltd., a Columbian firm, agrees to sell coffee beans to Barnaby Coffee Corporation, an American company. Barnaby accepts the beans, but refuses to pay Cordillera. Cordillera sues Barnaby in a Columbian court and is awarded damages, but Barnaby's assets are in the United States and cannot be reached unless the Columbian court's judgment is enforced in a U.S. court. Under what circumstances would a U.S. court enforce a foreign court judgment?

4. Exporting involves selling products manufactured in one country to buyers in other countries. Because the Constitution prohibits taxes on U.S. exports, Congress cannot impose any export taxes. There are other devices that Congress may use to control exports. What are some of the devices that Congress may use to restrict or bolster exports?

5. Demetrio Corporation and Conakry Coffeemakers, Inc. are U.S. firms Demetrio patents in the United States a unique type of coffeemaker that is designed for use in restaurants and in other commercial settings. Conakry begins selling a nearly identical coffeemaker abroad. Can Demetrio obtain an injunction against Conakry, on grounds that Conakry's sales violate U.S. patent law?

 Key Points

The **key points** in this chapter include:

1. The objective theory of contracts.

2. The requirements of an offer.

3. The difference between mistakes as to value and their effect on contracts.

4. Contracts that must be in writing to be enforceable.

5. Assignments and delegations.

Chapter 9:
Contracts: Part I

WHAT THIS CHAPTER IS ABOUT

Contract law is concerned with the formation and keeping of promises, the excuses our society accepts for breaking such promises, and what promises are considered to be contrary to public policy and therefore legally void. This chapter provides an introduction to many of the terms and concepts of contract law.

CHAPTER OUTLINE

I. BASIC REQUIREMENTS OF A CONTRACT
(1) Agreement, (2) consideration, (3) contractual capacity, and (4) legality (all four are outlined below).

II. THE OBJECTIVE THEORY OF CONTRACTS
Intention to enter into a contract is judged by objective facts as interpreted by a reasonable person, rather than by a party's subjective intention. Objective facts include (1) what the party said when entering into the contract, (2) how the party acted or appeared, and (3) the circumstances surrounding the transaction.

III. TYPES OF CONTRACTS

A. BILATERAL VERSUS UNILATERAL CONTRACTS
Bilateral contract—a promise for a promise (to accept the offer, the offeree need only promise to perform). **Unilateral contract**—a promise for an act (the offeree can accept only by completing performance).

B. EXPRESS VERSUS IMPLIED CONTRACTS
Express contract—the terms of the agreement are fully and explicitly stated in words (oral or written). **Implied contract**—implied from the conduct of the parties.

C. QUASI CONTRACTS—CONTRACTS IMPLIED IN LAW
In the absence of an actual contract, a quasi contract is imposed by a court to avoid the unjust enrichment of one party at the expense of another (under the doctrine of *quantum meruit*—"as much as he deserves").

D. EXECUTED VERSUS EXECUTORY CONTRACTS
Executed contract—a contract that has been fully performed on both sides. **Executory contract**—a contract that has not been fully performed by one or more of the parties.

E. VALID, VOID, VOIDABLE, AND UNENFORCEABLE CONTRACTS
Valid contract—has all elements necessary to entitle at least one party to enforce it. **Void contract**—produces no legal obligations on the part of any of the parties. **Voidable contract**—valid contract that can be avoided by one or more of the parties. **Unenforceable contract**—contract that cannot be enforced because of certain legal defenses.

IV. MUTUAL ASSENT

A. REQUIREMENTS OF THE OFFER
An offer is a promise or commitment to do or refrain from doing some specified thing in the future. The elements for an offer to be effective are—

1. **Intention**
The offeror must intend to be bound by the offer. Intent is determined by what a reasonable person in the offeree's position would conclude the offeror's words and actions meant.

   a. **Nonoffers**
   Nonoffers include: (1) expressions of opinion, (2) statements of intention, (3) preliminary negotiations, and (4) advertisements, catalogues, price lists, and circulars.

   b. **Agreements to Agree**
   Agreements to agree to a material term of a contract at some future date may be enforced if the parties clearly intended to be bound.

2. **Definiteness**
All major terms must be stated with reasonable definiteness in the offer (or, if the offeror directs, in the offeree's acceptance). Courts are sometimes willing to supply a missing term when the parties have clearly manifested an intent to form a contract.

3. **Communication**
The offer must be communicated to the offeree.

B. TERMINATION OF THE OFFER

1. **Termination by Action of the Parties**

   a. **Revocation of the Offer by the Offeror**
   The offeror can revoke an offer by express repudiation or by performance of acts that are inconsistent with the offer and that are

made known to the offeree. A revocation becomes effective when the offeree or offeree's agent actually receives it.

b. Irrevocable Offers

1) Option Contract
A promise to hold an offer open for a specified period of time (if no time is specified, a reasonable time is implied).

2) Detrimental Reliance
An offer may be irrevocable if the offeree justifiably relies on it to his or her detriment. Many courts will not allow an offeror to revoke an offer after the offeree has performed some substantial part of his or her duties under a unilateral contract.

c. Rejection of the Offer by the Offeree
An offer may be rejected by the offeree by words or conduct evidencing an intent not to accept the offer. Asking about an offer is not rejecting it. Rejection is effective only when it is received by the offeror or the offeror's agent.

d. Counteroffer by the Offeree
The offeree's attempt to include different terms is a rejection of the original offer and a simultaneous making of a new offer. The **mirror image rule** requires the acceptance to match the offer exactly.

2. Termination by Operation of Law
An offer terminates automatically when the time specified in the offer has passed (if no time is specified, a reasonable time is implied).

C. ACCEPTANCE
The offeree must accept the offer unequivocally.

1. Silence as Acceptance
Occurs if (1) an offeree receives the benefit of offered services even though he or she had an opportunity to reject them and knew that they were offered with the expectation of compensation, or (2) the offeree had prior dealings with the offeror that led the offeror to understand that silence will constitute acceptance.

2. Communication of Acceptance
A bilateral contract is formed when acceptance is communicated. In a unilateral contract, communication is unnecessary, unless the offeror requests notice or has no adequate means of determining if the act has been performed, or the law requires notice.

V.   CONSIDERATION
Consideration is the value given in return for a promise.

A. ELEMENTS OF CONSIDERATION

1. A Bargained-for Exchange
The promise must induce the value, and the value must induce the promise. Situations that lack this element include moral obligations and "past" consideration (promises made with respect to events that have already taken place are unenforceable).

2. **Something of Legal Value**
Must be given in exchange for a promise. It may be a return promise. If it is performance, it may be (1) an act (other than a promise); (2) a forbearance (refraining from action); or (3) the creation, modification, or destruction of a legal relation.

a. **Adequacy of Consideration**
Generally, a court will not evaluate the adequacy of consideration (the fairness of a bargain), unless it is so grossly inadequate as to "shock the conscience" of the court.

b. **Preexisting Duty Rule**
A promise to do what one already has a legal duty to do does not constitute consideration.

B. **DETRIMENTAL RELIANCE, OR PROMISSORY ESTOPPEL**
In some states, a promisor cannot assert a lack of consideration as a defense if (1) a promise given by one party induces another party to rely (justifiably) on that promise to his or her detriment, and (2) the promisor knew or had reason to believe that the promisee would likely be induced to change position (in a substantial way).

VI. CAPACITY

Persons who are minors, intoxicated, or mentally incompetent but not yet adjudicated officially as such, have capacity to enter into a contract; but they can normally avoid liability under the contract.

VII. GENUINENESS OF ASSENT

A. **MISTAKES**

1. **Unilateral Mistakes**
A unilateral mistake (as to a material fact) does not afford a mistaken party relief. Exceptions: (1) if the other party knows or should have known of the mistake or (2) if the mistake was due to a mathematical error and was done inadvertently and without gross negligence.

2. **Mutual Mistakes**
When both parties make a mistake as to a material fact, the contract can be rescinded by either party. The same rule applies if the parties attach materially different meanings to a word or term in the contract that may be subject to more than one reasonable interpretation. A mistake as to value will almost never justify voiding a contract.

B. **FRAUDULENT MISREPRESENTATION**
If an innocent party is fraudulently induced to enter into a contract, the contract normally can be avoided. Fraud consists of: (1) misrepresentation of a material fact, (2) an intent to deceive, and (3) the innocent party's justifiable reliance on the misrepresentation. To collect damages, a party must also have suffered an injury.

C. **NONFRAUDULENT MISREPRESENTATION**
If a person misrepresents a material fact without the intent to defraud (he or she believes the statement to be true), the person may be guilty of innocent or negligent misrepresentation. The party who relied on the statement to his or her detriment can rescind the contract.

D. **Undue Influence**

Occurs when a contract enriches a party at the expense of another who is dominated by the enriched party. The contract is voidable. The essential feature is that the party taken advantage of does not exercise free will.

E. **Duress**

Duress involves forcing a party to enter into a contract by threatening the party with a wrongful act. The threatened act must be wrongful or illegal.

F. **Adhesion Contracts and Unconscionability**

To avoid a contract, an adhering party must show that the parties had substantially unequal bargaining positions and that enforcement would be unfair or oppressive.

VIII. LEGALITY

To be enforceable, a contract must not violate any statutes or public policy.

IX. STATUTE OF FRAUDS

The Statute of Frauds stipulates what types of contracts must be in writing to be enforceable. If a contract is not in writing, it is not void but the Statute of Frauds is a defense to its enforcement.

A. **Contracts That Must Be in Writing to Be Enforceable**

Contracts involving interests in land, contracts that cannot be performed within one year of formation, collateral promises, promises made in consideration of marriage, contracts for sales of goods priced at $500 or more.

B. **Exceptions**

An oral contract may be enforced if (1) a promisor makes a promise on which the promisee justifiably relies to his or her detriment, (2) the reliance was foreseeable to the promisor, and (3) injustice can be avoided only by enforcing the promise.

X. THIRD PARTY RIGHTS

A. **Assignments**

The transfer of a contract right to a third person is an assignment. No consideration is necessary, but if an assignment was made for consideration, the assignor normally cannot revoke it.

1. **Rights That Cannot Be Assigned**

Rights cannot be assigned if a statute prohibits assignment, a contract is personal (unless all that remains is a money payment), the assignment materially increases or alters the risk or duties of the obligor, or the contract provides that it cannot be assigned.

2. **Exceptions**

A contract cannot prevent an assignment of (1) a right to receive money, (2) rights in real property, (3) rights in negotiable instruments (checks and notes), or (4) a right to receive damages for breach of a sales contract or for payment of an amount owed under the contract (even if the contract prohibits it).

B. **Delegations**

Duties are not assigned; they are delegated. A delegation does not relieve the delegator of the obligation to perform if the delegatee fails to perform.

1. **Duties That Cannot Be Delegated**

   Any duty can be delegated unless (1) performance depends on the personal skill or talents of the obligor, (2) special trust has been placed in the obligor, (3) performance by a third party will vary materially from that expected by the obligee, or (4) the contract prohibits it.

2. **Effect of a Delegation**

   The obligee must accept performance from the delegatee, unless the duty is one that cannot be delegated. If the delegatee fails to perform, the delegator is still liable.

C. **THIRD PARTY BENEFICIARIES**

   There are two types of third party beneficiaries: intended and incidental. An intended beneficiary is one for whose benefit a contract is made; if the contract is breached, he or she can sue the promisor. The benefit that an incidental beneficiary receives from a contract between other parties is unintentional; an incidental beneficiary cannot enforce the contract.

STUDY TIP ☞   <u>MY LEG</u>

Contracts that must be in writing to be enforceable under the Statute of Frauds include: (1) promises made in consideration of *marriage* ; (2) contracts that cannot by their terms be performed within one *year* from the date of formation; (3) con tracts involving interests in *land* ; (4) collateral contracts, including promises by an *executor* or administrator of an estate personally to pay a debt of the estate and promises to answer for the debt or duty of another; and (5) under the UCC, contracts for the sale of *goods* priced at $500 or more. These contracts can be remembered in shorthand as Marriage, Year, Land, Executor's promise, and Goods, which can be represented by the mnemonic **MY LEG**.

TRUE-FALSE QUESTIONS (Answers at the Back of the Book)

____ 1. An agreement includes an offer and acceptance—one party must offer to enter into an agreement, and the party must accept the terms of the offer.

____ 2. The seriousness of an offeror's intent is determined by what a reasonable person in the offeree's position would conclude the offeror's words and actions meant.

____ 3. Ordinarily, courts evaluate the adequacy of consideration, as well as its legal sufficiency.

____ 4. With exceptions, minors have the right to disaffirm their contracts, and an adult who enters into a contract with a minor can also avoid contractual duties even if the minor does not disaffirm the contract.

____ 5. To commit nonfraudulent misrepresentation, one party must intend to mislead another.

____ 6. An adhesion contract is a contract that is subject to hard bargaining.

FILL-IN QUESTIONS (Answers at the Back of the Book)

Whether or not a party intended to enter into a contract is determined by the _____ (objective/ subjective) theory of contracts. The theory is that a party's intention to enter into a contract is judged by _____ (objective/ subjective) facts as they would be interpreted by a reasonable person. A party's _____ (objective/ subjective) intentions are not at issue. _____ (Objective/ Subjective) facts include: (1) what the party said; (2) what the party _____ (did/ secretly believed); and (3) the _____ (circumstances surrounding/ party's personal thoughts concerning) the transaction.

MULTIPLE-CHOICE QUESTIONS (Answers at the Back of the Book)

____ 1. Before opening her new sporting goods store, Liza places an ad in the newspaper showing tennis shoes at certain prices. Within hours of opening for business, the store is sold out of some of the shoes. Gina arrives later and is angry that a specific shoe is sold out. If Gina sues Liza, Liza will

   a. win, because Liza's ad was only an invitation seeking offers.
   b. win, because anyone who offered money for the shoes was entitled to buy.
   c. lose, because Liza's ad was an offer that Gina accepted.
   d. lose, because anyone who offered money for the shoes was entitled to buy.

____ 2. Ritten Corporation offers employees $50 for any suggestion put into practice. On March 1, Mei-Ling makes a suggestion. On March 15, Ritten decides to increase the amount to $100 on April 1 without an advance announcement. On March 31, Mei-Ling's suggestion is put into practice, and Mei-Ling is paid $50. On April 1, Ritten raises the amount for suggestions put into use to $100. Is Mei-Ling entitled to an additional $50?

   a. Yes, because before Mei-Ling's suggestion was used, Ritten decided to increase the amount.
   b. Yes, because Mei-Ling's suggestion was in practice when Ritten increased the amount.
   c. No, because the new offer had not been communicated to Mei-Ling when she made her suggestion.
   d. No, because the new offer had not been communicated to Mei-Ling when she was paid $50.

____ 3. Hazzard Chemical Corporation stores chemicals at its plants. Some of the chemicals are hazardous and have been declared illegal. In shutting down one of the plants, Hazzard attempts to sell the chemicals. Ohio Steel Company signs a contract to buy some of the chemicals, but later refuses to accept delivery. If Hazzard sues, the court will

   a. enforce the entire contract.
   b. order Ohio Steel to pay for the chemicals, but refuse to order Hazzard to deliver.
   c. order Hazzard to deliver the chemicals, but refuse to order Ohio Steel to pay.
   d. refuse to enforce the entire contract.

____ 4. Bernaise has a right to $100 against Hollandaise. Bernaise assigns her right to Tabasco. Bernaise is the assignor, Hollandaise is the obligor, and Tabasco is the assignee. Tabasco has

    a. the right to demand performance from Hollandaise, because a right to the payment of money is assignable.
    b. the right to demand performance from Hollandaise, because the $100 was consideration for the assignment.
    c. no right to demand performance from Hollandaise, because there was no consideration for the assignment.
    d. no right to demand performance from Hollandaise, because a right to the payment of money is not assignable.

____ 5. Metro Transport asks six contractors to submit bids on a construction project. Metro Transport estimates that the cost will be $200,000, and five of the bids are between $200,000 and $250,000, but Richmond Construction's bid is $150,000. In totaling a column of figures, Richmond inadvertently omitted a $50,000 item. If it is determined that Metro Transport had reason to know of Richmond's mistake

    a. all bids must be recalculated and resubmitted.
    b. there is an enforceable contract between Metro Transport and Richmond Construction, and Richmond cannot alter the price.
    c. there is an enforceable contract between Metro Transport and Richmond Construction, but Richmond can increase the price.
    d. the contract is voidable by Richmond.

____ 6. To induce Flannery to buy amplifiers for her theaters, Dick, the president of Stat Sound Systems, Inc., writes a letter describing the amplifiers' output as "120 watts per channel." Dick's secretary mistypes the description as "210 watts per channel." Flannery buys the amplifiers. The misrepresentation is innocent. Which of the following statements is TRUE?

    a. Flannery cannot avoid the contract.
    b. Flannery can avoid the contract, if the misrepresentation is material.
    c. Flannery can avoid the contract, regardless of whether the misrepresentation is material.
    d. Flannery cannot enforce the contract.

SHORT ESSAY QUESTIONS

1. List and define the basic elements of a contract.

2. Discuss "non-offers."

ISSUE SPOTTERS (Answers at the Back of the Book)

1. Shorty signed and returned a letter from Buck referring to a certain saddle and its price. When Buck delivered the saddle, Shorty sent it back, claiming that they had no contract. Buck claimed that they did have a contract and sued. How will the court rule?

2. Cortland, an employee of Fidelity Corporation, gives a month's notice to quit. Fidelity offers Cortland's job to Brook, giving Brook a week to decide whether to

accept. Two days later, Cortland changes his mind and signs a new contract with Fidelity. The next day, Cortland tells Brook about the new contract. Brook quickly sends a letter of acceptance to Fidelity, who receives it before the end of the week. Do Fidelity and Brook have a contract?

3.   Before Manuela starts college, Don promises to give her $5,000 if she graduates. At the beginning of Manuela's senior year, she reminds Don of the promise. Don writes her a short note that says, "I revoke the promise." Is Don's promise binding?

4.   Michael, a famous and wealthy musician, dies in an swimming pool accident. His will states that all his property is to go to his wife Jessy. Jessy sells Michael's Virginia farm to Carlton, who asks what should be done with all the "junk" on the property. Jessy says that Carlton can do whatever he wants with it. Unknown to Jessy or Carlton, in the farmhouse are the master tapes for an unreleased album. Can Carlton keep the tapes?

5.   Remy and Brandt agree to go into the house painting business together as Rem, Brandt & Company. They agree, however, that the business is not to be begun unless they can raise $10,000 in capital to buy supplies, including an old truck. The raising of the capital is a *condition* of the duties of Remy and Brandt. What does this mean?

Chapter 10:
Contracts: Part II

WHAT THIS CHAPTER IS ABOUT

This chapter begins with a discussion of performance and discharge of contracts. Performance of a contract discharges it. Discharging a contract terminates it. Breach of contract is the failure to perform what a party is under a duty to perform. When this happens, the nonbreaching party can choose one or more remedies.

CHAPTER OUTLINE

I. PERFORMANCE AND DISCHARGE

A. CONDITIONS
If performance is contingent on a condition and the condition is not satisfied, the obligations of the parties are discharged.

B. DISCHARGE BY PERFORMANCE
Most contracts are discharged by the parties' doing what they promised.

1. Tender of Performance
Discharge can be accomplished by an unconditional offer to perform by one who is ready, willing, and able to do so. If the other party then refuses to perform, the party making the tender can sue for breach.

2. Degree of Performance Required

a. Complete Performance
Express conditions fully occur in all aspects. Any deviation operates as a discharge.

b. **Substantial Performance**
Performance that does not vary greatly from the performance promised in the contract. The other party is obligated to perform (but may obtain damages for the deviations).

 3. **Breach of Contract**
A breach of contract is the nonperformance of a contractual duty. A breach is material when performance is not at least substantial; the nonbreaching party is excused from performing. If a breach is minor, the nonbreaching party's duty to perform may be suspended.

4. **Time for Performance**
If a specific time is stated, the parties must perform by that time. If no time is stated, a reasonable time is implied. If time is construed to be "of the essence," a deadline must be complied with. Otherwise, a delay will not destroy the performing party's right to payment.

C. **DISCHARGE BY AGREEMENT**

1. **Discharge by Rescission**
Rescission is the process by which a contract is canceled and the parties are returned to the positions they occupied prior to forming it.

2. **Discharge by Novation or Substituted Agreement**

a. **Novation**
Occurs when the parties to a contract and a new party get together and agree to substitute the new party for one of the original parties.

b. **Substitution of a New Contract Between the Same Parties**

3. **Discharge by Accord and Satisfaction**
The parties agree to accept performance that is different from the performance originally promised.

D. **DISCHARGE BY OPERATION OF LAW**

1. **Alteration of the Contract**
An innocent party can treat a contract as discharged if the other party materially alters a term (such as quantity or price) without consent.

2. **Statutes of Limitations**
Statutes of limitations limit the period during which a party can sue based on a breach of contract. (2 years, cant be 2 years and a day!)

3. **Bankruptcy**
A discharge in bankruptcy (see Chapter 16) will ordinarily bar enforcement of most of a debtor's contracts.

4. **Discharge by Impossibility or Impracticability**

a. **Impossibility of Performance**
A contract may be discharged if, after it is made, performance becomes objectively impossible (death or incapacity of one of the parties, specific subject matter of the contract is destroyed, or change in the law that renders performance illegal.)

   b. **Commercial Impracticability**
   Performance may be excused if it becomes much more difficult or expensive than contemplated when the contract was formed.

   c. **Frustration of Purpose**
   A contract will be discharged if supervening circumstances make it impossible to attain the purpose the parties had in mind.

   d. **Temporary Impossibility**
   An event that makes it temporarily impossible to perform will suspend performance until the impossibility ceases.

II.   BREACH OF CONTRACT AND REMEDIES

A. **DAMAGES**
   Damages compensate a nonbreaching party for the loss of a bargain and, under special circumstances, for additional losses. Generally, the party is placed in the position he or she would have occupied if the contract been performed.

   1. **Types of Damages**

      a. **Compensatory Damages**
      Damages compensating a party for the loss of a bargain.

         1) **Contract for a Sale of Goods**
         The usual measure is the difference between the contract price and the market price. If the buyer breaches and the seller has not yet made the goods, the measure is lost profits on the sale.

         2) **Contract for a Sale of Land**
         If specific performance is unavailable, or if the buyer breaches, the measure of damages is usually the difference between the land's contract price and its market price.

      b. **Consequential Damages**
      Damages giving the injured party the entire benefit of the bargain—foreseeable losses caused by special circumstances beyond the contract. The losses flow from the consequences of the breach.

   2. **Mitigation of Damages**
   The nonbreaching party has a duty to mitigate damages. For example, persons whose employment has been wrongfully terminated have a duty to seek other jobs. The damages they receive are their salaries, less the income they received (or would have received) in similar jobs.

   3. **Liquidated Damages versus Penalties**

      a. **Liquidated Damages**
      A liquidated damages provision specifies a certain amount to be paid in the event of a breach. Such provisions are enforceable.

      b. **Penalties**
      Penalties specify a certain amount to be paid in the event of a breach (to penalize the breaching party). Such provisions are not enforceable.

B. RESCISSION AND RESTITUTION

1. Rescission
Rescission is an action to undo a contract—to return the contracting parties to the positions they occupied prior to the transaction. If fraud, mistake, duress, undue influence, misrepresentation, lack of capacity, or a party's failure to perform is present, unilateral rescission is available. Recission may also be available by statute.

2. Restitution
To rescind a contract, the parties must make restitution by returning to each other goods, property, or money previously conveyed.

C. SPECIFIC PERFORMANCE
This remedy calls for the performance of the act promised in the contract.

1. When Specific Performance Is Available
Damages must be an inadequate remedy. If goods are unique, a court will decree specific performance. Specific performance is granted to a buyer in a contract for the sale of land (every parcel of land is unique).

2. When Specific Performance Is Not Available
Contracts for a sale of goods (other than unique goods) rarely qualify, because substantially identical goods can be bought or sold elsewhere. Courts normally refuse to grant specific performance of personal service contracts.

D. REFORMATION
Used when the parties have imperfectly expressed their agreement in writing. Allows the contract to be rewritten to reflect the parties' true intentions.

E. RECOVERY BASED ON QUASI CONTRACT
Quasi contract provides a basis for relief when no enforceable contract exists. The courts use this theory to prevent unjust enrichment. The law implies a promise to pay the reasonable value (fair market value) for benefits received by the party accepting the benefits.

F. ELECTION OF REMEDIES DOCTRINE
The doctrine has been eliminated in contracts for the sale of goods [UCC 2–703, 2–711]. Remedies under the UCC are cumulative, although parties may still not recover twice for the same harm.

G. WAIVER OF BREACH
A nonbreaching party may be willing to accept a defective performance of the contract. This relinquishment of a right to full performance is a waiver. A waiver keeps the contract going, but the nonbreaching party can recover damages caused by defective or less-than-full performance.

H. CONTRACT PROVISIONS LIMITING REMEDIES

1. Exculpatory Clauses
A provision excluding liability for fraudulent or intentional injury or for illegal acts will not be enforced. An exculpatory clause for negligence contained in a contract made between parties who have roughly equal bargaining positions usually will be enforced.

2. **Limitation-of-Liability Clauses**
A clause excluding liability for negligence may be enforced.

STUDY TIP ☞ Analytical Models

As an aid to remembering this topic's major points, you may find it helpful to keep a brief analytical model in mind. For example, the material covered in the contracts chapters can be condensed and divided into points to use as a framework for study: (1) If there is an offer and acceptance, (2) supported by consideration, and (3) no defenses to formation, (4) there is an enforceable contract. (5) If the duties are absolute promises, there's an immedi - ate duty to perform. (6) If they are promises subject to conditions, the conditions must occur or be excused first. (7) If the duties have not been discharged by agreement or by operation of law, they must be performed. (8) If not, there's been a breach. (9) If so, what remedies are available?

TRUE-FALSE QUESTIONS (Answers at the Back of the Book)

___   1.   A condition is a possible future event, the occurrence or nonoccurrence of which will trigger the performance of a legal obligation or terminate an existing obligation under a contract.

___   2.   Complete performance occurs when performance is within or slightly below the bounds of reasonable expectations.

___   3.   Even if a breach is not material, it discharges a nonbreaching party's duty to perform.

___   4.   When a contract states that a certain time for performance is essential, the time must ordinarily be strictly complied with.

___   5.   An innocent party is not discharged when another party to the contract materially alters it without the innocent party's consent.

___   6.   Damages are designed to compensate a nonbreaching party for the loss of the contract or to give a nonbreaching party the benefit of the contract.

FILL-IN QUESTIONS (Answers at the Back of the Book)

Most contracts are discharged by performance—by doing what was promised. Any contract can be discharged by agreement of the parties. _____ (Rescission/ Novation) is the process by which a contract is canceled and the parties are returned to the positions they occupied before forming it. _____ (Rescission/ Novation) substitutes a new party for an original party by agreement of all the parties. _____ (Substitution of a new contract/ Accord and satisfaction) revokes and discharges a prior contract. _____ (A substitution/ An accord) suspends a contractual duty that has not been discharged. Once the _____ (substitution/accord) is performed, the original contractual obligation is discharged.

MULTIPLE-CHOICE QUESTIONS (Answers at the Back of the Book)

____ 1. Doyle Company contracts to build a store for Lonigan, Ltd., for $500,000, with payments in installments of $50,000 as building progresses. Doyle completes performance except for a cover over a compressor on the roof. A cover can be installed for $500. Lonigan refuses to pay the last installment. Doyle sues. If the court determines that Doyle's breach is not material

   a. Doyle has a claim against Lonigan for $50,000.
   b. Lonigan has a claim against Doyle for damages for Doyle's breach of its duty to put a cover over the compressor.
   c. both a and b.
   d. neither a nor b.

____ 2. Russ Services contracts with Locasta Concessions, Inc., to service Locasta's vending machines. Later, Russ wants to sell to Dean Services Company the Locasta contract. Dean agrees to assume Russ's duties to Locasta if Locasta agrees to accept Dean's assumption in substitution for Russ's duty. Locasta agrees. The process of substituting Dean for Russ is called

   a. rescission.
   b. accord and satisfaction.
   c. alteration of contract.
   d. novation.

____ 3. Molloy owes Moran $10,000. Molloy promises to deliver to Moran a "Destroyers" video-game machine within fifteen days and Moran agrees to accept the machine in lieu of other payment for the debt. This is called

   a. rescission.
   b. accord and satisfaction.
   c. alteration of contract.
   d. novation.

____ 4. Gil contracts to produce a movie for Big Pictures, Inc. As Big knows, Gil's only source of funds for the filming is a $500,000 deposit in Commerce International Bank (CIB). CIB fails. Gil loses $400,000 and fails to produce the film. Gil's duty to produce the movie is

   a. discharged on grounds of impossibility.
   b. discharged on grounds of commercial impracticability.
   c. suspended on grounds of temporary impossibility.
   d. not discharged, and Gil is liable to Big for breach of contract.

____ 5. Salomon contracts to sell a Borling derivator to Aziz for $100,000, payable in advance. Aziz pays the money, which Salomon deposits in First Bank of Lahore. The bank fails, and Salomon refuses to perform. Aziz is entitled to

   a. rescind the contract.
   b. restitution of the $100,000.
   c. rescind the contract and get restitution of the $100,000.
   d. nothing.

___ **6.** Spencer contracts to sell Spencer's Michigan warehouse operation—including the warehouse, loading docks, garage, parking lot, offices, and land on which everything is located—to Davis. Spencer repudiates the contract, and Davis sues. Under which theory can Spencer be required to convey the land and buildings?

    a. Rescission and restitution
    b. Specific performance
    c. Reformation
    d. Quasi contract

SHORT ESSAY QUESTIONS

1. Discuss material breach of contract and the effect a material breach and a nonmaterial breach has on the nonbreaching party.

2. Discuss what damages are designed to do in a breach of contract situation.

ISSUE SPOTTERS (Answers at the Back of the Book)

1. Aloha Construction Company contracts with Ho to build a store on Ho's lot. The work is to begin on May 1 to be completed by November 1, so that Ho can stock the store and open the day after Thanksgiving for the pre-Christmas buying season. Aloha does not start the work until May 11, but finishes November 6. Ho opens as planned, but due to the delay the store is slightly understocked, which causes the loss of some sales. Is Ho's duty to pay for the construction of the store discharged?

2. Lynda's Foods, Inc., contracts to buy from Bree Distributors, Inc., two hundred carloads of frozen pizzas. Before Lynda or Bree start performing, can their representatives get together and call off the deal? What if Bree has already shipped the pizzas?

3. The Brood contract with Howard to perform the last concert in the Brood's World Tour in Indianapolis. The night before the concert, the Brood are killed in a fiery plane crash. How do their deaths affect their duty to perform under the contract?

4. Anna contracts to sell her ranch to Rachel and to give Rachel possession on June 1. Anna delays the transfer until August 1. Rachel incurs expenses in providing for cattle that she bought to stock the ranch. When they made the contract, Anna had no reason to know of the cattle. Is Anna liable for Rachel's expenses in providing for the cattle?

5. Sal contracts to sell Sal's racing sloop *Dharma Bum* to Dean. The sloop is one of a class of similar boats made by Jack Boats, Inc. Other boats of the class are easily obtainable, but their racing characteristics differ considerably, and *Dharma Bum* is regarded as superior to the others. Sal repudiates the contract. If Dean sues Sal, can Dean get *Dharma Bum*?

 Key Points

The **key points** in this chapter include:

1. Formation of a sales contract.

2. Title, risk, and insurable interest under Article 2.

3. The buyer's and seller's obligations regarding performance.

4. The parties' remedies for breach of contract.

5. Warranties under Article 2.

Chapter 11:
Sales

WHAT THIS CHAPTER IS ABOUT

The Uniform Commercial Code (UCC) provides a framework of rules to deal with all the phases arising in an ordinary sales transaction from start to finish—from sale to payment. This chapter outlines the principles of Article 2, which covers sales of goods.

CHAPTER OUTLINE

I. FORMATION OF A SALES CONTRACT

The following sections summarize how UCC provisions *change* the effect of the common law of contracts.

A. OFFER

Verbal exchanges, correspondence, and the actions of the parties may not reveal exactly when a binding contractual obligation arises. An agreement sufficient to constitute a contract can exist even if the moment of its making is undetermined [UCC 2–204(2)].

1. Open Terms

A sales contract will not fail for indefiniteness even if one or more terms are left open, as long as (1) the parties intended to make a contract and (2) there is a reasonably certain basis for the court to grant an appropriate remedy [UCC 2–204(3)].

2. Merchant's Firm Offer

If the merchant gives assurances in a signed writing that an offer will remain open, the offer is irrevocable, without consideration for the stated period of time, or if no definite period is specified, for a reasonable period (neither period to exceed three months) [UCC 2–205].

B. ACCEPTANCE

1. **Promise to Ship or Prompt Shipment**
   The UCC permits acceptance of an offer to buy goods for current or prompt shipment by either a promise to ship or prompt shipment of the goods to the buyer [UCC 2–206(1)(b)]. Shipment off nonconforming goods is both an acceptance and a breach.

2. **Communication of Acceptance**
   To accept a unilateral offer, the offeree must notify the offeror of performance if the offeror would not otherwise know [UCC 2-206(2)].

3. **Additional Terms**
   If the offeree's response indicates a definite acceptance of the offer, a contract is formed, even if the acceptance includes terms in addition to, or different from, the original offer [UCC 2–207(1)]. If both parties are merchants, the terms may become part of the contract [UCC 2–207(2)].

II. CONSIDERATION

"[A]n agreement modifying a contract needs no consideration to be binding" [UCC 2–209(1)]. Modification must be sought in good faith [UCC 1–203]. Good faith in a merchant is honesty in fact and observance of reasonable commercial standards of fair dealing in the trade [UCC 2–103(1)(b)].

III. STATUTE OF FRAUDS

The UCC requires a writing for a contract to be enforceable when the price of the goods is $500 or more [UCC 2–201].

A. TRANSACTIONS BETWEEN MERCHANTS

The requirement of a writing is satisfied if one merchant sends a signed written confirmation to the other, unless the merchant who receives the confirmation gives written notice of objection within ten days of receipt.

B. EXCEPTIONS

If proved to exist, a contract for a sale of goods for the price of $500 or more will be enforceable despite the absence of a writing if [UCC 2–201(3)] (1) manufacture of special goods has begun, (2) the party against whom enforcement is sought admits in court proceedings that a contract was made, or (3) some payment has been made and accepted or some goods have been received and accepted (enforceable to that extent).

IV. TITLE, RISK, AND INSURABLE INTEREST

A. IDENTIFICATION

To pass an interest in specific goods from seller to buyer, the goods must be identified to the contract [UCC 2–105(2)]. Identification is designating goods as the subject matter of the contract. When a quantity is to be taken from a larger mass, identification can be made only by separating the goods.

B. WHEN TITLE PASSES

1. **According to the Parties' Agreement**
   Parties can agree on when and under what conditions title will pass.

2. **At the Time and Place at Which the Seller Performs**
   If the parties do not specify a time, title passes on delivery [UCC 2–401(2)]. The delivery terms determine when this occurs.

C. RISK OF LOSS
The question of who suffers a financial risk if goods are damaged, destroyed, or lost is resolved under UCC 2–509 and 2–319.

1. **Passage of Risk of Loss under the Parties' Agreement**
   Risk of loss can be assigned in an agreement by the parties if at the time, the goods are in existence and identified to the contract.

2. **Passage of Risk of Loss Absent a Breach of Contract**
   In the absence of agreement, risk of loss generally passes to the buyer when the seller delivers or tenders delivery of the goods to the buyer.

   a. **Delivery of Goods to the Buyer**
      When goods are to be delivered by truck or other paid transport, in a shipment contract risk passes to the buyer when the goods are delivered to a carrier [UCC 2–509(1)(a)]. In a destination contract, risk passes to the buyer when the goods are tendered to the buyer at the destination.

   b. **Delivery Without Movement of the Goods**
      When goods are to be picked up from the seller by the buyer, if the seller is a merchant, risk passes only on the buyer's taking possession of the goods. If the seller is not a merchant, risk passes on the seller's tender of delivery [UCC 2–509(3)].

3. **Risk of Loss in a Breached Sales Contract**
   Generally, the party in breach bears the risk of loss.

D. INSURABLE INTEREST
A buyer has an insurable interest in goods the moment they are identified to the contract, even before risk of loss passes [UCC 2–501(1)]. A seller has an insurable interest in goods as long as he or she retains title or holds a security interest in the goods [UCC 2–501(2)].

V. PERFORMANCE AND OBLIGATION

A. SELLER'S OBLIGATION—PERFECT TENDER OF DELIVERY
The seller must have and hold goods that conform exactly to the description of the goods in the contract at the buyer's disposal and give the buyer notice reasonably necessary to take delivery [UCC 2–503(1)]. If goods or tender fail in any respect, the buyer can accept the goods, reject them, or accept part and reject part [UCC 2–601]. Exceptions—

1. **Agreement of the Parties**
   For example, that the seller can repair or replace any defective goods within a reasonable time.

2. **Cure**
   If nonconforming goods are rejected, the seller can notify the buyer of intent to repair or replace the goods and can then do so in the contract time for performance [UCC 2–508(1)].

3. **Substitution of Carriers**

   When an agreed-on manner of delivery becomes impracticable or unavailable through no fault of either party, a commercially reasonable substitute is sufficient [UCC 2–614(1)].

4. **Commercial Impracticability**

   Delay or nondelivery is not a breach if performance is impracticable "by the occurrence of a contingency the nonoccurrence of which was a basic assumption on which the contract was made" [UCC 2–615(a)]. The seller must give notice.

5. **Destruction of Identified Goods**

   When goods are destroyed (through no fault of a party) before risk passes to the buyer, the parties are excused from performance [UCC 2–613(a)]. If goods are only partially destroyed, a buyer can treat a contract as void or accept damaged goods with a price allowance.

B. **BUYER'S OBLIGATIONS**

   The buyer must (1) furnish facilities reasonably suited for receipt of the goods [UCC 2–503(1)(b)] and (2) make payment at the time and place of delivery, even if it is the same as the place of shipment [UCC 2–310(a)].

C. **ANTICIPATORY REPUDIATION**

   Occurs if, before the time for either party's performance, one communicates to the other an intent not to perform. The other party can (1) treat the repudiation as a final breach by pursuing a remedy (see Chapter 23) or (2) wait, hoping that the repudiating party will decide to honor the contract [UCC 2–610]. If the party decides to wait, the repudiating party can retract the repudiation [UCC 2–611].

VII. **REMEDIES OF THE BUYER AND SELLER FOR BREACH**

A. **REMEDIES OF THE SELLER**

1. **The Right to Recover Damages**

   If a buyer repudiates a contract or wrongfully refuses to accept, the seller can recover the difference between the contract price and the market price (at the time and place of tender), plus incidental damages [UCC 2–708]. If the market price is less than the contract price, the seller gets lost profits.

2. **The Right to Recover the Purchase Price**

   A seller can bring an action for the price when (1) the buyer accepts and does not revoke acceptance; (2) the goods are lost or damaged after the risk of loss passes to the buyer; or (3) the buyer breaches after the goods are identified to the contract and the seller is unable to resell [UCC 2–709(1)]. The buyer gets the goods, unless the seller resells before collection of the judgment (proceeds of a resale are credited to the buyer).

3. **The Right to Withhold Delivery**

   A seller can withhold delivery if a buyer wrongfully rejects or revokes acceptance, fails to pay, or repudiates [UCC 2–703].

B. **REMEDIES OF THE BUYER**

1. **The Right of Rejection**

   If goods or tender fail to conform to the contract. If some of the goods conform, the buyer can keep those and reject the rest [UCC 2–601].

2. **The Right to Obtain Specific Performance**
A buyer can obtain specific performance if goods are unique [UCC 2–716(1)].

3. **The Right to Recover Damages**
If the seller wrongfully fails to deliver or repudiates the contract, the buyer can recover the difference between the contract price and, when the buyer learned of the breach, the market price (at the place of delivery), plus incidental and consequential damages, minus expenses saved as a result of the seller's breach [UCC 2–713].

VIII. SALES WARRANTIES

A. WARRANTIES OF TITLE

1. **Warranties**
Sellers warrant that (1) they have good title to the goods and transfer of the title is rightful [UCC 2–312(1)(a)]; (2) the goods are free of a security interest (see Chapter 16) or other lien of which the buyer has no knowledge [UCC 2–312(1)(b)]; and (3) the goods are free of any third person's patent, trademark, or copyright claims [UCC 2–312(3)].

2. **Disclaimers**
Title warranty can be disclaimed or modified only by specific contractual language (although the circumstances of a sale may indicate clearly that no assurance of title is being made [UCC 2–312(2)]).

B. EXPRESS WARRANTIES

1. **When Express Warranties Arise**
A seller warrants that goods will conform to [UCC 2–313] (1) affirmations or promises of fact (found on a label or in a contract, an advertisement, a brochure, or promotional material); (2) descriptions (for example, on a label or in a contract, an advertisement, a brochure, or promotional material); and (3) samples or models.

2. **Statements of Opinion and Value**
If a seller makes a statement that relates to the value or worth of the goods or makes a statement of opinion or recommendation about the goods, the seller is not creating an express warranty [UCC 2–313(2)], unless the seller is an expert and gives an opinion as an expert.

3. **Disclaimers**
A seller can avoid making express warranties by not promising or affirming anything, describing the goods, or using of a sample or model [UCC 2–313]. A written disclaimer in language that is clear and conspicuous, and called to a buyer's attention, can negate all oral warranties not included in the written contract [UCC 2–316(1)].

C. IMPLIED WARRANTIES
An implied warranty is derived by implication or inference from the nature of a transaction or the relative situations or circumstances of the parties.

1. **Implied Warranty of Merchantability**
This warranty automatically arises in every sale of goods by a merchant who deals in such goods [UCC 2–314(1)]. Goods that are merchantable are "reasonably fit for the ordinary purposes for which such goods are used" [UCC 2–314(2)].

2. **Implied Warranty of Fitness for a Particular Purpose**
   Arises when a seller (merchant or nonmerchant) knows or has reason to know the particular purpose for which a buyer will use goods and knows the buyer is relying on the seller to select suitable goods [UCC 2–315]. Goods can be merchantable but not fit for a buyer's particular purpose.

3. **Implied Warranty from Course of Dealing, Etc.**
   When the parties know a well-recognized trade custom, it is inferred that they intended it to apply to their contract [UCC 2–314(3)].

4. **Disclaimers**
   Implied warranties can be disclaimed by the expression "as is" or a similar phrase [UCC 2–316(3)(a)]. Implied warranty of fitness for a particular purpose: disclaimer must be in writing and be conspicuous Implied warranty of merchantability: disclaimer must mention merchantability; if it is in writing, it must be conspicuous.

STUDY TIP ☞ <u>Keeping the Law of Sales in Perspective</u>

It may be helpful to remember that a contract for the sale of goods is governed by the same common law applicable to all contracts. That is, the law that you studied in Unit Two also applies to contracts for the sales of goods. The law concerning sales of goods—commonly referred to simply as "sales"—has developed specialized aspects, however. It is these aspects that you should emphasize in your study of the Uniform Commercial Code. In particular, merchants are treated specially in a number of instances. For these reasons, it is important that you know the definitions of *goods* and *merchant* .

TRUE-FALSE QUESTIONS (Answers at the Back of the Book)

_____ 1. Unlike the common law rule, the UCC requires that an agreement modifying a contract must be supported by new consideration to be binding.

_____ 2. To satisfy the UCC's Statute of Frauds, a writing must include all material terms, except quantity, and be signed by both parties.

_____ 3. If the parties do not specify identification in their contract, identification occurs in most cases when goods are marked, shipped, or somehow designated by the seller as the goods to pass under the contract.

_____ 4. Performance of a sales contract is controlled by the agreement between the seller and the buyer.

_____ 5. Ordinarily, an award of damages to a buyer for a seller's breach is considered inappropriate if specific performance can be obtained.

_____ 6. An express warranty is derived by implication or inference from the nature of a transaction or parties' relative circumstances.

FILL-IN QUESTIONS (Answers at the Back of the Book)

1. A seller's obligations include holding _____ (conforming/ nonconforming) goods at a buyer's disposal _____ (and/ or) giving notice reasonably necessary for the buyer to take delivery.

2. A buyer's obligations include _____ (accepting/ rejecting) the goods and paying for them according to _____ (the buyer's total obligations/ the contract). Unless the parties have agreed otherwise, the _____ (seller/ buyer) must provide facilities reasonably suited for _____ (delivery/ receipt) of the goods. Also, unless the parties have agreed otherwise, a buyer must pay at the time and place of receipt, _____ (even if/ unless) the place of shipment is the place of delivery.

MULTIPLE-CHOICE QUESTIONS (Answers at the Back of the Book)

_____   **1.** On Monday, Stanley buys a mountain bike from Oliver, Stanley's neighbor. Oliver says, "The bike is ready to go. You can take it with you, if you want." Stanley says, "I'll leave it in your garage until Friday." On Wednesday, Rosie steals the bike from Oliver's garage. Who bore the risk and suffered the loss?

   a. Stanley
   b. Oliver
   c. Rosie
   d. Both a and b

_____   **2.** Andersen Gambling Supplies Company, whose office is in Fargo, North Dakota, contracts to ship 500,000 plastic silver dollars to Zenith Games, Inc., whose office is in Rapid City, South Dakota. The dollars are located in Warrenton Trucking Company's warehouse in Moorehead, Minnesota. Zenith plans to use the dollars in Lead, Colorado. The parties' agreement says that Zenith will pick the dollars up, but says nothing about the place. The place of delivery is

   a. Fargo.
   b. Rapid City.
   c. Moorehead.
   d. Lead.

_____   **3.** Wayne's World Globe Company contracts to sell to Garth's Map Shop fifty globes for a total of $500, payment to be on delivery. Wayne tenders delivery as agreed, but Garth refuses to accept the globes or to pay for them. If Wayne sues Garth for damages, Wayne could recover the difference between the contract price and the market price at the time and place of

   a. contracting.
   b. tender.
   c. contracting—plus, if the market price is less than the contract price, lost profits.
   d. tender—plus, if the market price is less than the contract price, lost profits.

    4. Elroy's Game Town orders virtual reality helmets from Imagination, Inc. Imagination delivers the helmets, but Elroy rejects the shipment because it does not include gloves, one of which is necessary for each helmet. Elroy does not tell Imagination the reason for the rejection. If Imagination had known the reason, Imagination could have had the gloves at Elroy's within hours. If Elroy sues Imagination for damages, Elroy will

    a. win, because Imagination's tender did not conform to the contract—Imagination did not deliver the gloves.

    b. win, because Imagination's tender did not conform to the contract, and Imagination made no attempt to cure—Imagination should have asked Elroy the reason for the rejection.

    c. lose, because Elroy's rejection was unjustified—Imagination could have cured, and thus Elroy cannot rely on the lack of gloves as a basis for a claim for damages.

    d. lose, because Elroy's claim is unjustified—a buyer cannot reject *and* sue for damages.

    5. Pietra's goods—miniature glass dinosaurs—are stored in Andrei's warehouse. Pietra has a negotiable warehouse receipt for the dinosaurs. On Tuesday, Pietra signs her name on the back of the receipt and sells it to Nicolai. On Wednesday, the warehouse collapses in an earthquake and the dinosaurs are destroyed. Who bore the risk and suffered the loss?

    a. Pietra
    b. Andrei
    c. Nicolai
    d. Both b and c

    6. Noel's Ski Shop sells to Ford a pair of skis. On Ford's first use of the skis, the skis snap in two. The cause of the break is attributable to something that Noel's did not know about and that Noel's could not have discovered. If Ford sues Noel's, Ford will

    a. win, because Noel's breached the merchant's implied duty of inspection.

    b. win, because Noel's breached the implied warranty of merchantability.

    c. lose, because Noel's knew nothing about the defect that made the skis unsafe.

    d. lose, because consumers should reasonably expect to find on occasion that a product will not work as warranted.

SHORT ESSAY QUESTIONS

1. In certain phases of sales transactions involving merchants, the UCC imposes special business standards because of the merchants' degree of commercial expertise. Discuss who, for these purposes, is a merchant.

2. Discuss the UCC's implied warranty of merchantability and implied warranty of fitness for a particular purpose—how each arises and the difference between them.

ISSUE SPOTTERS (Answers at the Back of the Book)

1. Leah, an automobile dealer, writes to Sandy that "I have a 1989 Honda Civic that I will sell to you for $7,600. The offer will be kept open for one week." Six days later,

Pam tells Sandy that Leah sold the car that morning for $8,000. Did Lea breach any contract?

2. Lou's Clothing, Inc., in Manhattan, Kansas, contracts to sell certain items of lingerie to Silk n' Satin Stores, Inc., in Oklahoma City. Lou carefully packs the lingerie and ships it by rail to Silk. In transit across Kansas, a tornado derails the train carrying the goods and scatters and shreds the lingerie across miles of cornfields. Lou claims that Silk bore the risk that something like that would happen and must pay for the goods. Silk says the risk belonged to Lou. What are the consequences if Lou is right? If Silk is right?

3. The Captain's Fruit Stand orders seventy-nine cases of fresh peaches from Eat-a-Peach, Inc. If Eat-a-Peach delivers seventy-eight cases instead of seventy-nine, does The Captain's have the right to reject the entire shipment and hold Eat-a-Peach in breach?

4. Angelina Machinery Company contracts to manufacture for Lilian & Daughters, Inc., specially made thermoformers. Except as scrap, the thermoformers would be useless to anyone but Lilian, and Angelina has no marketing expertise anyway—in other words, Angelina would be unable to resell them. What recourse does Angelina have if, on delivery of the thermoformers, Lilian refuses to pay? If, on delivery, Lilian refuses to accept? If, after the risk of loss has passed to Lilian but before Lilian pays, the thermoformers are destroyed in an explosion, and Lilian refuses to pay?

5. Makoto Construction Company tells Gindin Industrial Supplies, Inc., that Makoto needs an adhesive to do a particular job. After Makoto describes the circumstances in detail, Gindin provides a five-gallon bucket of Bulldog Industrial Adhesive and says, "Here you go." When Bulldog does not perform to Makoto's specifications, Makoto sues Gindin. Gindin claims, "We didn't expressly promise anything." What should Makoto argue?

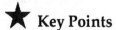 **Key Points**

The **key points** in this chapter include:

1. The differences between torts and crimes.

2. The elements of intentional torts that involve wrongs against persons and the defenses to these torts.

3. The elements of intentional torts that involve wrongs against property and the defenses to these torts.

4. The elements of negligence and the defenses to negligence.

5. The doctrine of strict liability.

Chapter 12:
Torts and Strict Liability

WHAT THIS CHAPTER IS ABOUT

Wrongful conduct by one person that causes injury to another is covered by the law of **torts**. *Tort* is French for "wrong." For acts that cause physical injury or that interfere with physical security and freedom of movement, tort law provides remedies, typically damages (money).

This chapter outlines intentional torts, negligence, and strict liability. Torts that are more specifically related to business are outlined in Chapter 13.

CHAPTER OUTLINE

I.   THE BASIS OF TORT LAW

Two notions serve as the basis of all torts: wrongs and compensation. Tort law recognizes that some acts are wrong because they cause injuries to others. Most crimes involve torts, but not all torts are crimes. A tort action is a *civil* action in which one person brings a personal suit against another.

II.   INTENTIONAL TORTS AGAINST PERSONS

Intentional torts involve acts that were intended to bring about the consequences that are the basis of the tort. The tortfeasor (the one committing the tort) must intend to commit an act, the consequences of which interfere with the personal or business interests of another in a way not permitted by law.

A. ASSAULT AND BATTERY

1. Assault
An intentional act that creates in another person a reasonable apprehension or fear of immediate harmful or offensive contact.

2. Battery
An intentional and harmful or offensive physical contact. Physical injury need not occur. Whether the contact is offensive is determined by the reasonable person standard.

3. Defenses

a. Consent
When a person consents to an act that damages him or her, there is generally no liability for the damage.

b. Self-Defense
An individual who is defending his or her life or physical well-being can claim self-defense.

c. Defense of Others
An individual can act in a reasonable manner to protect others who are in real or apparent danger.

d. Defense of Property
Reasonable force may be used in attempting to remove intruders from one's home, although force that is likely to cause death or great bodily injury can never be used just to protect property.

B. FALSE IMPRISONMENT

1. What False Imprisonment Is
The intentional confinement or restraint of another person without justification. The confinement can be accomplished through the use of physical barriers, physical restraint, or threats of physical force.

2. Defense: Probable Cause
In some states, a merchant is justified in delaying a suspected shoplifter if the merchant has probable cause. The detention must be conducted in a reasonable manner and for only a reasonable length of time.

C. INTENTIONAL INFLICTION OF EMOTIONAL DISTRESS

1. What Intentional Infliction of Emotional Distress Is
An intentional act that amounts to extreme and outrageous conduct resulting in severe emotional distress to another.

2. How It Is Committed
Annoyance alone is usually not enough; repeated annoyances, coupled with threats, may be. Some physical symptom or emotional disturbance documented by a medical professional may be required.

D. DEFAMATION

1. What Defamation Is
Wrongfully hurting another's good reputation through false statements. Doing it orally is **slander**; doing it in writing or in other forms of communication (such as pictures, signs, or films) is **libel**.

2. **Slander** *Per Se*

Proof of injury is not required when one falsely states that another has a loathsome communicable disease, has committed improprieties while engaging in a profession or trade, or has committed or been imprisoned for a serious crime, or that an unmarried woman is unchaste.

3. **The Publication Requirement**

To be defamatory, statements must be published—that is, they must be communicated to third parties. Anyone who republishes or repeats defamatory statements is liable, even if the person reveals the source of the statements.

4. **Defenses**

a. **Truth**

The statement is true. It must be true in whole, not in part.

b. **Public Figure**

The statement is about a public figure, made in a public medium, and related to a matter of general public interest. To recover damages, a public figure must prove that the statement was made with **actual malice** (with knowledge of its falsity or a reckless disregard for the truth).

c. **Privilege**

The statement is privileged: absolutely (made in a judicial or legislative proceeding) or conditionally (for example, made by one corporate director to another and was about corporate business).

E. **INVASION OF THE RIGHT TO PRIVACY**

Four acts qualify as invasions of privacy:

1. The use of a person's name, picture, or other likeness for commercial purposes without permission.

2. Intrusion on an individual's affairs or seclusion.

3. Publication of information that places a person in a false light.

4. Public disclosure of private facts about an individual that an ordinary person would find objectionable.

F. **FRAUDULENT MISREPRESENTATION**

Fraud is the use of misrepresentation and deceit for personal gain.

1. **The Elements of Fraudulent Misrepresentation**

a. **Misrepresentation** of material facts or conditions with knowledge that they are false or with reckless disregard for the truth.

b. **Intent** to induce another to rely on the misrepresentation.

c. **Justifiable reliance** by the deceived party.

d. **Damages** suffered as a result of reliance.

e. **Causal connection** between the misrepresentation and the injury.

2. Puffery
Seller's talk, or puffery, is not fraud.

III. INTENTIONAL TORTS AGAINST PROPERTY

A. TRESPASS TO PERSONAL PROPERTY

1. What Trespass to Personal Property Is
When an individual unlawfully harms the personal property of another or interferes with the owner's right to exclusive possession and enjoyment of the property.

2. Defenses
Defenses include that the interference was **warranted**.

B. CONVERSION

1. What Conversion Is
An act depriving an owner of personal property without the owner's permission and without just cause. Conversion is the civil side of crimes related to theft.

2. Liability for Buying Stolen Goods
A buyer of stolen goods is liable to the owner of the goods in conversion even if the buyer did not know that the goods were stolen.

3. Defenses

a. The purported **owner does not own** the property or does not have a right to possess it that is superior to the right of the holder.

b. **Necessity** (for example, the property was taken to protect the public).

C. TRESPASS TO LAND

1. What Trespass to Land Is
When a person, without permission, enters onto, above, or below the surface of land that is owned by another; causes anything to enter onto the land; or remains on the land or permits anything to remain on it.

2. Defenses

a. Trespass was **warranted** (the trespasser entered, for instance, to assist someone in danger).

b. The purported **owner had no right to possess** the land in question.

IV. NEGLIGENCE

A. THE ELEMENTS OF NEGLIGENCE

Test 7

1. What Negligence Is
Negligence is the failure to exercise reasonable care, creating a risk of certain harmful consequences. The risk must be foreseeable (the negligent person knows or should know of the risk), and the conduct must be unreasonable in light of the nature of the possible harm.

2. **The Elements of Negligence**
   The elements of negligence are: (1) duty of care, (2) breach of the duty of care, (3) causation (the breach must cause damage or injury), and (4) damage or injury.

B. **DUTY OF CARE**
   The duty of care is measured by the reasonable person standard (how a reasonable person would have acted in the same circumstances). Landowners, landlords, and business persons are expected to exercise reasonable care (guard against some risks and warn of others) to protect from harm persons coming onto their property.

C. **BREACH OF THE DUTY OF CARE**

1. **Factors for Determining a Breach**
   To determine whether there is a breach of a duty of care, consider the nature of the act (whether it is outrageous or commonplace), the manner in which the act is performed (cautiously versus heedlessly), and the nature of the injury (whether it is serious or slight).

2. **A Professional's Breach**
   In deciding whether a professional breached a duty, consider his or her knowledge, skill, and intelligence.

3. **Failing to Rescue**
   Failing to rescue a stranger in peril is not a breach of a duty of care.

D. **CAUSATION**

1. **The Elements of Causation**

   a. **Causation in Fact**
      "But for" the breach of the duty of care, the injury would not have occurred.

   b. **Proximate Cause**
      There must be a connection between the negligent act and the injury strong enough to justify imposing liability. Generally, the harm or the victim of the harm must have been foreseeable in light of all of the circumstances.

2. **Superseding Intervening Force**
   A superseding intervening force breaks the connection between the breach of the duty of care and the injury or damage. Taking a defensive action (such as swerving to avoid an oncoming car) does not break the connection. Nor does someone else's attempt to rescue the injured party.

E. **DAMAGE OR INJURY**
   To recover damages (receive compensation), the plaintiff must have suffered some loss, harm, wrong, or invasion of a protected interest.

F. **DEFENSES TO NEGLIGENCE**

1. **Assumption of Risk**
   A plaintiff who voluntarily enters into a risky situation, knowing the risk, cannot recover. This does not include a risk different from or greater than the risk normally involved in the situation.

2. **Contributory Negligence**
    In some states, a plaintiff cannot recover for an injury if both parties have been negligent and their negligence has combined to cause the injury. The **last-clear-chance doctrine** allows a plaintiff to recover despite failing to exercise care if the defendant had the "last clear chance" to avoid causing damage.

3. **Comparative Negligence**
    In most states, the plaintiff's and the defendant's negligence is compared and the damages pro rated. Some states allow a plaintiff to recover if his or her fault is greater than that of the defendant. In many states, the plaintiff recovers nothing if he or she was more than 50 percent at fault.

G. SPECIAL NEGLIGENCE DOCTRINES AND STATUTES

1. *Res Ipsa Loquitur*
    If negligence is very difficult to prove, a court may infer it, and the defendant must prove he or she was *not* negligent. This is only if the event causing the harm is one that normally does not occur in the absence of negligence and is caused by something within the exclusive control of the defendant.

2. **Negligence *Per Se***
    A person who violates a statute providing for a criminal penalty is liable when the violation causes another to be injured, if (1) the statute sets out a standard of conduct, and when, where, and of whom it is expected; (2) the injured person is in the class protected by the statute; and (3) the statute was designed to prevent the type of injury suffered.

V. STRICT LIABILITY
Under this doctrine, liability for injury is imposed for reasons other than fault.

A. ABNORMALLY DANGEROUS ACTIVITIES

1. **The Basis Behind the Doctrine**
    The basis for imposing strict liability on an abnormally dangerous activity is that the activity creates an extraordinary risk. Balancing the risk against the potential for harm, it is fair to ask the person engaged in the activity to pay for injury caused by that activity.

2. **The Elements of an Abnormally Dangerous Activity**

    a. **Potential harm, of a serious nature**, to persons or property.

    b. **A high degree of risk** that cannot be completely guarded against by reasonable care.

    c. **Not commonly performed** in the community or area.

B. ANIMALS
A person who keeps a wild animal is strictly liable for any harm inflicted by the animal. An owner of a domestic animal (such as a dog) is strictly liable for harm caused by the animal if the owner knew, or should have known, that the animal had a propensity to harm others.

C. PRODUCT LIABILITY

A significant application of strict liability is in the area of product liability—liability of manufacturers, sellers, and others for harmful or defective products. Product liability is outlined in Chapter 14.

STUDY TIP ☞ Mnemonic Devices

A mnemonic device is a method that many students use to remember legal principles. A mnemonic device may be a word, a formula, or a rhyme. As an aid to remembering the elements of a cause of action in negligence, for example, you might use "ABCD"—

A   A duty of care,
B   Breach of the duty of care,
C   Causation (the breach must cause an injury), and
D   Damage (injury or harm).

TRUE-FALSE QUESTIONS (Answers at the Back of the Book)

____   1.   In contrast to criminal law, the function of tort law is to provide an injured person with a remedy.

____   2.   An intentional tort requires that the actor intend the consequences of his or her act or know with substantial certainty that certain consequences will result.

____   3.   Immediate harmful or offensive contact is an essential element of assault.

____   4.   Immediate harmful or offensive contact is an essential element of battery.

____   5.   A single indignity or annoyance is usually enough to support an action for the intentional infliction of emotional distress.

____   6.   The tort of defamation does not occur unless a defamatory statement is made in writing.

____   7.   If Edison does not believe that he is the best plumber in town, his telling customers that "I'm the best plumber in town" can form the basis for the tort of fraudulent misrepresentation.

____   8.   A customer who deliberately breaks merchandise on display for sale in a store is guilty of conversion.

____   9.   Seller's talk, or puffery, is not fraud.

____   10.   Under negligence theory, the same duty of care must be exercised by all individuals, regardless of their knowledge, skill, or intelligence.

____   11.   Under the doctrine of strict liability, liability is imposed for reasons other than fault.

FILL-IN QUESTIONS (Answers at the Back of the Book)

1.   Basic defenses to _____ (negligence/trespass) include the last-clear-chance doctrine, comparative negligence, contributory negligence, and assumption of risk.

2.   One who voluntarily and knowingly enters into a risky situation normally cannot recover damages. This is the _____ (last-clear-chance doctrine/ defense of assumption of risk). The _____ (failure/ assumption) can be express, or it can be implied by a plaintiff's knowledge of the risk and subsequent conduct. This defense does not involve the _____ (creation/ assumption) of a risk different from or greater than the risk normally carried by an activity.

3.   When both parties' failure to use reasonable care combines to cause injury, in some states the injured party's recovery is precluded by his or her own _____ (injury/ negligence). This is the _____ (comparative/ contributory) negligence doctrine.

4.   When both parties' failure to use reasonable care combines to cause injury, in most states damages are reduced by a percentage that represents the degree of the plaintiff's _____ (injury/ negligence).   This is the _____ (comparative/ contributory) negligence doctrine. In some states, a plaintiff can recover only if he or she was 49 percent or less at fault. In other states, a plaintiff's _____ (injury/ negligence) must be no greater than the defendant's. In still other states, a plaintiff can recover no matter how _____ (injured/ negligent) he or she was.

5.   When both parties' _____ (failure to use reasonable care/ voluntary assumption of the risk) combines to cause injury, in states that apply the contributory negligence doctrine, the person who _____ (had the last clear chance to avoid the accident and failed to do so/ assumed the risk) is liable.

MULTIPLE-CHOICE QUESTIONS (Answers at the Back of the Book)

____   1.   Which of the following statements is TRUE?

a.   Commission of a tort is always a crime.
b.   The state prosecutes tortfeasors.
c.   A tort action is a civil action in which one person brings a suit of a personal nature against another.
d.   A court may punish a tortfeasor with a jail term, a fine, or both.

____   2.   Feeble, a 99-pound weakling, clenches his fist, stands as if ready to throw a punch, and orally threatens to hit The Freezer, a 360-pound lineman for the Chicago Bears. Feeble is

a.   not guilty of assault, because words alone are not enough.
b.   not guilty of assault, because it is unlikely that The Freezer is afraid of Feeble.
c.   guilty of assault, because his words are accompanied by a threatening act.
d.   both a and b.

____ 3. Tonya owns Tonya's Ski Shop. One afternoon, Tonya believes that she sees Nancy, a customer, shoplifting. As Nancy is about to leave the shop, Tonya stops her and tells her that she won't be allowed to leave until Tonya checks her bag. If Nancy sues Tonya for false imprisonment, Nancy will

a. win, because a merchant cannot delay a customer on a mere suspicion.
b. win, because a merchant can increase prices to spread the cost of a lawsuit.
c. lose, because a merchant may delay a suspected shoplifter for a reasonable time.
d. lose, because Tonya did not intend to commit a tort.

____ 4. A music critic writes in a review that Madonna performed as if she were drunk. If Madonna sues the critic for defamation, Madonna will

a. win, because Madonna is a public figure.
b. win, if Madonna can prove that the statement was made with actual malice.
c. lose, because music reviews are absolutely privileged.
d. lose, because the critic is a public figure.

____ 5. During a trial, a judge calls an attorney unethical. If the attorney sues the judge for defamation, the attorney will

a. win, because the attorney is a public figure.
b. win, if the attorney can prove that the statement was made with actual malice.
c. lose, because the judge's statement was absolutely privileged.
d. lose, because the judge is a public figure.

____ 6. A landlord installs two-way mirrors in his tenants' bedrooms through which he watches their activities without their knowledge. The landlord is guilty of

a. using another's likeness for commercial purposes without permission.
b. public disclosure of private facts about another.
c. publication of information that places another in false lights.
d. intrusion on another's affairs or seclusion.

____ 7. Fred returns home from a hard day at work to find Barney camped in Fred's backyard. Fred says, "Get off my property." Barney says, "I'm not leaving." Fred forcibly drags Barney off the property. If Barney sues Fred, Barney will

a. win, because Fred used too much force.
b. win, because Barney told Fred that he was not leaving.
c. lose, because Fred had a hard day at work.
d. lose, because Barney is a trespasser.

____ 8. Gus sends a letter to Paco in which he accuses Paco of embezzling. Paco's secretary Tina reads the letter to Paco. If Paco sues Gus for defamation, Paco will

a. win, because Tina's reading of the letter satisfies the publication element.
b. win, because Gus's writing of the letter satisfies the publication element.
c. lose, because the letter is not proof that Paco is an embezzler.
d. lose, because the publication element is not satisfied.

_____ 9. Wandering through Oscar's air-conditioned market on a hot summer day with her sisters, seven-year-old Silvia drops her popsicle on the floor near the dairy case. Two hours later, Janet stops to buy milk on her way home from work, slips on the popsicle puddle, and breaks her arm. Oscar is

   a. liable, because Janet's injury was the fault of Silvia's sisters.
   b. liable, if Oscar failed to take all reasonable precautions against Janet's injury.
   c. not liable, if Oscar failed to take all reasonable precautions against Janet's injury.
   d. not liable, because Janet's injury was the fault of Silvia's sisters.

_____ 10. Driving his car negligently, Efrem crashes into an electrical pole. The crash fells the pole, knocking out electrical power in the area, which includes a hospital. The hospital's emergency power system fails. Karl, who was connected to electronic life-sustaining equipment, dies. But for Efrem's negligence, Karl would not have died. Efrem's negligence is the

   a. cause in fact of Karl's death.
   b. proximate cause of Karl's death.
   c. intervening cause of Karl's death.
   d. superseding cause of Karl's death.

_____ 11. Strict liability is applied to abnormally dangerous activities because of their extreme risk. Abnormally dangerous activities involve

   a. potentially serious harm to persons or property.
   b. a high degree of risk that cannot be completely guarded against by the exercise of reasonable care.
   c. activities not commonly performed in the area.
   d. all of the above.

_____ 12. To be prepared to deal with potential legal problems, a retailer should

   a. obtain liability insurance.
   b. post warnings for all potential hazards.
   c. attempt to reason with individuals claiming to have been injured on the premises.
   d. all of the above.

_____ 13. To be held liable for negligence, a defendant's act must be

   a. the cause in fact of the harm.
   b. the proximate cause of the harm.
   c. both a and b.
   d. none of the above.

SHORT ESSAY QUESTIONS

1. Define tort.

2. Identify and describe the elements of a cause of action based on negligence.

ISSUE SPOTTERS (Answers at the Back of the Book)

1.   While Eve is asleep, Adam kisses the sleeve of her pajamas, something that she would not have allowed had she been awake. Is Adam guilty of a tort?

2.   A bartender refuses to serve any more drinks to Andy, who has been drinking heavily in the bar.   Andy argues with the bartender who tells two bouncers to "sober this guy up." The bouncers take Andy into the restroom and threaten him with physical harm if he doesn't stay there until he sobers up. Has a tort been committed against Andy?

3.   If a student takes another student's business law textbook as a practical joke and hides it for several days before the final examination, has a tort been committed?

4.   Standing next to a gasoline truck, Joe lights a cigarette and tosses the match into the tank. The ensuing explosion and fire ends in the evacuation and destruction of downtown Richmond. During the evacuation, eleven-year-old Mandy is trampled by a fleeing mob. Is Joe liable for Mandy's injuries?

5.   Gary owns a dog that Gary knows can be unpredictably vicious. One afternoon while Gary is at work, nine-year-old Dennis is walking past Gary's house when the dog attacks Dennis, severely injuring the boy. Is Gary liable for Dennis's injuries?

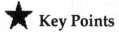
Chapter 13:
Torts and Crimes Related to Business

WHAT THIS CHAPTER IS ABOUT

Business torts are wrongful interferences with others' business rights. Business torts include the torts discussed in this chapter. This chapter also defines what makes an act a crime and describes crimes that affect business. Finally, there is a section on the application of the Racketeer Influenced and Corrupt Organizations Act (RICO) to fraudulent business activities.

CHAPTER OUTLINE

I. TORTS RELATED TO BUSINESS

A. WRONGFUL INTERFERENCE
Torts involving wrongful interference with another's business rights generally fall into the two categories outlined here.

1. Wrongful Interference with a Contractual Relationship

a. What Wrongful Interference with a Contractual Relationship Is
The plaintiff must prove that the defendant *induced* the breach of a contractual relationship, not merely that the defendant reaped the benefits of a broken contract.

b. Elements
(1) A **contract** between two parties, (2) a third party's **knowledge** of the contract, (3) the third party's intentionally causing either of the two parties to **break the contract**.

2. **Wrongful Interference with a Business Relationship**
If there are two yogurt stores in a mall, placing an employee of Store A in front of Store B to divert customers to Store A constitutes the tort of wrongful interference with a business relationship. This is an unfair trade practice.

3. **Defenses to Wrongful Interference**
A person is not liable if the interference is justified or permissible (such as bona fide competitive behavior). It is not illegal to negotiate secretly behind a rival's back, refuse to do business with a competitor, or refuse to deal with third parties until they stop doing business with a rival.

B. **WRONGFUL ENTRY INTO BUSINESS**
Business needs protection from abusive practices. Opening a business for the sole purpose of driving another firm out of business is predatory, simulated competition. Business activity that is not bona fide competition may be ruled by a court to be tortious.

C. **APPROPRIATION**
The use of one person's name or likeness by another, without permission and for the benefit of the user, constitutes **appropriation**. An individual's right to privacy includes the right to the exclusive use of his or her identity.

D. **DEFAMATION IN THE BUSINESS CONTEXT**
The tort of defamation occurs when an individual makes a false statement that injures another's reputation. **Defamation** is a business tort when the defamatory matter injures someone in a profession, business, or trade or when it adversely affects a business entity in its credit rating and other dealings.

E. **DISPARAGEMENT OF PROPERTY**
Disparagement of property occurs when economically injurious falsehoods are made about another's product or property. It is a general term for torts that can be more specifically referred to as **slander of quality** or **slander of title**.

II. CRIMES RELATED TO BUSINESS

A. **NATURE OF CRIMINAL LAW**
A crime is a wrong against society specifically set out in a statute and, if intentionally committed, punishable by society. Crimes are prosecuted by public officials, not by victims.

B. **CLASSIFICATION OF CRIMES**
Felonies—serious crimes that are punishable by death or by imprisonment in a federal or state penitentiary for more than a year. **Misdemeanors**—a crime that is not a felony is a misdemeanor—punishable by a fine or by confinement (in a local jail) for up to a year.

C. **ESSENTIALS OF CRIMINAL LIABILITY**

1. **A Criminal Act**
A criminal statute prohibits certain behavior—an act of commission (doing something) or an act of omission (not doing something that is a legal duty). A criminal act is an *actus reus*.

2. **A State of Mind (Criminal Intent)**

   The mental state (*mens rea*) required to establish guilt of a crime is set out in a statute that describes the crime. The common forms of intent include purpose, knowledge, negligence, and recklessness.

D. CRIMES AFFECTING BUSINESS

1. **Forgery**

   Fraudulently making or altering any writing in a way that changes the legal rights and liabilities of another.

2. **Robbery**

   Forcefully and unlawfully taking personal property from another.

3. **Burglary**

   Breaking and entering the dwelling or other structure with the intent to commit a felony. Some states do not require a breaking.

4. **Larceny**

   Wrongfully or fraudulently taking and carrying away another person's personal property with the intent of depriving the owner permanently of the property (without the use of force or intimidation).

5. **Obtaining Goods by False Pretenses (Through Fraud or Deceit)**

6. **Receiving Stolen Goods**

   The recipient need not know the identity of the true owner of the goods.

7. **Embezzlement**

   Fraudulently appropriating another's property or money by one who has been entrusted with it (without force or intimidation).

8. **Bribery**

   a. **Bribery of Public Officials**

      Attempting to influence a public official to act in a way that serves a private interest by offering the official a bribe. The crime is committed when the bribe (anything the recipient considers valuable) is offered.

   b. **Commercial Bribery**

      Attempting, by a bribe, to obtain proprietary information, cover up an inferior product, or secure new business.

   c. **Bribery of Foreign Officials**

      Attempting, by bribing foreign officials, to obtain favorable business contracts. Prohibited by the Foreign Corrupt Practices Act of 1977 (see Chapter 8).

9. **Money Laundering**

   Transferring proceeds of criminal acts through legitimate businesses.

10. **Insider Trading**

    Using inside information (information not available to the general public) about a publicly traded corporation to profit from the purchase or sale of the corporation's securities (see Chapter 28).

11. **Corporate Crime**

 a. **Liability of the Corporate Entity**
 A corporation may be convicted if a crime is: (1) within the scope of employment of the agent or employee who commits it; (2) a failure to perform a duty imposed on corporations by law; and (3) authorized, requested, commanded, committed, or recklessly tolerated by one of the corporation's high managerial agents.

 b. **Liability of Corporate Officers and Directors**
 Liability may be imposed if an officer was in a "responsible relationship" to the firm with the power to prevent the violation. An officer's control over corporate operations may be so pervasive that, in effect, the officer is an employer and may be convicted of crimes under statutes that provide for the convictions of "employers."

III. RICO

If a person commits two of the offenses under the Racketeer Influenced and Corrupt Organizations Act (RICO) of 1970, he or she is guilty of "racketeering activity."

A. ACTIVITIES PROHIBITED BY RICO

 1. Use income from racketeering activity to buy an interest in an enterprise.
 2. Acquire or maintain such an interest through racketeering activity.
 3. Conduct or participate in an enterprise through racketeering activity.
 4. Conspire to do any of the above.

C. CIVIL LIABILITY UNDER RICO
Civil penalties include divestiture of a defendant's interest in a business or dissolution of the business. Private individuals can recover treble damages, plus attorneys' fees, for business injuries.

D. CRIMINAL LIABILITY UNDER RICO
Criminal penalties include fines of up to $25,000 per violation, imprisonment for up to twenty years, or both, and forfeiture of any interest gained in any enterprise as a result of a violation.

STUDY TIP ☞ Defamation—Libel and Slander

Defamatory statements made in written or printed form are libel, and defamatory statements made orally are slander. A shorthand reference that you might use to remember the distinction is: If the defamatory statement is made in writing, it is "literature," and the applicable term is libel. If the statement is made orally, it is "spoken," and the applicable term is slander.

TRUE-FALSE QUESTIONS (Answers at the Back of the Book)

F **1.** To commit the tort of interference with a contractual relationship, a party must act in bad faith or with malice.

F **2.** There are no legitimate defenses to wrongful interference torts.

T **3.** Opening a business for the sole purpose of driving another firm out of business may be ruled by a court to be tortious.

T **4.** The Racketeer Influenced and Corrupt Organizations Act (RICO) created no new types of crimes.

T **5.** Under RICO, the government can seek divestiture of a defendant's interest in a business or dissolution of the business.

T **6.** Criminal law is primarily statutory.

F **7.** All criminal statutes, and thus all crimes, require an act of commission—an *actus reus*, or guilty act.

F **8.** Burglary is the taking of another's personal property, from his or her person or immediate presence, by force or intimidation.

FILL-IN QUESTIONS (Answers at the Back of the Book)

RICO makes reference to twenty-six _____ (federal/state) crimes and nine _____ (federal/state) felonies. If a person commits _____ (two/four) of these offenses, he or she is guilty of racketeering activity. Under RICO, it is a federal crime (1) to acquire or _____ (maintain/sell) an interest in a business, or (2) to conduct or _____ (participate in/ignore) a business through commission of these offenses—that is, through racketeering activity. It is also a crime (3) to use funds gained through _____ (racketeering/business) activity to buy an interest in any business. Finally, it is a crime (4) to conspire to do any of these things.

MULTIPLE-CHOICE QUESTIONS (Answers at the Back of the Book)

____ **1.** RICO prohibits

a. operation by organized crime of legitimate businesses.
b. operation by organized crime of illegal businesses.
c. operation by anyone of any business with funds obtained through racketeering activity.
d. none of the above.

____ **2.** Under RICO, a defendant

a. may be subject to a civil action only.
b. may be subject to a criminal action only.
c. may be subject to a civil action or a criminal action.
d. must be criminally prosecuted before being subjected to a civil action.

___ 3. A shopping mall contains three fast food restaurants—Big Food, Royal Dogs, and Giant Chicken. Big's manager sends Big employees to the entrances of Royal and Giant to divert customers to Big with free samples. If Royal and Giant sue Big for wrongful interference with a business relationship, Big will be held

a. liable, because Big interfered unreasonably with their attempts to do business.
b. liable, because Big Food is not as good as Royal Dogs and Giant Chicken.
c. not liable, because Big Food is not as good as Royal Dogs and Giant Chicken.
d. not liable, because Big was not competing unfairly.

___ 4. Joe is liable for the tort of appropriation when he

a. uses Grace's name or likeness, with Grace's permission, for Joe's benefit.
b. uses Grace's name or likeness, without Grace's permission, for Joe's benefit.
c. makes a false statement, with Grace's permission, that harms her reputation.
d. makes a false statement, without Grace's permission, that harms her reputation.

___ 5. Grace is liable for the tort of defamation when she

a. uses Joe's name or likeness, with Joe's permission, for Joe's benefit.
b. uses Joe's name or likeness, without Joe's permission, for Joe's benefit.
c. makes a true statement, with Joe's permission, that harms his reputation.
d. makes a false statement, without Joe's permission, that harms his reputation.

___ 6. In a jewelry store, Augustine takes a Rolex from the counter and puts it in her pocket. Augustine walks three steps toward the door before the security guard stops her. If Augustine is arrested and charged with larceny, she will be

a. acquitted, because she was entrapped.
b. acquitted, because there was no larceny—she was stopped before she got to the door.
c. convicted, because she was properly apprehended.
d. convicted, because she committed larceny.

___ 7. Kevin decides to take home the company-owned personal computer (PC) that he uses in his office. Leaving the office building, Kevin tells the security guard that the computer is Kevin's. Kevin has committed the crime of

a. larceny.
b. embezzlement.
c. obtaining goods by false pretenses.
d. receiving stolen goods.

SHORT ESSAY QUESTIONS

1. Discuss the category of business tort known as "wrongful interference with a business relationship."

2. Discuss the circumstances under which a corporate officer can be held personally liable for crimes of the corporation or of corporate employees.

3.   Discuss civil liability under the Racketeer Influenced and Corrupt Organizations Act (RICO)—its causes and results.

ISSUE SPOTTERS (Answers at the Back of the Book)

1.   After less than a year in business, Muscle Health Club surpasses Fitness Club in number of memberships. Attributable to aggressive advertising and marketing strategies, the membership includes many former Fitness members. Does Fitness have any recourse against Muscle for this interference with its profits?

2.   When Mike applied for credit with First National Bank, Pedestrian Credit Reporting Agency reported that Mike had failed to pay several previous obligations. Mike told the bank that this was not true and offered proof, but the bank refused to grant Mike credit. Does Mike have any recourse against Pedestrian?

3.   John uses Paul's name and photo, without Paul's permission, in a promotion for John's Photography Studio. When Paul objects, John claims that Paul's identity is not actually Paul's—a person's identity is public and can be used by others for harmless purposes. Paul sues. What will the court say?

4.   With James's permission, Elmore signs James's name to several traveler's checks that were issued to James and cashes them. James reports that the checks are stolen and receives replacements. Has Elmore committed forgery?

5.   Maxy takes her roommate's credit card, intending to charge to it the expenses that she expects to accrue on a cross-country vacation. Maxy's first stop is a gas station, where she presents the card to pay for gas put into her car. The station accepts the card, and Maxy drives off. With respect to the gas station, what crime has Maxy committed?

 **Key Points**

The **key points** in this chapter include:

1. Negligence as the basis of liability in a product liability suit.

2. Strict liability in a product liability context.

3. Limitations on the application of the doctrine of strict liability.

4. Extended and expanded applications of the doctrine of strict liability.

5. Defenses to theories of liability in product liability suits.

Chapter 14:
Product Liability

WHAT THIS CHAPTER IS ABOUT

Manufacturers, processors, and sellers can be held liable to consumers, users, and bystanders for physical harm or property damage that is caused by defective goods. This is product liability, and it includes the contract theory of warranty and tort theories of negligence, misrepresentation, and strict liability.

CHAPTER OUTLINE

I. WARRANTY LAW
Warranty law (see Chapter 11) is an important part of product liability law.

II. NEGLIGENCE
If the failure to exercise reasonable care in the creation or marketing of a product causes an injury, the basis of liability is negligence.

A. BASIC ELEMENTS
The plaintiff must prove that (1) a duty of care existed, (2) the duty was breached, (3) the plaintiff suffered a legally recognizable injury, and (4) the injury was proximately caused by the breach (see Chapter 12).

1. **Privity of Contract Between Plaintiff and Defendant Is Not Required**

2. **Manufacturer's Duty of Care**
   Due care must be exercised in (a) designing a product and selecting materials and production processes; (b) assembling and testing; (c) inspecting and testing products bought for use in the final product; and (d) placing warnings on the label to inform users of dangers of which an ordinary person might not be aware (including foreseeable misuses).

3. **Breach of the Duty, Causation, and Injury**
    A manufacturer is liable for its failure to exercise due care to any person who sustains an injury proximately caused by a negligently made (defective) product. (How to analyze whether a product is sufficiently defective is outlined in the section on strict liability below.)

B. **VIOLATION OF STATUTORY DUTY**
Manufacturers of cosmetics, drugs, foods, toxic substances, and flammable materials have statutory duties relating to descriptions of contents, labeling, branding, advertising, and selling. In a tort action for damages, a violation of a statutory duty is often held to constitute negligence *per se* .

C. **DEFENSES TO NEGLIGENCE**

1. **Defendant Used Due Care in the Manufacture of Its Product**

2. **No Causation**
    The plaintiff fails to prove the defendant's act caused his or her injury.

3. **Plaintiff's Negligence**
    If a plaintiff misuses a product or fails to make a reasonable effort to preserve his or her own welfare, a manufacturer or seller can claim that the plaintiff negligently contributed to causing the injuries.

    a. **Contributory Negligence**
        In some states, contributory negligence is an absolute defense for the defendant-manufacturer or seller.

    b. **Comparative Negligence**
        In some states, the negligence of both parties is compared. Damages are based on the proportion of negligence attributed to each.

III. **MISREPRESENTATION**

A. **BASIC ELEMENTS**
A misrepresentation (1) must be of a material fact; (2) must have been intended to induce a buyer's reliance; and (3) the buyer must rely on it.

1. **Material Fact**
    A fact concerning the quality, nature, or appropriate use of a product on which a buyer may be expected to rely.

2. **The Element of Intent**
    Misrepresentation on a label or advertisement shows an intent to induce the reliance of anyone who may use the product.

3. **The Buyer's Reliance**
    If the buyer is not aware of the misrepresentation or if it does not influence the transaction, there is no liability.

B. **FRAUDULENT MISREPRESENTATION**
Misrepresentation must have been made knowingly or with reckless disregard for the facts (such as intentionally concealing product defects).

C. **NONFRAUDULENT MISREPRESENTATION**
Occurs when a merchant innocently misrepresents the character or quality of goods (misrepresentation need not be made knowingly).

D. NO PROOF OF DEFECTS NECESSARY
A plaintiff does not have to show a product was defective or malfunctioned.

IV. STRICT LIABILITY
A defendant may be held liable for the result of his or her act regardless of intention or exercise of reasonable care (see Chapter 12).

A. REQUIREMENTS OF STRICT PRODUCT LIABILITY
Under the Restatement (Second) of Torts, Section 402A—

1. **Product Is in a Defective Condition When the Defendant Sells It**

2. **Defendant Is Normally in the Business of Selling the Product**

3. **Defect Makes the Product Unreasonably Dangerous**
   A product may be so defective if either—

   a. **Product Is Dangerous Beyond the Ordinary Consumer's Expectation**

   b. **There Was a Less Dangerous, Economically Feasible Alternative**
      But the manufacturer failed to use it.

      1) **Factors That Courts Consider**
         Product's utility; availability of safer products; known dangers; probability of injury; avoidability of injury (including warnings); viability of removing the danger without impairing the function or making the product too expensive.

      2) **Reasonably Foreseeable Misuses**
         Suppliers are generally required to design products that are either safe when misused or sold with some protective device.

4. **Plaintiff Incurs Harm to Self or Property by Use of the Product**

5. **Defect Is the Proximate Cause of the Harm**

6. **Product Was Not Substantially Changed After It Was Sold**
   Between the time the product was sold and the time of the injury.

B. OTHER IMPORTANT POINTS

1. **To Whom Section 402A Applies**
   Sellers of goods, including manufacturers, processors, assemblers, packagers, bottlers, wholesalers, distributors, and retailers.

2. **Privity of Contract Not Required**
   The injured party does not have to be a buyer or a third party beneficiary (as in an action based on warranty).

3. **Proof of a Failure to Exercise Due Care Not Required**
   A plaintiff does not have to prove that there was a failure to exercise due care (as in an action based on negligence).

4. **Liability May Be Virtually Unlimited**

C. LIABILITY SHARING
Some courts hold that all firms that manufactured and distributed DES (diethylstilbestrol) during a certain period are liable for injuries in proportion to the firms' respective shares of the market.

1. **Lack of Proof**

   In such cases, plaintiffs are unable to prove which of the distributors supplied the particular product that caused the injuries.

2. **Elements**

   (1) The product must be identical in design and defect to products manufactured and sold by several firms; (2) the inability to prove the cause of the harm must not be the plaintiff's fault; and (3) the manufacturer that made the particular product must be unidentifiable.

D. LIMITATIONS ON RECOVERY

1. **Type of Injury or Loss**

   Some courts limit recovery to personal injuries. Recovery for economic loss is rarely available. Recovery for breach of warranty may be available, depending on the type of injury (see UCC 2–318).

2. **Statutes of Limitations**

   A statute of limitations provides that an action must be brought within a specified period of time after the cause of action accrues (after some damage occurs or after a harmed party discovers the damage).

3. **Statutes of Repose**

   A statute of repose limits the time in which a suit can be filed. It runs from an earlier date and for a longer time than a statute of limitations.

4. **Type of Goods or Lack of Recognition**

   Some states limit the application of strict liability to new goods. Others refuse to recognize strict product liability. In these states, recovery is gained through breach of warranty or negligence theory.

E. STRICT LIABILITY TO BYSTANDERS

All courts extend the availability of strict liability to injured bystanders (limited in some cases to those whose injuries are reasonably foreseeable).

F. CRASHWORTHINESS DOCTRINE

Some courts apply this doctrine to impose liability for defects in the design or construction of motor vehicles that increase the extent of injuries if an accident occurs (even when the defects do not actually cause the accident).

G. OTHER APPLICATIONS OF STRICT LIABILITY

Suppliers of component parts and lessors may be liable for injuries caused by defective products. (Some courts base liability on the contract theory of warranty, not the tort theory of strict liability.)

H. DEFENSES TO STRICT LIABILITY

1. **Assumption of Risk**

   In some states, this is a defense if (1) the plaintiff voluntarily engaged in the risk, (2) the plaintiff knew and appreciated the risk created by the defect, and (3) the decision to undertake the risk was unreasonable.

2. **Misuse of the Product**

   The use must not be the one for which the product was designed and the misuse must not be reasonably foreseeable.

3. **Comparative Fault**

   Most states consider the plaintiff's actions in apportioning liability.

STUDY TIP ☞   <u>A Collision As a Foreseeable Misuse</u>
<u>of a Car</u>

Suppliers are generally required to expect reasonably
foreseeable misuses and to design products that are either safe
when misused or marketed with some protective device. You
may find it helpful to consider the crashworthi ness doctrine as
an application of this principle. That is, in states that apply
the crashworthiness doctrine, car crashes are generally
regarded as foreseeable misuses of cars. Thus, under the
crashworthiness doctrine, cars must be designed so as not to
subject drivers or passengers to enhanced injuries from
unreasonably dangerous features during a collision.

TRUE-FALSE QUESTIONS (Answers at the Back of the Book)

____ 1. At one time, privity of contract was not required to hold a manufacturer liable in a product liability action based on negligence, but today privity of contract is required.

____ 2. Failure to comply with a statute may be an automatic breach of the duty to exercise reasonable care and be held to constitute negligence *per se.*

____ 3. In an action based on strict liability, as in a negligence action, a plaintiff must prove that there was a failure to exercise due care.

____ 4. Under the crashworthiness doctrine, liability is imposed for defects in the design or construction of motor vehicles that cause injuries to passengers only if the defects also cause the accident.

____ 5. Strict liability for personal injuries caused by defective goods does not extend to those who lease the goods.

____ 6. In a comparative negligence jurisdiction, in a strict liability case, an injured party's failure to take precaution against a known defect will be considered in apportioning liability.

FILL-IN QUESTIONS (Answers at the Back of the Book)

Statutes of limitations and statutes of repose restrict the time within which an action may be brought. A statute of _____ (limitations/ repose) typically provides a specified period after a cause of action accrues within which an action must be brought. Sometimes the running of this period _____
(does not begin until/ ends when) the injured party discovers, or should have discovered, the injury. A statute of _____ (limitations/ repose) provides a time limit on filing a claim, whether or not a cause of action has accrued, so that a defendant will not be vulnerable to a lawsuit indefinitely. Usually, a statute of _____ (limitations/ repose) begins to run at an earlier date and runs for a longer time than a statute of _____ (limitations/ repose).

MULTIPLE-CHOICE QUESTIONS (Answers at the Back of the Book)

____ 1. Exercise Forever, a retailer, sells a treadmill to Humphrey without warning him of the fact, known to Exercise, that the safety shut-off device does not work. In using the treadmill, Humphrey discovers this defect. Later, while running on the treadmill, Humphrey's shoelace is caught in the gears, which do not shut off, and Humphrey's foot is injured. If Humphrey sues Exercise, Exercise may be held

   a. liable, because Exercise voluntarily assumed the risk of the harm.
   b. liable, because the non-functioning safety device was an intervening cause.
   c. not liable, because Humphrey voluntarily assumed the risk of the harm.
   d. not liable, because the non-functioning safety device was an intervening cause.

____ 2. Bea tells the pharmacist at Evergreen Pharmacy that Bea needs something to cure her cough. In reaching for a bottle of cough medicine, the pharmacist unintentionally selects a bottle of poison, which Bea buys and uses. Bea is seriously injured. If Bea sues Evergreen, Evergreen will be held

   a. liable, because Evergreen's selection of the bottle of poison was an intervening cause.
   b. liable, because Evergreen misrepresented the character of the contents of the bottle.
   c. not liable, because Bea voluntarily assumed the risk of the harm when she asked the pharmacist for advice.
   d. not liable, because Evergreen unintentionally selected the bottle of poison.

____ 3. Strict liability is imposed as a matter of public policy. This public policy rests on all of the following assumptions EXCEPT

   a. consumers who are injured can reasonably expect to be compensated.
   b. consumers should be protected against unsafe products.
   c. manufacturers and distributors should not escape liability for faulty products simply because they are not in privity of contract with the ultimate users of those products.
   d. manufacturers and sellers of products are in a better position to bear the costs associated with injuries caused by their products.

____ 4. While using a grain auger manufactured by Silo Implements, Inc., Curly fell into an opening on the top of the machine, injuring his legs and feet. Around the opening were several warning labels. Natural Farms, Inc., Curly's employer, subsequently welded a grid over the top to prevent future similar events. The grid did not interfere with the efficiency of the auger. If Curly sues Silo, on grounds of strict liability, Silo will be held

   a. liable, because Silo manufactured the machine.
   b. liable, because a less dangerous alternative (than the unguarded opening) was economically feasible, but Silo failed to produce it.
   c. not liable, because several warning labels were around the opening.
   d. not liable, because a less dangerous alternative (than the unguarded opening) was economically feasible, but both Curly and Natural failed to produce it.

_____ 5. For purposes of applying the doctrine of strict liability, which of the following is a product so defective as to be unreasonably dangerous?

   a. Ordinary sugar, because it is a deadly poison to diabetics
   b. Ordinary tobacco, because the effects of smoking are harmful
   c. Ordinary tobacco laced with bits of radioactive dust, because it is dangerous to an extent beyond that which the ordinary consumer would expect
   d. All of the above

_____ 6. Brigitte is standing in line at a convenience store near a bottle of Bolt Cola, which is on the floor about six inches from where she is standing. The bottle of Bolt explodes, and Brigitte's legs are severely injured. If Brigitte sues Bolt Cola Company, on grounds of strict liability, Bolt will be held

   a. liable, because it was reasonably foreseeable that a bystander would be injured by the defective bottle of Bolt.
   b. liable, because the explosion was an intervening cause of Brigitte's injury.
   c. not liable, because Brigitte assumed the risk that the Bolt might explode— Brigitte was voluntarily standing in line.
   d. not liable, because there was no less dangerous, economically feasible alternative that the manufacturer could have produced.

_____ 7. In those states in which assumption of risk is a defense in an action based on strict liability, all of the following elements must be shown EXCEPT

   a. the injured party voluntarily engaged in the risk while realizing the potential danger.
   b. the injured party knew and appreciated the risk created by the defect.
   c. the injured party's decision to undertake the known risk was unreasonable.
   d. the injured party used the product for something for which it was not designed.

SHORT ESSAY QUESTIONS

1. Discuss what distinguishes strict liability as a theory for recovery in a product liability case from other bases for recovery.

2. Discuss how defective a product must be to support a cause of action in strict liability in a product liability suit, particularly the factors that a court will look at when considering whether a less dangerous alternative was economically feasible.

ISSUE SPOTTERS (Answers at the Back of the Book)

1. Ferry MacGruder, Inc., manufactures automobile wheels, which it sells to Empire Automobile Corporation. Empire incorporates the wheels in the manufacture of its cars. One set of the wheels is made of defective materials, which an inspection of the wheels before putting them on a car would reveal. Empire does not inspect the wheels. The car is sold through Westland Corporation, an independent distributor, to Lovett's Automotive Sales, Inc. Keith buys the car. A defective wheel collapses while Keith is driving the car, causing Keith to crash into Woody's car. Keith, Woody, and their passengers Mick and Charlie suffer injury. To whom is Empire liable?

2. Powell Candies, Inc., manufactures and packs a box of candy, which Powell sells to Hasty Wholesalers, Inc. Hasty sells the candy to Jimmy Jingle Concessions Company, a distributor of concession items to theaters, and Jimmy Jingle sells it to Skylight Mall Cinemas. Tamara buys the box from Skylight one afternoon, but instead of eating the candy, gives it to Verley later that day. Verley offers some to Marie. While eating the candy, Marie breaks a tooth on a stone that is the same size, shape, and color of a piece of the candy. No reasonable inspection could have discovered the stone. Although there is no negligence on the part of Powell, Hasty, Jimmy Jingle, or Skylight, can they be held liable to Marie?

3.   Thompson-Edison Products, Inc., manufactures furniture polish. Thompson-Edison does not intend that little children drink the polish, but the company does not include warnings to that effect on the label, and it does not market the polish with a child-proof cap. Charlene uses the polish and leaves it capped on a table near her baby's crib. The baby drinks it and dies. Can Thompson-Edison be held liable for failing to guard against a reasonably foreseeable "misuse" of its product?

4.   Anchor Corporation manufactures prewrapped mattress springs. Through the carelessness of one of Anchor's employees, a spring is not properly wrapped. Anchor sells the spring to Bloom Manufacturing Company, which uses it in the manufacture of a mattress. Bloom sells the mattress to Mattress Madness, Inc., a retail store. Mattress Madness sells it to Kay. While sleeping on the mattress, Kay is stabbed in the back by the spring. The wound becomes infected, and Kay becomes seriously ill. Can Anchor be held liable?

5.   Goodlettsville Lock Company manufactures automobile door locks. Premiere Motors Corporation installs one of Goodlettsville's locks on Premiere's automobiles. Chad buys one of Premiere's automobiles. Later, driving home after a party, Chad does not wear a seat belt, and in a one-car accident, Chad is thrown from the car when the door flies open. Chad is killed. Chad's spouse Evelyn sues Goodlettsville and Premiere, on a theory of strict liability, alleging that the door lock was defective. Can Goodlettsville and Premiere contend that Chad's failure to wear a seat belt was negligent and contributed to Chad's death?

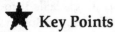 **Key Points**

The **key points** in this chapter include:

1. Patents and patent infringement.

2. Copyright law.

3. Trademarks and related property.

4. Trade secrets and the applicable law.

5. Computer crime and responses to it.

Chapter 15:
Intellectual Property and Computer Law

WHAT THIS CHAPTER IS ABOUT

Intellectual property consists of the products of intellectual, creative processes. Many of these products (such as inventions, books, television shows, computer programs, movies, and songs) are protected by the law of trademarks, patents, copyrights, and related concepts. The first half of this chapter outlines the laws that protect these products.

Intellectual property protection for computers and computer programs is new— the generations who drafted the intellectual property laws never envisioned a computerized world. The second half of this chapter covers how the intellectual property laws apply to computers and touches on another topic unique to the end of the twentieth century: computer crime.

CHAPTER OUTLINE

I. **TRADEMARKS AND RELATED PROPERTY**

A. **TRADEMARKS**

1. **What a Trademark Is**
   A distinctive mark, motto, device, or emblem that a manufacturer stamps, prints, or otherwise affixes to the goods it produces to distinguish them from the goods of other manufacturers.

2. **Requirements for Trademark Protection**
   The extent to which the law protects a trademark is normally determined by how **distinctive** the mark is. This may depend on whether it

114

has acquired a **secondary meaning** (which means that customers associate the mark with the source of a product).

  a. Fanciful, Arbitrary, or Suggestive Trademarks
  Generally considered to be the most distinctive trademarks.

  b. Descriptive Terms, Geographic Terms, and Personal Names
  Not inherently distinctive and not protected until they acquire a secondary meaning, which depends on how extensively the product is advertised, its market, the number of sales, and other factors.

  c. Colors
  A shade of color may be protected if it meets the requirements (this is rare).

  d. Generic Terms
  Terms such as *bicycle* or *computer* receive no protection, even if they acquire secondary meaning.

3. **Trademark Registration**
  A trademark may be registered with a state or the federal government (renewable between the fifth and sixth years and every twenty years, as long as it remains distinctive and is used). Whoever registers a mark is entitled to its exclusive use for marketing purposes. Trademarks do not need to be registered to be protected.

4. **Trademark Revision Act of 1988**
  Allows a trademark to be filed with the federal Patent and Trademark Office on the basis of (1) use or (2) the bona fide intention to use the mark in commerce within six months (which may be extended to thirty months). At the end of the six months, it must be proved that the mark was put into commerce.

5. **Trademark Infringement**
  When a trademark is copied to a substantial degree or used in its entirety by another, the trademark is infringed.

B. **SERVICE, CERTIFICATION, AND COLLECTIVE MARKS**
The same policies and restrictions that apply to trademarks normally apply to service, certification, and collective marks.

1. **Service Marks**
  Used to distinguish the services of one person or company from those of another. Registered in the same manner as trademarks.

2. **Certification Marks**
  Used by one or more persons, other than the owner, to certify the region, materials, mode of manufacture, quality, or accuracy of the owner's goods or services.

3. **Collective Marks**
  Certification marks used by members of a cooperative, association, or other organization.

C. **TRADE NAMES**
Used to indicate part or all of a business's name. Trade names cannot be registered with the federal government but may be protected under the common law if they are used as trademarks or service marks.

II.   PATENTS

A. WHAT A PATENT IS
A grant from the federal government that conveys and secures to an inventor the exclusive right to make, use, and sell an invention for a period of seventeen years (a lesser period for a design).

B. REQUIREMENTS FOR A PATENT
An invention, discovery, or design must be genuine, novel, useful, and not obvious in light of the technology of the time.

C. PATENT INFRINGEMENT
Making, using, or selling another's patented design, product, or process without the patent owner's permission (even if not all features or parts of an invention are copied). The owner may sue for an injunction, damages, the destruction of all infringing copies, attorneys' fees, and court costs.

D. PATENTS FOR COMPUTER SOFTWARE
The basis for software is often a mathematical equation or formula, which is not patentable. It is possible, however, to obtain a patent for a process that incorporates a computer program. Many patents have been issued for software-related inventions.

E. INTERNATIONAL PATENT PROTECTION
International patent protection is governed by the patent laws in each country in which an inventor seeks protection. Patent laws differ in different countries. In the United States, for example, most patents are granted only to the first inventor. In most other countries, patents are granted to the first party to apply.

III.   COPYRIGHTS

A. WHAT A COPYRIGHT IS
An intangible right granted by statute to the author or originator of certain literary or artistic productions.

1. Copyright Protection
Automatic for the life of the author plus fifty years. Copyrights owned by publishing houses expire seventy-five years from the date of publication or a hundred years from the date of creation, whichever is first. For works by one or more authors, the copyright expires fifty years after the death of the last surviving author.

2. What this Protection Means
A party who does not hold a copyright must obtain the permission of the copyright holder to use the copyrighted work and pay him or her royalties (fees for the privilege of reproducing the work).

B. REQUIREMENTS FOR COPYRIGHT PROTECTION

1. Works of Expression
To be protected, a work of expression must meet the following requirements:

a. Original
A work must be original.

b. Fit a Certain Category

A work must be a (1) literary work; (2) musical work; (3) dramatic work; (4) pantomime or choreographic work; (5) pictorial, graphic, or sculptural work; (6) film or other audiovisual work; or (7) a sound recording. The Copyright Act also protects computer software and architectural plans.

c. Fixed in a Durable Medium

A work must be "fixed in a durable medium" from which it can be perceived, reproduced, or communicated.

2. Compilations of Facts

A compilation is "a work formed by the collection and assembling of preexisting materials of data that are selected, coordinated, or arranged in such a way that the resulting work as a whole constitutes an original work of authorship" [Copyright Act, Section 103] To be copyrightable, a compilation must meet the above requirements.

C. WHAT IS NOT PROTECTED

1. Ideas and Related Concepts

No protection for any "idea, procedure, process, system, method of operation, concept, principle or discovery, regardless of the form in which it is described, explained, illustrated, or embodied" [Copyright Act, Section 102]. If an idea and an expression cannot be separated, the expression cannot be copyrighted.

2. Facts and Related Concepts

No protection for facts widely known to the public, page numbers (because they follow a sequence known to everyone), or mathematical calculations.

D. COPYRIGHT INFRINGEMENT

A copyright is infringed if a work is copied without the copyright holder's permission. A copy does not have to be exactly the same as the original—copying a substantial part of the original is enough.

1. Penalties

Penalties include actual damages (based on the harm to the copyright holder) or statutory damages (under the Copyright Act, not to exceed $100,000) and criminal proceedings for willful violations (which may result in fines or imprisonment).

2. Exception—Fair Use Doctrine

The Copyright Act, Section 107, permits the fair use of a work for purposes such as criticism, comment, news reporting, teaching (including multiple copies for classroom use), scholarship, or research. Permission is not necessary and royalties do not have to be paid.

E. COPYRIGHT PROTECTION FOR COMPUTER SOFTWARE

The Computer Software Copyright Act of 1980 protects computer programs.

1. What Is Protected

a. Binary Object Code

The part of a software program that is readable only by the computer.

    b. **Source Code**
        The part of a program that is readable by people.

    c. **Program Structure, Sequence, and Organization**
        The structure, sequence, and organization of a program.

2. **What May or May Not Be Protected**
    Based on court decisions, it is not clear whether the "look and feel"—the general appearance, command structure, video images, menus, windows, and other displays—of a program is protected by copyright.

    a. **Menu Command Structure**
        Lotus's menu command structure—including the choice of command terms, the structure and order of those terms, their presentation on the screen, and the long prompts—was held to be copyrightable.

    b. **User Interface, Windows, Icons, and Menus**
        The user interface of Apple's Macintosh computer and Apple's use of windows, icons, and menus (generally the images that Apple calls a "desktop metaphor") were held to be unprotectable "ideas."

    c. **The Test**
        Divide a program into its component parts and determine whether each part is (1) protectable as an expression of an idea or (2) unprotectable because it is an idea or a technique dictated by utilitarian considerations.

3. **Mask Works**
    The Semiconductor Chip Protection Act of 1984 protects a mask work (a series of images related to the pattern formed by the layers of a semiconductor-chip).

    a. **Requirements for Protection**
        A mask work must be fixed in the product and within two years of taking commercial advantage of the mask work, the owner must register it with the Copyright Office.

    b. **What the Protection Means**
        On registration, the owner obtains the exclusive right, for ten years, to reproduce, import, or distribute the work or a semiconductor-chip product that contains it.

F. **INTERNATIONAL COPYRIGHT PROTECTION**
    The United States is a party to a number of international copyright treaties, including the Berne Convention and the Universal Copyright Convention.

1. **Protection for Citizens of Countries That Have Signed the Berne Convention**
    If, for example, an American writes a book, his or her copyright in the book is recognized by every country that has signed the convention.

2. **Protection for Citizens of Countries That Have Not Signed the Berne Convention**
    If a citizen of a country that has not signed the convention publishes a book first in a country that has signed, all other countries that have signed the convention recognize that author's copyright.

IV. TRADE SECRETS

A. WHAT A TRADE SECRET IS

Customer lists, formulas, plans, research and development, pricing information, marketing techniques, production techniques, and generally anything that provides an opportunity to obtain an advantage over competitors who do not know or use it.

B. TRADE SECRET PROTECTION

Virtually all law with respect to trade secrets is common law. Protection of trade secrets extends both to ideas and their expression. Liability extends to those who misappropriate trade secrets by any means (breach of contract, industrial espionage).

V. COMPUTER CRIME

Computer crime is any act that is directed against computers or computer parts, that uses computers as instruments of crime, or that involves computers and constitutes abuse.

A. TYPES OF COMPUTER CRIME

1. Financial Crimes

Unauthorized transfer of monies among accounts. Unauthorized alteration of computer records.

2. Software Piracy

The theft of software; the unauthorized copying of computer programs; the rental, leasing, or lending of computer software without the express permission of the copyright holder.

3. Property Theft

The theft of computer equipment (hardware). Computer-related theft also may involve goods that are controlled and accounted for by means of a computer applications program. The theft of equipment and the theft of goods with the aid of computers are subject to the same criminal and tort laws as thefts of other property.

4. Vandalism and Destructive Programming

Smashing or damaging computer equipment; walking past computer storage banks with a large electromagnet; designing a computer program to rearrange, replace, or destroy data.

5. Theft of Data or Services

Using another's computer, computer information system, or data without authorization is generally considered larceny (theft). Breaking a computer's security code and perusing the information in the system's records is known as hacking.

B. DETECTING AND PROSECUTING COMPUTER CRIME

1. Federal Law

a. What Is Prohibited

The Counterfeit Access Device and Computer Fraud and Abuse Act of 1984 prohibits the unauthorized use of certain types of information, including restricted government information, information in a financial institution's records, and information in a consumer reporting agency's files on consumers.

b. **Penalties**
Up to five years' imprisonment and a fine of up to $250,000 or twice the amount that was gained or lost as a result of the crime.

2. **State Law**
Several states have laws addressing the problem of computer crime.

VI. PRIVACY RIGHTS AND COMPUTERS

Information in computer files is to a great extent unprotected by the law, and how to control computer use and abuse remains a significant challenge.

A. FEDERAL LAW
The Privacy Act of 1974 regulates government records and recording practices.

B. STATE LAW

1. **Legislation**
Many state laws regulating government records and recording practices are based on the federal Privacy Act of 1974. Many state laws enacted to address computer crime are also concerned to some extent with the issue of privacy.

2. **Common Law**
Tort damages may be awarded for unauthorized intrusion into another's private records or unauthorized examination of another's bank account. The difficulty is showing that private records have been invaded when there has been no physical intrusion into one's home or place of business.

STUDY TIP ☞ **Analyzing Intellectual Property Problems**

In analyzing problems that focus on topics discussed in the intellectual property portion of this chapter, there are three steps that you should follow. First, determine if the party who is bringing the suit has a protectable interest (that is, ask whether the subject matter of the plaintiff's interest is appropriate for copyright protection, patent protection, trademark protection, or whatever the case may be). Second, determine whether the other party—the defendant—has interfered with those rights. Third, consider what remedy is appropriate.

TRUE-FALSE QUESTIONS (Answers at the Back of the Book)

1. To obtain a patent, an applicant must satisfy the patent office that the invention, discovery, or design is genuine, novel, useful, and not obvious in light of contemporary technology.

____   2. To obtain a copyright, an author or originator of a work must satisfy the copyright office that the work is genuine, novel, useful, and not a copy of another copyrighted work.

____   3. Copyright infringement of software can occur even when there is no substantial similarity between computer programs' literal elements.

____   4. Personal names, words, or places that describe an article or its use can be trademarked if they are used in an uncommon or fanciful way.

____   5. The same policies and restrictions that apply to copyrights apply to service, certification, and collective marks.

____   6. Like copyright and trademark protection, protection of trade secrets extends only to the expression of ideas, not to the ideas themselves.

____   7. A computer crime may be difficult to prosecute, because its particular form of abuse may fall outside the traditional definition of a crime.

____   8. Software piracy consists of decoding and making unauthorized copies of software.

____   9. Although legislation is pending, damages may not yet be recovered for unauthorized intrusion into private records or unauthorized examination of a bank account.

FILL-IN QUESTIONS (Answers at the Back of the Book)

The Semiconductor Chip Protection Act of 1984 provides _____ (patent/ copyright) protection for _____ (mask works/ spreadsheet format designs), which are defined as series of images related to patterns formed by the layers of a semiconductor-chip product. A ____-_____ (mask work/ spreadsheet format design) must be fixed in the product to qualify, and within two years of initially taking commercial advantage of the work, the owner must register it with the U.S. _____ (Patent/ Copyright) Office. On registration, the owner of the protected work obtains an exclusive right, for ten years, to reproduce, import, or distribute the work or a semiconductor-chip product that contains it.

MULTIPLE-CHOICE QUESTIONS (Answers at the Back of the Book)

____   1. Without McCormick's permission, O'Reilly makes and sells widgets that are identical to McCormick's patented widget, except for cosmetic differences in the handle. If McCormick sues O'Reilly for patent infringement, McCormick will

    a. win, because O'Reilly is making and selling McCormick's widget without McCormick's permission.
    b. win, because patent infringement litigation is costly.
    c. lose, because of the differences between the widgets' caps and handles.
    d. lose, because O'Reilly is making fair use of McCormick's widget.

____   2.   Software products are often NOT patentable because

a.   much software simply automates procedures that can be performed manually.
b.   the basis for software is often a mathematical equation or formula.
c.   the technology changes too rapidly.
d.   both a and b.

____   3.   Grey Street Directories, Inc., compiles a directory listing all persons living in the Detroit area organized by the name of the street on which they live. In compiling the directory, Grey uses, without permission, Detroit-area telephone directories published by Yellow Ball, Inc.   In Yellow's suit against Grey for copyright infringement, Yellow will

a.   win, because once a compiler has selected and arranged facts in a certain way, the facts are as protected as the selection and arrangement.
b.   win, because Grey's directory renders Yellow's directories less useful.
c.   lose, because a compiler's selection and arrangement may be protected, but raw facts can be copied without liability.
d.   lose, because Grey's directory has no effect on the utility of Yellow's directories.

____   4.   The Computer Software Copyright Act of 1980 extended Copyright Act protection to computer programs.   In applying and interpreting this act, courts have NOT extended protection to

a.   a computer program's source code—the part of a program readable by humans.
b.   a computer program's structure, sequence, and organization.
c.   menu command structure—including the choice of command terms, the structure and order of those terms, their presentation on the screen, and the long prompts.
d.   a computer program's "look and feel"—the general appearance, command structure, video images, menus, windows, and other screen displays.

____   5.   Mark Corporation uses a monkey symbol in marketing its Monkey Man jeans, but has never registered the symbol with any government office.   Lladro, Inc., imports jeans manufactured in Hong Kong and markets them with the monkey symbol, although it does not register the symbol with a government office.   If Mark sues Lladro for trademark infringement, Mark will

a.   win, because Lladro had no right to trade on Mark's good will.
b.   win, because Lladro did not register the symbol with the federal trademark office.
c.   lose, because Mark did not register the symbol with the federal trademark office.
d.   lose, because Lladro did not manufacture the jeans, it only imported them.

____   6.   Which of the following is FALSE?

a.   Computer hardware is patentable.
b.   Some software is copyrightable as the expression of an idea.
c.   Computer hardware that is not patentable may be protected under trademark laws.
d.   Software that is not copyrightable may be protected as a trade secret.

___ 7. Rocket Construction Company has defaulted on a number of bank loans due to a couple of slow business years, but has recently been awarded a contract that Bob Rocket, the company's president, believes will turn Rocket's prospects around. To obtain loans that might not otherwise be obtainable, Bob accesses a credit reporting agency's computers and removes Rocket's bad credit history. If Rocket Construction Company is charged with larceny, Rocket will be

   a. acquitted, because a business firm cannot be convicted of larceny.
   b. acquitted under the common law definition of larceny.
   c. convicted under the common law definition of larceny.
   d. convicted, because Bob acted in Rocket's interest.

___ 8. Sven signs a contract with Peterssen Silk-Screening Company, promising not to divulge any process that Sven uses while in Peterssen's employ. After three years, Sven leaves Peterssen to go into business for himself, copying Peterssen's unique silk-screening technique. If Peterssen sues Sven for misappropriation of a trade secret, Peterssen will

   a. win, because Peterssen has been in the silk-screening business at least three years longer than Sven.
   b. win, because Sven committed theft of a trade secret.
   c. lose, because silk-screening techniques are not protected as trade secrets at common law.
   d. lose, because Sven is making fair use of what he learned.

___ 9. The Counterfeit Access Device and Computer Fraud and Abuse Act prohibits the use of

   a. a computer to obtain information contained in a financial institution's records or a consumer reporting agency's files on consumers.
   b. a computer to obtain information contained in a private educational institution's records or a private national testing service's files on students.
   c. a stolen ATM card to conduct an electronic fund transfer to obtain anything of value.
   d. any computer to commit any crime.

___ 10. When a computer is involved, an individual's right to privacy may be protected by

   a. traditional tort law.
   b. federal and state legislation.
   c. federal legislation only.
   d. both a and b.

___ 11. Jonathan Livingston Taylor invents a superior light bulb that lasts twice as long as the ordinary light bulb. To prevent others from making, using, or selling this invention or its design, Taylor should obtain a

   a. trademark.
   b. copyright.
   c. patent.
   d. none of the above.

SHORT ESSAY QUESTIONS

1.   Discuss what a copyright does and does not protect.

2.   Define trade secrets and discuss how they are protected.

ISSUE SPOTTERS (Answers at the Back of the Book)

1.   A video game manufacturer develops a gladiators video game with distinctive graphics, featuring the Mimeo brothers. Can the developer prevent a competitor from producing another game that is based on gladiators? Can the developer prevent competitors from copying the graphics?

2.   Maldo writes, copyrights, and publishes in the United States a book in Spanish titled *En la Casa del Tigre*. What copyright protection does Maldo have in other countries?

3.   Crabb Apple Ball Company makes and sells Crabb's Apple Balls, a distinctively flavored candy. Over time, some consumers come to refer to all similar candies as apple balls. Green Candy Corporation begins making and marketing "Green's Apple Balls." Can Crabb prevent Green from using the words Apple Balls for its candy?

4.   Burley Seed Company discovers that it can extract data from the computer of Northern King Hybrids, Inc., its major competitor, by making a series of telephone calls over a high-speed modem. When Burley uses its discovery to extract Northern King's customer lists, without Northern King's permission, what recourse does Northern King have?

5.   Bret discovers that he can extract data from the computer of Jennifer, who, as Bret knows, is an extraordinarily successful investor. When Bret uses his discovery to track Jennifer's investment decisions, without Jennifer's permission, what recourse does Jennifer have?

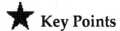 **Key Points**

The **key points** in this chapter include:

1. A lien creditor's priority.

2. Prejudgment attachment and postjudgment writs of execution.

3. What property is exempt from levy of execution or attachment.

4. Suretyship and guaranty.

5. The basic steps in the bankruptcy process.

Chapter 16:
Creditor-Debtor Relations and Bankruptcy

WHAT THIS CHAPTER IS ABOUT

This chapter sets out the rights and remedies available to a creditor, when a debtor defaults. Among those remedies are rights afforded by liens, and surety and guaranty agreements. This chapter also covers bankruptcy law, based on the Bankruptcy Reform Act of 1978 (the Code).

CHAPTER OUTLINE

I. LAWS ASSISTING CREDITORS

A. MECHANIC'S LIEN
A **mechanic's lien** is placed by a creditor on real property when a person contracts for labor, services, or material to make improvements on the property but does not immediately pay for the improvements.

B. ARTISAN'S LIEN
An **artisan's lien** is a security device by which a creditor can recover from a debtor for labor and materials furnished in the repair of personal property.

C. JUDICIAL LIENS
A debt must be past due before a creditor can commence legal action. Once an action is brought, the debtor's property may be seized to satisfy the debt.

1. Attachment
Attachment is a court-ordered seizure and taking into custody of property before the entry of a final judgment for a past-due debt.

2. Writ of Execution

A **writ of execution** is an order, usually issued by the clerk of the court, directing the sheriff to seize and sell any of the debtor's nonexempt property within the court's geographical jurisdiction.

E. GARNISHMENT

Garnishment is when a creditor collects a debt by seizing property of the debtor (such as wages or money in a bank account) that is being held by a third party (such as an employer or a bank).

F. MORTGAGE FORECLOSURE

A mortgagor can foreclose on the mortgaged property if the debtor defaults. The usual method is a judicial sale. The proceeds are applied to the debt.

1. Equity of Redemption

A mortgagor can redeem the property any time before the sale (and, in some states, within a certain period of time after the sale).

2. Deficiency Judgment

If the proceeds do not cover the foreclosure costs and the debt, the mortgagee can recover the difference from the mortgagor by obtaining a deficiency judgment (in a separate legal action after the foreclosure).

II. SURETYSHIP AND GUARANTY

A. SURETYSHIP

Suretyship is a promise by a third person to be responsible for a debtor's obligation. Does not have to be in writing. A surety is primarily liable—a creditor can demand payment from the surety the moment the debt is due.

B. GUARANTY

A **guaranty** is a promise to be secondarily liable for the debt or default of another. A guarantor pays only after the debtor defaults and the creditor has made an attempt to collect from the debtor. A guaranty must be in writing unless the main-purpose exception applies.

C. DEFENSES OF THE SURETY AND THE GUARANTOR

1. The Contract Between the Debtor and the Creditor Is Modified

Without obtaining the consent of the surety (guarantor), a gratuitous surety is discharged completely and a compensated surety is discharged to the extent that the surety suffers a loss.

2. The Principal Obligation Is Paid or Valid Tender Is Made

The surety (guarantor) is discharged from the obligation.

3. Most of the Defenses of the Principal Debtor

Defenses that a surety cannot use: the debtor's incapacity, bankruptcy, and the statute of limitations.

4. A Surety or Guarantor's Own Defenses

For example, fraud by the creditor to induce the surety (guarantor) to guarantee the debt (such as the creditor's failure to inform the surety of facts that would substantially increase the surety's risk).

5. A Creditor's Surrender or Impairment of the Collateral

Without the surety's (guarantor's) consent, releases the surety to the extent of any loss suffered from the creditor's actions.

D. RIGHTS OF THE SURETY AND THE GUARANTOR
If the surety (guarantor) pays the debt—

1. Right of Subrogation
The surety (guarantor) may pursue any remedies that were available to the creditor against the debtor.

2. Right of Reimbursement
The surety is entitled to receive from the debtor all outlays made on behalf of the suretyship arrangement.

3. Co-Sureties' Right of Contribution
A surety who pays more than his or her proportionate share on a debtor's default is entitled to recover from the co-sureties the amount paid above the surety's obligation.

III. PROTECTION FOR DEBTORS

A. PROPERTY EXEMPT FROM CREDITORS' ACTIONS

1. Homestead
Each state permits a debtor to retain the family home (in some states only if the debtor has a family) in its entirety or up to a specified dollar amount.

2. Personal Property
Often exempt: household furniture up to a specified dollar amount; clothing and other personal possessions; a vehicle (or vehicles) (up to a specified dollar amount); certain animals, usually livestock but including pets; and equipment that the debtor uses in a business or trade.

B. SPECIAL PROTECTION FOR CONSUMER DEBTORS
A Federal Trade Commission rule limits the rights of a holder in due course (HDC) who holds a negotiable promissory note executed by a consumer as part of a consumer transaction. Other laws include the Truth-in-Lending Act, which protects consumers by requiring creditors to disclose certain information when making loans (see Chapter 23).

IV. BANKRUPTCY AND REORGANIZATION

A. LIQUIDATION PROCEEDINGS (CHAPTER 7)
A debtor in a liquidation proceeding declares his or her debts and turns all assets over to a trustee, who sells the nonexempt assets and distributes the proceeds to creditors. Most debts are discharged.

1. Who Can File for a Liquidation
Any "person"—individuals, partnerships, and corporations (spouses can file jointly)—except railroads, insurance companies, banks, savings and loan associations, and credit unions.

2. Filing the Petition
Filing a petition constitutes an order for relief. A court can dismiss a petition if granting it would constitute substantial abuse [11 U.S.C. Section 707(b)]. In some case, creditors can force bankruptcy proceedings.

3. Automatic Stay
When a petition is filed, an **automatic stay** suspends all action by creditors against the debtor. The **adequate protection doctrine** protects se-

cured creditors by requiring payments, or other collateral or relief, to the extent that the stay may cause the value of collateral to decrease.

4. **Property of the Estate**

With some exceptions, most property acquired after the filing of the petition is not included.

5. **Creditors' Meeting and Claims**

Within "not less than ten days or more than thirty days," the court calls a meeting of creditors, at which the debtor answers questions. Within ninety days of the meeting, a creditor must file a proof of claim.

6. **Property Exempt from a Liquidation**

a. **Federal Law**

Exempts such property as interests in a residence to $7,500, a motor vehicle to $1,200, household goods to $4,000, and tools of a trade to $750, and the rights to receive Social Security and other benefits.

b. **State Law**

Most states preclude the use of federal exemptions; others allow a debtor to choose between state and federal. State exemptions may include different value limitations and exempt different property.

7. **The Trustee**

After the order for relief, an interim trustee is appointed to preside over the debtor's property until the first meeting of creditors, when a permanent trustee is elected. A trustee's duty is to collect and reduce to money the property of the estate and distribute the proceeds.

8. **Distribution of Property**

a. **Secured Creditors**

Within thirty days of the petition or before the first creditors' meeting (whichever is first), a debtor must state whether he or she will retain secured collateral (or claim it as exempt, etc.). The trustee must enforce the statement within forty-five days.

b. **Unsecured Creditors**

Paid in the order of priority. Each class is paid before the next class is entitled to anything. The order of priority is—

1) Administrative expenses (court costs, trustee and attorney fees).
2) In an involuntary bankruptcy, expenses incurred by the debtor in the ordinary course of business from the filing of the petition to the appointment of the trustee or the issuance of an order for relief.
3) Unpaid wages, salaries, and commissions earned within ninety days of the petition, to $2,000 per claimant. A claim in excess is a claim of a general creditor (no. 8 below).
4) Unsecured claims for contributions to employee benefit plans, limited to services performed within 180 days before the petition and $2,000 per employee.
5) Claims by farmers and fishers, to $2,000, against storage or processing facilities.

6) Consumer deposits to $900 given to the debtor before the petition to buy, lease, or rent property or services that were not received. A claim over $900 is a claim of a general creditor.
7) Taxes and penalties due to the government.
8) Claims of general creditors.

c. Debtors
Any amount remaining is turned over to the debtor.

9. Discharge
A Chapter 7 discharge is granted only to individuals (corporations and partnerships may use Chapter 11). A discharge does not affect the liability of a co-debtor. A court can revoke a discharge within a year, if the debtor acts fraudulently or dishonestly during the proceedings.

10. Reaffirmation
A debtor's agreement to pay a dischargeable debt must be made before a discharge is granted and must usually be approved by the court.

B. REORGANIZATIONS (CHAPTER 11)
The creditors and debtor formulate a plan under which the debtor pays a portion of the debts, is discharged of the rest, and continues in business.

1. Who Is Eligible for Relief Under Chapter 11
Any debtor (except a stockbroker or a commodities broker) eligible for Chapter 7. The same principles apply that govern liquidation.

2. Why a Case May Be Dismissed
Creditors may prefer a workout to bankruptcy proceedings, or there may be other reasons (inability to effect a plan, etc.).

3. Debtor in Possession
On entry of an order for relief, the debtor continues to operate his or her business as a debtor in possession (DIP). The court may appoint a trustee (or receiver) if that is in the best interests of the estate.

4. Creditors' Committees
A committee of unsecured creditors is appointed to consult with the trustee or DIP. Other committees may represent creditors.

5. The Reorganization Plan

a. What the Plan Must Do
Conserve and administer the debtor's assets in the hope of a return to solvency; be fair and equitable; designate classes of claims and interests; specify the treatment to be afforded the classes; and provide an adequate means for execution.

b. Who Can File a Plan
Only the debtor within the first 120 days after the date of the order for relief. Any other party, if the debtor does not meet the deadline or fails to obtain creditor consent within 180 days.

c. The Plan Is Submitted to Creditors for Acceptance
Each class adversely affected by a plan must accept it (two-thirds of the total claims must approve). If only one class accepts, the court may confirm it if it "does not discriminate unfairly" against

any creditors. The plan is binding on confirmation, and the debtor is given a discharge from all claims not within the plan (except those that would be denied in a liquidation).

C. INDIVIDUALS' REPAYMENT PLANS (CHAPTER 13)

1. Who Is Eligible

Individuals (not partnerships or corporations) with regular income and unsecured debts of less than $100,000 or secured debts of less than $350,000. With a few exceptions, all debts are dischargeable.

2. Voluntary Filing Only

A Chapter 13 case can be initiated by the filing of a voluntary petition only. A trustee is appointed.

3. The Repayment Plan

The plan must provide for (1) turnover to the trustee of the debtor's future income, (2) full payment of all claims entitled to priority, and (3) the same treatment of each claim within a particular class.

4. Discharge

After completion of payments, all debts under the plan are discharged. A discharge obtained by fraud can be revoked within one year.

STUDY TIP 👉 Why Study?

Sometimes forgotten in the activity of studying are the reasons for studying in the first place. You may find it helpful, from time to time, to remind yourself of your own reasons for studying business law—you may be studying, for example, to be ready for tomorrow's class, to be prepared for the final examination, to attain a certain grade, to be awarded a degree, and ultimately to obtain a position in an occupational field that you believe you will enjoy.

TRUE-FALSE QUESTIONS (Answers at the Back of the Book)

____ 1. Statutes permit a holder of a mechanic's lien or an artisan's lien to foreclose on property (after notice to the owner) and sell it to satisfy the debt.

____ 2. If a creditor's suit is successful, the court enters a judgment against the debtor, but if the debtor does not or cannot pay, there is nothing that the creditor can do.

____ 3. Federal and state laws limit the amount that can be garnished from wages, and state laws often provide for larger exemptions, but state and federal statutes cannot be applied together to determine how much is exempt from garnishment.

____ 4. Generally, to avoid liability, a surety or a guarantor can use only his or her own defenses—that is, a surety or guarantor cannot use any defenses that the principal might have to liability.

____ 5. Under the adequate protection doctrine, debtors are protected from losing the value of their property as a result of the automatic stay.

____ 6. Generally, in a bankruptcy proceeding, any creditor's claim is allowed automatically unless contested by the trustee, the debtor, or another creditor.

FILL-IN QUESTIONS (Answers at the Back of the Book)

1. A contract of _____ (suretyship/ guaranty) is a promise to a creditor made by a third person to be responsible for a debtor's obligation. A _____ (guarantor/ surety) is primarily liable: The creditor can hold the _____ (guarantor/ surety) responsible for payment of the debt when the debt is due, without first exhausting all remedies against the debtor. A contract of _____ (suretyship/ guaranty) also includes a promise to answer for a principal's obligation, but a _____ (guarantor/ surety) is secondarily liable.

2. A contract of _____ (suretyship/ guaranty) does not have to be in writing to be enforceable. A contract of _____ (suretyship/ guaranty) must be in writing to be enforceable unless the "main purpose" exception applies.

MULTIPLE-CHOICE QUESTIONS (Answers at the Back of the Book)

____ 1. Under Chapter 11, creditors and debtor plan for the debtor to pay some debts, be discharged of the rest, and continue in business. Which of the following is FALSE about Chapter 11?

a. A Chapter 11 plan must designate classes of claims and interests and provide adequate means for execution.
b. Even if all creditors accept a plan, the court may reject it if it is not "in the best interests of the creditors."
c. Even if only one class of creditors accepts a plan, the court may confirm it.
d. Under Chapter 11, a debtor cannot reject a collective bargaining agreement.

____ 2. Under Chapter 7, a debtor may be denied a discharge on any of the following grounds EXCEPT

a. concealing property with the intent to defraud a creditor.
b. fraudulently destroying financial records.
c. obeying a lawful bankruptcy court order.
d. obtaining a bankruptcy discharge within six years of the petition.

____ 3. Grand Turk Concessions wants to borrow money from Bank of Athena. Athena refuses to lend Grand Turk the money unless Rocky cosigns the note. Rocky cosigns the note. Grand Turk makes the first six installment payments under the note. When the seventh payment is due, Athena can seek payment from

a. Grand Turk, not Rocky, because Rocky is a guarantor.
b. Grand Turk, not Rocky, because Grand Turk is a surety.
c. Grand Turk or Rocky, because Rocky is a surety.
d. Grand Turk or Rocky, because Rocky is a guarantor.

____ **4.** Bruel obtains a judgment for $30,000 and a writ of execution against Ugo. On enforcement of the writ, Ugo's family's home is sold for $60,000. The state's homestead exemption is $35,000. All of Ugo's personal property is exempt under the state's exemption laws, except a pair of motorcycles that are sold for $5,000. After applying the appropriate amounts to payment of the judgment debt, how much of the debt will remain?

   a. $25,000
   b. $10,000
   c. $5,000
   d. $0

____ **5.** Under the Bankruptcy Code, within thirty days of an order for relief, a trustee is appointed or elected to reduce the debtor's estate to money. To collect the property of the estate, a trustee can set aside a transfer of the debtor's property on all of the following grounds EXCEPT

   a. any ground that the debtor could use.
   b. the ground that the transfer was made within ninety days of the filing of the petition in preference to one creditor over others.
   c. the ground that the transfer was made as a payment within the ordinary course of business.
   d. the ground that the transfer was fraudulent and made within a year of the filing of the petition or made with the intent to hinder, delay, defraud a creditor.

____ **6.** The differences between Chapter 7 and Chapter 11 proceedings and Chapter 13 plans include all of the following EXCEPT

   a. under Chapter 13, only a debtor can file a petition.
   b. under Chapter 13, only individuals with regular income and certain levels of debt can file a petition.
   c. under Chapter 13, unlike Chapters 7 and 11, a debtor continues in possession of a business.
   d. a Chapter 13 filing is less expensive than a Chapter 7 liquidation or a Chapter 11 proceeding.

SHORT ESSAY QUESTIONS

1. Define a lien, list four ways under which a lien can arise, and discuss a lienholder's priority.

2. Compare contracts of suretyship and guaranty contracts.

ISSUE SPOTTERS (Answers at the Back of the Book)

1. Sanford owes Sinclair Suburban Credit Company $6,000. The debt is past due, and Sinclair files suit. While the wheels of justice grind, Sinclair discovers that Sanford has removed some of his property from the state, has hidden other property, and has assigned still other property in fraud of her creditors, including Sinclair. Sinclair justifiably believes that Sanford is about remove, hide, and assign the rest of his property to defeat the creditors' claims. What can Sinclair do to assure that there will be some assets to satisfy the debt once Sinclair wins the suit?

2.   Eli owes Oran $2,500, and the debt is past due. Eli owns no house and has very little personal property, but Eli has a checking account, a savings account, and a job, for which, of course, Eli is paid wages. All of these assets are in the hands of third parties, however—in the case of the accounts, Eli's bank and, in the case of the wages, Eli's employer. What can Oran do to reach these assets to satisfy the debt?

3.   Laura wants to borrow $10,000 from Twin Peaks Finance Company to buy a new Miata, but Twin Peaks refuses to lend the money to Laura unless Bob cosigns the note. Bob cosigns the note. When Laura fails to make three payments, Bob pays Twin Peaks. Can Bob get the money for these three payments from Laura?

4.   Jerry's monthly income is $2,500, Jerry's monthly expenses are $2,100, and Jerry's debts total nearly $15,000. Although Jerry's debts seem large to Jerry, if Jerry diligently applied the difference between his income and expenses to paying off the debts, the debts could be eliminated within three years. Are there any provisions in the bankruptcy laws for individuals in Jerry's position?

5.   After graduating from college, for which Dirk paid by taking out loans, Dirk works briefly as an investment counselor before filing for bankruptcy. As part of his bankruptcy petition, Dirk reveals his only debts as the student loans, taxes accruing within the three previous years, and a claim against him based on misuse of clients' funds during his employment. Are these debts dischargeable in a bankruptcy proceeding?

Chapter 17:
Business Organizations

WHAT THIS CHAPTER IS ABOUT

This chapter sets out the basic features of sole proprietorships, partnerships, corporations, and other forms for doing business, including limited liability companies. The chapter concludes with a discussion of private franchises.

CHAPTER OUTLINE

I. SOLE PROPRIETORSHIPS

The simplest form of business: the owner is the business. The proprietor takes all the profits; pays only personal income tax on profits. The proprietor has all the risk (unlimited liability for all debts); limited opportunity to raise capital; the business dissolves when the owner dies.

II. PARTNERSHIPS

Agreement between two or more persons to carry on a business for profit.

A. GENERAL PARTNERSHIPS

General partners jointly control the operation and share the profits. No particular form of agreement is necessary to create a general partnership; partners may agree to any terms. Partners are personally liable for partnership obligations; profit is taxed as individual income to partners.

B. LIMITED PARTNERSHIPS

Consist of at least one general partner and one or more limited partners. General partners run the business and are subject to personal liability for partnership obligations. Limited partners have limited liability. Generally, participating in management results in personal liability for partnership debts, if the creditor knew of the participation.

III. CORPORATIONS

Corporations consist of shareholders, who own the business; a board of directors, who are elected by the shareholders to manage the business; and officers, who oversee day-to-day operations.

A. CORPORATE FORMATION

1. Promotional Activities

Promoters take the first steps in organizing a corporation and are personally liable on preincorporation contracts, unless the contracting party agrees otherwise. This liability continues after incorporation unless the third party releases the promoter or the corporation assumes the contract by novation.

2. Articles of Incorporation

Include basic information about a corporation and serve as a primary source of authority for its organization and functions. Incorporators must sign the articles when they are submitted to the state; often this is their only duty.

3. Certificate of Incorporation (Charter)

The articles of incorporation are sent to the appropriate state official (usually the secretary of state). Many states issue a certificate of incorporation authorizing the corporation to conduct business.

B. IMPROPER INCORPORATION

1. *De Jure* Existence

Occurs if there is substantial compliance with all requirements for incorporation. In most states, the certificate of incorporation is evidence that all requirements have been met, and neither the state nor a third party can attack the corporation's existence.

2. *De Facto* Existence

The existence of a corporation cannot be challenged by third persons (except the state) if (1) there is a statute under which the firm can be incorporated, (2) the parties made a good faith attempt to comply with it, and (3) the firm has attempted to do business as a corporation.

3. Corporation by Estoppel

If an association that is neither an actual corporation nor a *de facto* or *de jure* corporation holds itself out as being a corporation, it will be estopped from denying corporate status in a lawsuit by a third party.

C. DISREGARDING THE CORPORATE ENTITY

A court may ignore the corporate structure (pierce the corporate veil), exposing the shareholders to personal liability, if—

1. A party is tricked or misled into dealing with the corporation rather than the individual.
2. The corporation is set up never to make a profit or always to be insolvent, or it is too thinly capitalized.
3. Statutory corporate formalities are not followed.
4. Personal and corporate interests are commingled to the extent that the corporation has no separate identity.

D. CORPORATE MANAGEMENT—DIRECTORS

1. Election of Directors

Set in a corporation's articles or bylaws. Corporations with fewer than fifty shareholders can have no directors [RMBCA 8.01]. The first board (appointed by the incorporators or named in the articles) serves until the first shareholders' meeting. Subsequent directors are elected by a majority vote of the shareholders (see below).

2. Removal of Directors

A director can be removed for cause by shareholder action (or the board may have the power). In most states, a director cannot be removed without cause, unless the shareholders have reserved the right.

3. Board of Directors' Meetings

A board conducts business by holding formal meetings with recorded minutes. Quorum requirements vary. If the firm specifies none, in most states a quorum is a majority of the number of directors authorized in the articles or bylaws. Voting is done in person, one vote per director.

4. Directors' Management Responsibilities

Major corporate policy decisions; financial decisions; appointment, pay, supervision, and removal of officers and other managerial employees. Most states permit a board to elect an executive committee from among the directors to handle management between board meetings.

E. CORPORATE MANAGEMENT—SHAREHOLDERS

Shareholders own the corporation. Regular meetings must occur annually; special meetings can be called to handle urgent matters.

1. Shareholders' Meetings

At the meeting, a quorum must be present. A majority vote of the shares present is usually required to pass resolutions. Fundamental changes (amending the articles of incorporation and bylaws, merging or dissolving the corporation, selling all or substantially all of the corporation's assets) require a higher percentage.

2. Voting Techniques

Each common shareholder has one vote per share. The articles can exclude or limit voting rights.

a) Cumulative Voting

The number of members of the board to be elected is multiplied by the total number of voting shares. This is the number of votes a shareholder has and can be cast for one or more nominees.

b) Shareholder Agreements

A group of shareholders can agree to vote their shares together.

1) Proxies

A shareholder can vote by proxy. Any person can solicit proxies. Normally revocable, unless designated otherwise.

2) Shareholder Proposals

When a company sends proxy materials to its shareholders, it must include proposals to be considered and give shareholders the opportunity to vote by returning proxy cards.

c) **Voting Trust**

Exists when legal title (recorded ownership on the corporate books) is transferred to a trustee who is responsible for voting the shares. The shareholder retains all other ownership rights.

IV. OTHER ORGANIZATIONAL FORMS

A. JOINT VENTURE

A relationship in which two or more persons combine their efforts or property for a single transaction or project, or a related series of transactions or projects. Unless otherwise agreed, members share profits and losses equally.

B. SYNDICATE

A group of individuals financing a project; may exist as a corporation, a partnership, or no legally recognized form.

C. JOINT STOCK COMPANY

Usually treated like a partnership (formed by agreement, members have personal liability, etc.), but members are not agents of one another, and has many characteristics of a corporation: (1) ownership by shares of stock, (2) managed by directors and officers, and (3) perpetual existence.

D. BUSINESS TRUST

Legal ownership and management of the property of the business is in one or more trustees; profits are distributed to beneficiaries, who are not personally responsible for the debts of the trust. Resembles a corporation.

E. COOPERATIVE

An association that is organized to provide an economic service without profit to its members (or shareholders).

F. THE LIMITED LIABILITY COMPANY (LLC)

A hybrid form of business enterprise that offers the limited liability of the corporation with the tax advantages of a partnership.

V. PRIVATE FRANCHISES

A **franchise** is any arrangement in which the owner of a trademark, a trade name, or a copyright has licensed others to use it in selling goods or services.

A. THE LAW OF FRANCHISING

1. **Federal Regulation of Franchising**

   a. **Automobile Dealers' Franchise Act of 1956**
   Dealership franchisees are protected from manufacturers' bad faith termination of their franchises.

   b. **Petroleum Marketing Practices Act (PMPA) of 1979**
   Prescribes the grounds and conditions under which a gasoline station franchisor may terminate or decline to renew a franchise.

   c. **Federal Antitrust Laws**
   May apply if there is an illegal price-fixing agreement (see Chapters 26 and 27) between a franchisor and franchisee.

   d. **Federal Trade Commission (FTC) Regulations**
   Franchisors must disclose material facts necessary to a prospective franchisee's making an informed decision concerning a franchise.

2. **State Regulation of Franchising**
   Similar to federal law. When a franchise exists primarily for the sale of products manufactured by the franchisor, Article 2 of the Uniform Commercial Code applies (see Chapter 11).

B. **THE FRANCHISE AGREEMENT**
A franchise relationship is created by a contract between the franchisor and the franchisee.

1. **Paying for the Franchise**
   The franchisee ordinarily pays (1) an initial fee for the franchise license, (2) separate fees for products bought from or through the franchisor, (3) a percentage of sales, and (4) sometimes a percentage of advertising and administrative costs.

2. **Location of the Franchise**
   Typically, the franchisor will determine the territory to be served and its exclusivity. The agreement may specify whether the premises for the business must be leased or purchased and who is to supply equipment and furnishings for the premises.

3. **Price Controls**
   A franchisor may require a franchisee to buy certain supplies from the franchisor at an established price. A franchisor can suggest retail prices for the goods but cannot insist on them (see Chapters 26 and 27).

4. **Business Organization and Quality Controls**
   A franchisor may specify (1) particular requirements for the form and capital structure of the business; (2) standards of operation (such as quality standards); and (3) the training of personnel.

5. **Termination of the Franchise**
   Determined by the parties. Usually, termination must be "for cause" (such as breach of the agreement, etc.) and notice must be given. A franchisee must be given reasonable time to wind up the business.

STUDY TIP 👉 <u>Agency Relationships</u>

The principles of agency law (Chapter 19) can have considerable impact in situations involving business organizations. Any but the smallest of small businesses must do business through its employees or others—thus, even a sole proprietor must have agents. As you will discover in the next chapters, a partnership relationship is subject to the principles of agents—each partner is an agent of the other partners. A corporation could not do business without its representatives—its agents. Even a franchise may be deemed a principal-agent relationship, if there is a close relationship between franchisor and franchisee.

TRUE-FALSE QUESTIONS (Answers at the Back of the Book)

_____ 1. In a sole proprietorship, the owner is the business.

_____ 2. A partnership is an association of two or more persons to carry on, as co-owners, a business for profit.

_____ 3. Unlike a sole proprietorship and many partnerships, a corporation is not a legal entity separate and distinct from its owners.

_____ 4. Failing to follow statutory corporate formalities, such as calling required meetings, will never affect individual shareholders' protection from personal liability for corporate debts.

_____ 5. As a general rule, shareholders have no responsibility for the daily management of a corporation, although they are ultimately responsible for choosing the board of directors and must approve fundamental changes before they can be affected.

_____ 6. A franchise is any arrangement in which the owner of a trademark, a trade name, or a copyright has licensed others to use it in selling goods or services.

FILL-IN QUESTIONS (Answers at the Back of the Book)

A franchise operating under a franchisor's trade name and identified as a member of a select group of dealers that engage in the franchisor's business is a _____ (chain-style/ distributorship/ manufacturing) franchise. When a franchisor licenses a franchisee to sell its product in an exclusive territory, a _____ (chain-style/ distributorship/ manufacturing) franchise is established. When a franchisee is required to follow standardized or prescribed methods of operations and to deal exclusively with the franchisor to obtain materials and supplies, a _____ (chain-style/ distributorship/ manufacturing) franchise exists. When a franchisor transmits to a franchisee the essential ingredients or formula to make a particular product, which the franchisee then markets in accordance with the franchisor's standards, a _____ (chain-style/ distributorship/ manufacturing) franchise is created.

MULTIPLE-CHOICE QUESTIONS (Answers at the Back of the Book)

_____ 1. Which of the following statements about sole proprietorships is FALSE?

a. The proprietor receives all the profits.
b. The proprietor has complete discretion as to the business's management.
c. The proprietor's liability is limited to the amount of his or her investment.
d. The proprietor pays personal taxes on the business's income.

_____ 2. Which of the following statements about general partners is FALSE?

a. Each partner is a co-owner of the business.
b. Each partner has an equal voice in the business's management.
c. Each partner's liability is limited to the amount of his or her investment.
d. Each partner pays personal taxes on his or her share of the business's income.

____ 3. Which of the following statements about limited partnerships is FALSE?

a. A limited partnership is not formed until a special certificate is filed.
b. Each limited partner has a voice in the business's management.
c. Each limited partner's liability is limited to the amount of his or her commitment to investment.
d. Each limited partner pays personal taxes on his or her share of the business's income.

____ 4. Which of the following statements about corporations is FALSE?

a. Each shareholder is a co-owner of the corporation.
b. Each shareholder is a manager of the corporation.
c. Each shareholder's liability is limited to the amount of his or her investment.
d. Corporate income is taxed twice.

____ 5. Which of the following statements concerning directors' management responsibilities is FALSE?

a. Directors can declare and pay corporate dividends to shareholders.
b. Any one director can act individually in carrying routine corporate business.
c. Directors can bind the corporation in matters involving major corporate policy decisions.
d. Directors can appoint, supervise, and remove corporate officers and other managerial employees, and determine their compensation.

____ 6. Which of the following statements about other business forms is FALSE?

a. A joint venture is similar to a partnership but created in contemplation of a limited activity.
b. A syndicate may exist as a partnership or a corporation but is undertaken to finance a particular project.
c. A joint stock company is a hybrid of a partnership and a corporation but is usually treated like a partnership.
d. A business trust is similar to a corporation, but beneficiaries are personally liable for the trust's debts and obligations.

____ 7. A franchise agreement may require a franchisee to do all of the following EXCEPT

a. sell the franchisor's products at prices set by the franchisor.
b. pay a percentage of the franchisee's annual sales receipts to the franchisor.
c. pay a percentage of the franchise advertising costs and administrative expenses.
d. purchase certain supplies from the franchisor at established prices.

____ 8. A franchise agreement may allow a franchisor to do all of the following EXCEPT

a. terminate the franchise without notice.
b. set certain standards of operation.
c. periodically inspect the franchisee's premises.
d. specify particular requirements for the business form of the organization.

SHORT ESSAY QUESTIONS

1.   Discuss the principal characteristics of sole proprietorships, partnerships and corporations.

2.   Discuss how franchise agreements generally deal with the following areas of coverage: (1) payment for the franchise; (2) location of the franchise; (3) price controls; (4) quality control; and (5) termination of the franchise.

ISSUE SPOTTERS (Answers at the Back of the Book)

1.   Sullivan wants to open a sporting goods store. Sullivan plans to hire only Gilbert and Art to help customers and run the store. Sullivan plans to invest only his own capital in the business. Sullivan does not expect to make a profit for at least eighteen months and not to make much of a profit for the first three years. Sullivan hopes to expand eventually, but has no plans to do so in the first five years. Which form of business organization would be most appropriate for Sullivan's business?

2.   Flem, Ike, Manny, and Eula want to start a ranch. Between them, Flem and Ike have nearly twenty years' experience in day-to-day ranching, but little capital to invest. Manny and Eula have expertise in the administrative background necessary to manage and operate a ranch and considerable capital to invest, but no experience in day-to-day ranching. Which form of business organization would be most appropriate for their business?

3.   Five years ago, Chick started Frenchy's Fries, a small potato products company, as a sole proprietorship. Since the introduction of Frenchy's products, they have increased in popularity, and Chick is now receiving considerably more orders than the current operation can handle. Chick needs to buy more equipment, lease larger facilities, and hire more employees. Chick also his eye on acquiring Rondi's Pizzas, a small frozen-pizza maker. To expand and diversify, Chick needs more capital. Which form of business organization would be most appropriate for Chick's business?

4.   Jefferson Corporation is a small business. Incorporated in Missouri, its one class of stock is owned by twelve members of a single family. Ordinarily, corporate income is taxed at the corporate and shareholder levels—that is, a corporation is taxed on its profits, which are taxed again as income to shareholders when distributed in the form of dividends. Is there a way for Jefferson to avoid this incidence of double income taxation?

5.   Varner Automobiles, a dealership in Mink County, and Mallison Automobile Manufacturing Company (MAM) enter into a franchise agreement. The agreement provides that Varner has the right to buy MAM's cars for resale, but it does not provide that Varner has the exclusive right to do so within Mink County. MAM's area manager orally tells Varner that Varner will be the county's exclusive dealer. Eight months later, MAM grants another MAM dealership in Mink County to Snopes. Varner sues, claiming that MAM's action violates the Automobile Dealers' Day in Court Act. The act defines franchise as a "written agreement." Will Varner win the suit?

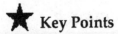 Key Points

The **key points** in this chapter include:

1. The role of officers and directors.

2. The effect of the business judgment rule on liability for managerial decisions.

3. The rights of shareholders, including a shareholder's right to bring a derivative suit.

4. Shareholders' duties and liabilities.

Chapter 18:
Rights and Duties within the Corporation

WHAT THIS CHAPTER IS ABOUT

This chapter outlines the rights and responsibilities of all participants—directors, officers, and shareholders—in the corporate enterprise. Also noted are the ways in which conflicts among these participants are resolved.

CHAPTER OUTLINE

I. **ROLE OF DIRECTORS AND OFFICERS**
The board of directors governs a corporation. Officers handle daily business.

A. **DUTIES OF DIRECTORS AND OFFICERS**
Directors and officers are fiduciaries of the corporation.

1. **Duty of Care**
Directors and officers must act in good faith, in what they consider to be the best interests of the corporation, and with the care that an ordinarily prudent person would exercise in similar circumstances.

a. **Being Honest and Using Prudent Business Judgment**
They must (1) exercise reasonable supervision when work is delegated to others, (2) act in accord with their knowledge and training, (3) attend board meetings, and (4) be informed on corporate matters and understand professional advice rendered to the board.

b. **Relying on Others' Advice**
Most states allow a director to make decisions in reliance on information furnished by competent officers or employees, professionals (such as accountants), or an executive committee, without being ac-

cused of acting in bad faith or failing to exercise due care if the information turns out to be faulty [RMBCA 8.30].

    c. **Business Judgment Rule**

    Honest mistakes of judgment and poor business decisions do not make directors and officers liable to the corporation for poor results, if the decision complies with management's fiduciary duties, has a reasonable basis, and is within managerial authority and the power of the corporation.

2. **Duty of Loyalty**

    a. **What Directors and Officers Must Do**

    Disclose fully any corporate opportunity or conflict of interest that might occur in a deal involving the corporation (and abstain from voting on, entering into, or supporting a deal in which there is a conflict of interest).

    1) **A Contract Involving a Conflict of Interest May Be Upheld**

    If it was fair and reasonable to the corporation at the time it was made, there was a full disclosure of the interest of the officers or directors involved, and it was approved by a majority of disinterested directors or shareholders.

    2) **Directors Can Sit on the Board of More Than One Corporation**

    b. **What Directors and Officers Cannot Do**

    Use corporate funds or confidential corporate information for their personal advantage. Specifically, they cannot (1) compete with the corporation, (2) usurp a corporate opportunity, (3) have an interest that conflicts with the interest of the corporation, (4) engage in insider trading (see Chapter 28), (5) authorize a corporate transaction that is detrimental to minority shareholders, or (6) sell control over the corporation.

II. RIGHTS OF DIRECTORS

A. PARTICIPATION AND INSPECTION

A director has a right to participate in corporate business. A director must have access to all corporate books and records to make decisions.

B. COMPENSATION AND INDEMNIFICATION

Officers receive compensation. Nominal sums may be paid to directors, and there is a trend to provide more. Most states permit a corporation to indemnify a director for costs and fees in defending against corporate-related lawsuits. Many firms buy insurance to cover indemnification.

III. RIGHTS OF MANAGERS AND OFFICERS

These individuals are employees; their rights are defined by employment contracts.

IV. RIGHTS OF SHAREHOLDERS

A. STOCK CERTIFICATES

Notice of shareholder meetings, dividends, and corporate reports are distributed to owners listed in the corporate books, not on the basis of possession of stock certificates (which most states do not require).

B. **PREEMPTIVE RIGHTS**

The articles generally define the scope of preemptive rights (if any). Such rights usually apply only to additional, newly issued stock sold for cash and must be exercised within a specified time (usually thirty days). When new shares are issued, each shareholder is given **stock warrants** (transferable options to acquire a given number of shares).

C. **DIVIDENDS**

Dividends can be paid in cash, property, or stock. Once declared, a cash dividend is a corporate debt. Dividends are payable only from (1) retained earnings, (2) current net profits, or (3) any surplus.

1. **Illegal Dividends**

A dividend paid when a corporation is insolvent is illegal and must be repaid. A dividend paid from an unauthorized account or causing a corporation to become insolvent may have to be repaid. In any case, the directors can be held personally liable.

2. **If the Directors Fail to Declare a Dividend**

Shareholders can ask a court to compel a declaration of a dividend.

D. **VOTING RIGHTS**

Shareholders exercise power through their voting rights (see Chapter 17).

E. **INSPECTION RIGHTS**

Shareholders (or their attorney, accountant, or agent) can inspect and copy corporate books and records for a proper purpose, if the request is made in advance. This right can be denied to prevent harassment or to protect confidential corporate information.

F. **TRANSFER OF SHARES**

Any restrictions on transferability must be noted on the face of a stock certificate. Restrictions must be reasonable—for example, a right of first refusal remains with the corporation or the shareholders for only a specified time or a reasonable time.

G. **RIGHT TO PETITION FOR DISSOLUTION**

Shareholders can petition a court to dissolve the corporation if—

1. The directors are deadlocked; shareholders are unable to break the deadlock; and there is or could be irreparable injury to the firm.
2. The acts of the directors or those in control of the corporation are illegal, oppressive, or fraudulent.
3. Corporate assets are being misapplied or wasted.
4. The shareholders are deadlocked in voting power and have failed, for a specified period (usually two annual meetings), to elect successors to directors.

H. **SHAREHOLDER'S DERIVATIVE SUIT**

If directors fail to sue in the corporate name to redress a wrong suffered by the firm, shareholders can do so (after complaining to the board). Any recovery normally goes into the corporate treasury.

V. **LIABILITY OF SHAREHOLDERS**

In most cases, if a corporation fails, shareholders lose only their investment. Exceptions include (see also Chapter 17)—

A. STOCK-SUBSCRIPTION AGREEMENTS

Once a subscription agreement is accepted, any refusal to pay is a breach, resulting in personal liability.

B. WATERED STOCK

When shares are sold by a corporation for less than par value (or the value set by the board or shareholders), the shares are "watered." In most cases, a shareholder who receives watered stock must pay the difference to the corporation. In some states, such shareholders may be liable to creditors of the corporation for unpaid corporate debts.

VI. DUTIES OF MAJORITY SHAREHOLDERS

A single shareholder (or a few acting together) who owns enough shares to control the corporation owes a fiduciary duty to the minority shareholders and creditors when they sell their shares.

STUDY TIP ☞   <u>Viewing a Corporation</u>

The simplest way of viewing a corporation is to think of it as an artificial entity independent of its owners (shareholders). It can do business in its own name just as a "real" person can. This view is sometimes criticized, however, because it seems to ignore that "real" persons are behind everything that a corporation does. From a realistic point of view, a corporation is only a way in which persons do business and share profits and losses.

TRUE-FALSE QUESTIONS (Answers at the Back of the Book)

____ 1. Both directors and officers may be immunized from liability for poor business decisions under the business judgment rule.

____ 2. Because their positions involve similar decision making and control, officers have the same duties and rights as directors.

____ 3. The rights of shareholders are established solely in the articles of incorporation.

____ 4. Stock can be paid for with cash, property, or services, and dividends can be paid in cash, property, or stock.

____ 5. Any damages recovered in a shareholder's derivative suit are normally paid to the shareholder or shareholders who exercised the derivative right.

____ 6. As a general rule, shareholders are not personally responsible for the debts of the corporation.

FILL-IN QUESTIONS (Answers at the Back of the Book)

A stock certificate may be lost or destroyed, _____
(and ownership is/ but ownership is not) destroyed with it. A new certificate
_____ (can/ cannot) be issued to replace one that has been lost or destroyed.
The actual certificate _____ (must/ need not) be indorsed and delivered to a
transferee to transfer the shares. Notice of meetings, dividends, and operational and
financial reports are all distributed according to _____
_____ (possession of the certificate/ recorded ownership in the corporation's books).

MULTIPLE-CHOICE QUESTIONS (Answers at the Back of the Book)

____   1.   Space, Inc., offers to buy Uni Corporation. Uni's board unanimously accepts
the offer without investigating the value of Uni and without determining
whether a higher price could be obtained. If Uni's shareholders sue the directors, and they are held liable, it will be because directors

a.   are expected to be informed on corporate matters.
b.   are expected to act in accord with their own knowledge and training.
c.   cannot rely on information furnished by officers or employees, professionals
such as attorneys and accountants, or an executive committee of the board.
d.   who do not dissent from board decisions are liable for mismanagement.

____   2.   Shareholders' rights include all of the following EXCEPT a right to

a.   one vote per share, subject to any exclusion or limitation in the articles.
b.   access to corporate books and records, subject to the firm's right to protect itself from potential abuse, including theft of confidential information.
c.   transfer shares, subject to any valid restriction, such as a corporate or
shareholder right of first refusal.
d.   take title to and sell corporate property when directors are mishandling
corporate assets, subject to any class limitation in the articles.

____   3.   Which of the following is NOT a shareholder's derivative suit?

a.   A suit alleging that corporate officers misused corporate assets
b.   A suit alleging that directors authorized improper dividends
c.   A suit alleging that the board's plan to merge with another corporation is
designed to dilute a shareholder's voting power
d.   A suit alleging that directors authorized an improper premium paid to a
majority shareholder

____   4.   In which of the following situations is a shareholder personally liable?

a.   A shareholder pays for stock by transferring title to an office building to
the corporation at the same time as unpaid corporate debts come due.
b.   A shareholder receives watered stock and does not pay the difference to
the corporation before unpaid corporate debts come due.
c.   A shareholder signs a subscription agreement, and when the corporation accepts, the shareholder pays before unpaid corporate debts come due.
d.   A shareholder sells a corporation's stock one week before its market price
plummets, and the corporation goes out of business, leaving unpaid corporate debts.

____ **5.** A director does *not* have a right to

a. participate in board meetings.
b. access to all corporate books and records.
c. compensation for his or her services.
d. indemnification for costs and fees associated with a firm-related lawsuit.

____ **6.** Honi Corporation's board announces that to accumulate funds for expansion, it will stop paying dividends for five years. Honi's minority shareholders sue to compel a dividend. If the shareholders win, it will be because

a. the board abused its discretion.
b. it is illegal not to declare a dividend.
c. dividends are like a debt—they must be paid.
d. there is sufficient surplus or earnings available to pay a dividend.

SHORT ESSAY QUESTIONS

1. Discuss the duty of care and the duty of loyalty and the ways in which they govern the conduct of directors and officers in a corporation.

2. Discuss the rights typically exercised by the shareholders of a corporation.

ISSUE SPOTTERS (Answers at the Back of the Book)

1. Wallace is a director and shareholder of Stevens Jar Corporation and of Tennessee Hills, Inc. If a resolution comes before the Stevens board to make an offer to contract with Tennessee, what is Wallace's responsibility? If a resolution comes before the Tennessee board to compete with Stevens, what is Wallace's responsibility?

2. Branden Corporation's chief financial officer resigns. To find a replacement, Branden's board appoints a committee to conduct a search for qualified individuals. After investigating candidates, the committee recommends three individuals. After its own investigation, the board elects Fred to the position. When Fred turns out to be dishonest, Branden's shareholders sue the board. What is the board's defense?

3. Opha Corporation's board of directors—among whom are Thom and Phil, officers of the firm—is deadlocked over whether to market a new product. Consequently, corporate investment is frozen. Ed, a minority shareholder, suspects that Thom and Phil are taking advantage of the deadlock to use corporate assets—offices, equipment, supplies, staff time—to initiate a competing enterprise. Is Ed powerless to intervene?

4. JKL Development Corporation has an opportunity to buy stock in De Jonge Properties, Inc. The directors decide that, instead of JKL buying the stock, the directors will buy it. After they buy the stock, Francisco, a JKL shareholder, learns of the circumstances and wants to sue the directors on JKL's behalf. Can he do so?

5. Greta is Mayer Corporation's majority shareholder. Greta owns enough stock in Mayer that if she were to sell it, the sale would be a transfer of control of the firm. Does Greta owe any duty to Mayer or the minority shareholders in selling her shares?

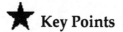
Chapter 19:
Agency

The **key points** in this chapter include:

1. The difference between employees and independent contractors.

2. The formation of an agency relationship.

3. The scope of an agent's authority.

4. The liability of a principal and an agent for contracts with third parties.

5. A principal's and an agent's liability for the agent's torts.

WHAT THIS CHAPTER IS ABOUT

This chapter covers agency relationships, including how they are formed and the duties involved. Agency relationships are essential to a corporation, which can function and enter into contracts only through its agents.

CHAPTER OUTLINE

I. **AGENCY RELATIONSHIPS**
The parties agree that the agent will act on behalf and instead of the principal in negotiating and transacting business with third persons.

A. **EMPLOYER-EMPLOYEE RELATIONSHIPS**
An employee is one whose physical conduct is controlled, or subject to control, by the employer. Normally, all employees who deal with third parties are deemed to be agents. Statutes covering workers' compensation and so on (see Chapter 20) apply only to employer-employee status.

B. **EMPLOYER–INDEPENDENT CONTRACTOR RELATIONSHIPS**
Those who hire independent contractors have no control over the details of their physical performance.

1. **Employee or Independent Contractor?**
The greater an employer's control over the work, the more likely it is that the worker is an employee. Another key factor is whether the employer withholds taxes from payments to the worker and pays unemployment and Social Security taxes covering the worker.

2. **Independent Contractors May Be Agents**

II. FORMATION OF THE AGENCY RELATIONSHIP

A. AGENCY AND THE ELEMENTS OF A CONTRACT
Consideration is not required. A principal must have capacity to contract; anyone can be an agent. An agency can be created for any legal purpose.

B. AGENCY BY AGREEMENT
Normally, an agency must be based on an agreement that the agent will act for the principal. Such an agreement can be an express written contract, can be implied by conduct, or can be oral. Exceptions to oral agency agreements:

1. Equal Dignity Rule
In most states, if the contract being executed is or must be in writing, the agent's authority must also be in writing.

2. Power of Attorney
A power of attorney can be special or general. An ordinary power terminates on the incapacity or death of the person giving it. A durable power is not affected by the principal's incapacity.

C. AGENCY BY RATIFICATION
A person who is not an agent (or who is an agent acting outside the scope of his or her authority) may make a contract on behalf of another (a principal). If the principal approves or affirms that contract by word or by action, an agency relationship is created by ratification.

D. AGENCY BY ESTOPPEL

1. The Principal's Actions
When a principal causes a third person to believe that another person is his or her agent, and the third person deals with the supposed agent, the principal is estopped to deny the agency relationship.

2. The Third Party's Reasonable Belief
The third person must prove that he or she reasonably believed that an agency relationship existed and that the agent had authority—that an ordinary, prudent person familiar with business practice and custom would have been justified in concluding that the agent had authority.

E. AGENCY BY OPERATION OF LAW
An agency relationship in the absence of a formal agreement may occur in family relationships or in an emergency, if the agent's failure to act outside the scope of his or her authority would cause the principal substantial loss.

III. DUTIES OF AGENTS AND PRINCIPALS
The principal-agent relationship is fiduciary.

A. AGENT'S DUTIES TO PRINCIPAL
(1) Perform with reasonable diligence and skill, (2) notify the principal of all matters that concerning the agency, (3) act solely for the benefit of the principal, (4) follow all lawful instructions of the principal, and (5) keep and make available to the principal an account of everything received and paid out on behalf of the principal.

B. PRINCIPAL'S DUTIES TO AGENT
(1) Pay the agent for services rendered, (2) reimburse the agent for money paid at the principal's request or for necessary expenses , (3) indemnify an

agent for liability incurred because of authorized acts, (4) cooperate with an agent, (5) provide safe working conditions.

C. SUBAGENTS' DUTIES
When an agent employs a subagent, a fiduciary duty exists between the subagent and principal, and between the subagent and agent. Subagents owe the same duties to agents and to principals as agents owe to principals.

IV. REMEDIES AND RIGHTS OF AGENTS AND PRINCIPALS

A. REMEDIES OF BOTH PARTIES
When one party violates his or her duty to the other, remedies available to the other party include damages, termination, injunction, and accounting.

B. AGENT'S RIGHTS AND REMEDIES AGAINST PRINCIPAL
The agent has a right to be compensated, reimbursed, and indemnified and to work in a safe environment. An agent also has a right to perform agency duties without interference by the principal. Breach of duty by the principal follow normal contract and tort remedies.

C. PRINCIPAL'S RIGHTS AND REMEDIES AGAINST AGENT
Constructive trust (if an agent retains benefits or profits that belong to the principal or takes advantage of the agency to obtain goods or property that the principal wants to purchase); if an agent breaches an agency agreement, the principal can avoid a contract with the agent; indemnification.

V. SCOPE OF AN AGENT'S AUTHORITY

A. ACTUAL AUTHORITY—EXPRESS AND IMPLIED
Express authority may be oral or in writing. Implied authority may be conferred by custom, can be inferred from the position an agent occupies, or is implied as reasonably necessary to carry out express authority.

B. APPARENT AUTHORITY AND ESTOPPEL
An agent has apparent authority when a principal, by word or action, causes a third party reasonably to believe that an agent has authority, though the agent has no authority. The principal may be estopped from denying it if the third party changes position in reliance.

C. EMERGENCY POWERS
If an emergency demands action by the agent, but the agent is unable to communicate with the principal, the agent has emergency power.

D. RATIFICATION
A principal can ratify an unauthorized contract or act, if he or she is aware of all material facts. Ratification can be done expressly or impliedly (by accepting the benefits of a transaction). An entire transaction must be ratified; a principal cannot affirm only part.

VI. LIABILITY FOR CONTRACTS

A. IF AN AGENT ACTS WITHIN THE SCOPE OF HIS OR HER AUTHORITY

1. Disclosed Principals' Contract Liability
The principal is liable to a third party for a contract made by the agent. The agent has no liability.

2. **Partially Disclosed Principals' Contract Liability**
   The principal is liable to a third party for a contract made by the agent. In most states, the agent is also liable for nonperformance. If so, the agent is entitled to indemnification by the principal.

3. **Undisclosed Principals' Contract Liability**
   The principal and the agent are liable. Exceptions—

   a. The principal was expressly excluded as a party in the contract.
   b. The contract is a negotiable instrument (check or note).
   c. The performance of the agent is personal to the contract.
   d. The third party would not have contracted with the principal had the third party known his or her identity, the agent or the principal knew this, and the third party rescinds the contract.

B. IF THE AGENT HAS NO AUTHORITY
The principal cannot be held liable in contract by a third party. The agent's liability to a third party is based on the theory of breach of implied warranty of authority. If the agent intentionally misrepresents his or her authority, then the agent can also be liable in tort for fraud.

VII. LIABILITY FOR AGENT'S TORTS

A. PRINCIPAL'S TORTIOUS CONDUCT
A principal may be liable for harm resulting from the principal's negligence or recklessness, which may include giving improper instructions; authorizing the use of improper materials or tools; establishing improper rules; or failing to prevent others' tortious conduct while they are on the principal's property or using the principal's equipment, materials, or tools.

B. PRINCIPAL'S AUTHORIZATION OF AGENT'S TORTIOUS CONDUCT
A principal who authorizes an agent to commit a tortious act may be liable.

C. MISREPRESENTATION
If an agent with authority to make statements makes false claims, the principal is liable. If an agent apparently acting within authority takes advantage of a third party, the principal who put the agent in the position is liable. If a principal knows an agent does not have the facts but does not correct the agent's or the third party's impressions, the principal is liable.

D. THE DOCTRINE OF *RESPONDEAT SUPERIOR*
An employer is liable for any harm caused (negligently or intentionally) to a third party by an employee acting within the scope of employment, without regard to the personal fault of the employer. An employee going to and from work or meals is considered outside the scope of employment.

1. **Employer's Liability for Torts Outside the Scope of Employment**
   An employer who knows or should know that an employee has a propensity for committing tortious acts is liable for the acts even if they are outside the scope of employment. Also, an employer is liable for permitting an employee to engage in reckless acts that can injure others.

2. **Employee's Liability for His or Her Own Torts**
   An employee is liable for his or her own torts. An employee who commits a tort at the employer's direction can be liable with the employer, even if he or she was unaware of the wrongfulness of the act.

VIII. LIABILITY FOR INDEPENDENT CONTRACTOR'S TORTS

An employer is not liable for physical harm caused to a third person by the tortious act of an independent contractor (except in cases of hazardous activities such as blasting operations, the transportation of highly volatile chemicals, and the use of poisonous gases, in which strict liability is imposed).

IX. LIABILITY FOR AGENT'S CRIMES

A principal is not liable for an agent's crime, unless the principal participated. In some jurisdictions, a principal may be liable for an agent's violating, in the course and scope of employment, such regulations as those governing sanitation, prices, weights, and the sale of liquor.

X. TERMINATION OF AN AGENCY

A. TERMINATION BY ACT OF THE PARTIES

An agency ends when the time specified in the agreement expires, its purpose is achieved, a specified event occurs, or by mutual agreement. Both parties have the *power* to terminate an agency, but they may not have the *right* and may therefore be liable for breach of contract.

B. TERMINATION BY OPERATION OF LAW

Circumstances under which an agency terminates by operation of law include death of insanity of either party, destruction of the subject matter of the agency, changed circumstances, bankruptcy of either party, and war between the principal's and agent's countries.

C. NOTICE REQUIRED FOR TERMINATION

If an agency terminates by operation of law because of death, insanity, or some other unforeseen circumstance, there is no duty to notify third persons, unless the agent's authority is coupled with an interest. If the parties themselves terminate the agency, the principal must inform any third parties who know of the agency that it has ended.

STUDY TIP 👉 <u>Agents Are Everywhere</u>

No area of the law is more pervasive than the law of agency. The law of agency affects virtually everyone everyday. When confronted with legal problems to analyze, you may find it helpful to remember how common agency relationships are. Agency law applies in the context of professional partnerships, for example. Also involved are travel, insurance, and other agencies; banks involved in the check collection process; corporate shareholders; and gas stations, car dealers, and other franchisors and franchisees.

TRUE-FALSE QUESTIONS (Answers at the Back of the Book)

____   1.   An agent can perform legal acts that bind the principal.

____ 2. An agency relationship may arise without an affirmative indication that the agent agrees to act for the principal and the principal agrees to have the agent act for him or her.

____ 3. An agency relationship is fiduciary—an agent and a principal owe each other a duty to act in good faith and to disclose material facts having a bearing on the relationship.

____ 4. A disclosed or partially disclosed principal is liable to a third party for a contract made by an agent acting within the scope of authority.

____ 5. An agent is liable for his or her own torts, but a principal who authorizes an agent to commit a tort is not liable to persons or property injured.

____ 6. An employer is generally not expected to bear responsibility for an independent contractor's torts unless exceptionally hazardous activities are involved.

FILL-IN QUESTIONS (Answers at the Back of the Book)

An agent must use reasonable diligence and skill. This is part of the agent's duty of _____ (obedience/ performance). An agent is required to inform a principal of all material matters that come to the agent's attention concerning the subject matter of the agency. This is an aspect of the agent's duty of _____ (accounting/ notification). An agent must act solely for the benefit of the principal and not in the interest of the agent or a third party. This is part of the agent's duty of _____ (loyalty/ performance). An agent must follow all lawful and clearly stated instructions of the principal. This is an aspect of the agent's duty of _____ (loyalty/ obedience). If an agent is required to keep and make available to the principal a record of all property and money received and paid out on behalf of the principal, this is part of the agent's duty of _____ (accounting/ notification).

MULTIPLE-CHOICE QUESTIONS (Answers at the Back of the Book)

____ 1. Ryan agrees to buy a certain amount of goods from O'Neal, Inc. Ryan will pay for and sell the goods at prices set by O'Neal, deposit 90 percent of the proceeds in an account for O'Neal, and return unsold goods. O'Neal will pay half of Ryan's expenses. Which of the following is FALSE?

a. Ryan is an agent.
b. O'Neal is a principal.
c. Both a and b
d. None of the above

____ 2. Six-Two-Four Corporation employs Mae to manage one of its stores. Six-Two-Four does not specify the extent, if any, of Mae's authority to contract with third parties. The express authority given by Six-Two-Four to Mae to manage the store implies authority to do whatever is reasonably required

a. as is customary to operate the business.
b. as can be inferred from the manager's position.
c. both a and b.
d. none of the above.

    3. Ivar is a real estate broker. Mandy asks Ivar to sell her land. Ivar learns that the price is rapidly appreciating. Instead of telling Mandy about the increase, Ivar tells Mandy that Ivar will buy the land himself. Before the contract is executed, Mandy sells the land to Kendal. If Ivar sues Mandy

    a. Ivar will win, because Mandy breached their contract.
    b. Ivar will win, because Mandy held the property in constructive trust.
    c. Mandy will win, because Ivar breached his fiduciary duties to Mandy, and thus Mandy could avoid the contract.
    d. Mandy will win, because they had no contract.

    4. Farrah, owner of Faucets & Fixtures, Inc., frequently sends Gerhard, Faucets's production manager, to Ormrod Bank to borrow money in amounts of $1,000 or more. One morning, Farrah sends Gerhard to Ormrod to borrow $3,000. Gerhard borrows $6,000. Later, Farrah refuses to repay $6,000. If Ormrod sues Farrah, Farrah will be held liable to repay

    a. $6,000, because Gerhard had apparent authority to borrow $6,000.
    b. $6,000, because Gerhard had actual authority to borrow $6,000.
    c. $3,000, because Gerhard had actual authority to borrow only $3,000.
    d. $3,000, because Gerhard had apparent authority to borrow only $3,000.

    5. In which of the following situations is the employer NOT liable under the doctrine of *respondeat superior*?

    a. Northwest Company employs Hugh to cut down specific trees. Hugh mistakenly cuts down an unspecified tree, negligently injuring Casey.
    b. Luther, owner of a farm, employs Henry as a milker of cows. In Luther's absence, Henry mows a field, negligently injuring Cordell.
    c. Weinberg Guns & Ammo, Inc., directs its salespersons never to load a gun during a sale. Elbert, a sales person, loads a gun during a sale, negligently injuring Kathryn.
    d. Swayne's Fast Food requires Noah, an employee, to clean the kitchen after work. Noah negligently fails to shut off the water, which floods Whitney's Card Shop next door.

    6. Madeleine's daughter Isabel passes her driving test and is granted a driver's license. Madeleine asks Sondra, an insurance agent, to obtain automobile insurance coverage for Madeleine and Isabel with Farmers State Insurance Company. Six months later, Isabel is in an accident, and Madeleine learns that Sondra failed to obtain the requested coverage. If Madeleine sues Sondra, and Madeleine wins, it will be because Sondra breached their agency contract by failing to satisfy an agent's duty of

    a. performance.
    b. notification.
    c. loyalty.
    d. accounting.

SHORT ESSAY QUESTIONS

1.   Compare relationships between principal and agent, employer and employee, and employer and independent contractor.

2. Identify, define, and discuss the categories of authority by which an agent can bind a principal and a third party in contract.

ISSUE SPOTTERS (Answers at the Back of the Book)

1. Chet contracts with Dee to buy a particular racehorse for Dee. Dee asks Chet not to disclose her identity. Chet arranges the purchase with Hammon Stables, the owner of the horse. Chet gives Hammon a down payment. Later, Dee decides that she does not want the horse and fails to pay the rest of the price. Hammon sues Chet for breach of contract. Can Dee be liable for whatever damages Chet may have to pay?

2. Young Development Corporation wants to build a new mall on a specific tract of land. Young contracts with Shoshana to purchase the property. When Shoshana learns of the difference between the price that Young is willing to pay and the price at which the owner is willing to sell, Shoshana wants to buy the land and sell it to Young herself. Can Shoshana do this?

3. Marguerite, owner of Consumer Merchandise Company, employs Fern as an administrative assistant. In Marguerite's absence, and without authority, Fern represents herself as Marguerite and signs a promissory note in Marguerite's name. Under what circumstance could Marguerite be held liable on the note?

4. First Union Bank of Fleming encourages its depositors to ask Fleming's advice concerning their investments. Ian, one of Fleming's investment counselors, advises Bond to invest in Spectre Corporation, although Ian knows that Spectre's financial situation is precarious. If Bond loses money on the deal, can Fleming be held liable?

5. United Delivery Service employs Otis as a driver. One afternoon, United tells Otis to deliver a certain package within the hour. While making the delivery, to bypass a traffic jam, Otis recklessly drives onto the sidewalk, injuring Bea. Is United liable to Bea? Is Otis liable to Bea?

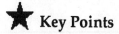 **Key Points**

The **key points** in this chapter include:

1. The employment-at-will doctrine and its exceptions.

2. FICA, FUTA, and the laws behind workers' compensation.

3. FLSA, OSHA, and ERISA—laws providing health and safety protection in the workplace, and retirement and security income outside the workplace.

Chapter 20:
Employment Relationships

WHAT THIS CHAPTER IS ABOUT

This chapter outlines significant laws regulating employment relationships. Other significant laws regulating the workplace—those prohibiting employment discrimination—are dealt with in Chapter 21. Labor law is the subject of Chapter 22.

CHAPTER OUTLINE

I. EMPLOYMENT AT WILL

A. THE EMPLOYMENT-AT-WILL DOCTRINE
Either party may terminate an employment relationship at any time and for any reason (unless a contract provides to the contrary).

B. STATUTORY EXCEPTIONS
An employer cannot fire an employee in violation of a federal or state statute. If so, the employee may bring an action for wrongful discharge. Some state and federal statutes protect whistleblowers from retaliation.

C. CONTRACT THEORY EXCEPTIONS

1. Implied Contract
Some courts have held that an implied contract exists between an employer and an employee (if, for example, a personnel manual states that no employee will be fired without good cause).

2. Implied Covenant of Good Faith
A few states have held that all employment contracts contain an implied covenant of good faith.

D. **PUBLIC-POLICY EXCEPTIONS**
An employer may not fire a worker for reasons that violate a public policy of the jurisdiction.

E. **TORT THEORY EXCEPTIONS**
Discharge may give rise to a tort action for wrongful discharge.

II. PRIVACY RIGHTS OF EMPLOYEES

A right to privacy has been inferred from constitutional guarantees provided by the First, Third, Fourth, Fifth, and Ninth Amendments to the Constitution.

A. **LIE-DETECTOR TESTS**
Under the Employee Polygraph Protection Act of 1988, employers cannot, among other things, require, request, or suggest that employees or applicants take lie-detector tests. Employers may use polygraph tests when investigating thefts.

B. **DRUG TESTING**

1. **Protection for the Privacy Rights of Private-Sector Employees**
Some state constitutions may prohibit private employers from testing for drugs. State statutes may restrict drug testing by private employers. Other sources of protection include collective bargaining agreements and tort actions for invasion of privacy (see Chapter 12).

2. **Protection for Public-Sector Employees**
Constitutional limitations (the Fourth Amendment) apply. Drug tests have been upheld when there was a reasonable basis for suspecting employees of using drugs, or when drug use could threaten public safety.

C. **PERFORMANCE MONITORING**

1. **Electronic Communications Privacy Act (ECPA) of 1986**
The ECPA bars the interception of any wire or electronic communication or the disclosure or use of information obtained by interception.

2. **Common Law Actions**
If an employee sues for invasion of privacy, a court may weigh the employee's reasonable expectation of privacy against the employer's need for surveillance. If a search (of a desk, files, or office) is conducted and the employee sues, a court may weigh the purposes of the search against its intrusiveness, and consider the availability of alternatives.

D. **PREEMPLOYMENT SCREENING PROCEDURES**
A key factor in determining whether preemployment screening tests violate privacy rights is whether there is a connection between the questions and the job for which an applicant is applying.

III. HEALTH AND SAFETY PROTECTION

A. **OCCUPATIONAL SAFETY AND HEALTH ACT OF 1970**

1. **Agencies That Enforce the Act**

a. **Occupational Safety and Health Administration (OSHA)**
Has authority to make inspections and issue standards governing workplace details and protecting employees against exposure to substances that may be harmful to their health.

    b. National Institute for Occupational Safety and Health
    Researches safety and health problems and recommends standards for OSHA to adopt.

    c. Occupational Safety and Health Review Commission
    Hears appeals from actions taken by OSHA administrators.

  2. Procedures
  Employees file complaints of OSHA violations (employers cannot retaliate); employers must keep injury and illness records; employers must file accident reports directly to OSHA. OSHA officers may inspect any establishment covered by the act (not without a warrant).

B. STATE WORKERS' COMPENSATION LAWS

  1. Requirements for Recovery
  (1) An employment relationship and (2) the injury must be (a) accidental and (b) occur on the job or in the course of employment.

  2. Excluded Employees
  Often excluded are domestic workers, agricultural workers, temporary employees, and employees of common carriers.

  3. Procedure
  An employee must notify his or her employer of an injury (usually within thirty days), and file a claim with a certain state agency within a certain period (sixty days to two years) from the time the injury is first noticed.

  4. Acceptance of Workers' Compensation Benefits Bars Suits
  An employee's acceptance of benefits bars the employee from suing for injuries caused by the employer's negligence.

IV. RETIREMENT AND SECURITY INCOME

A. OLD AGE, SURVIVORS, AND DISABILITY INSURANCE
The Social Security Act of 1935 provides retirement, survivors, and disability insurance. Employers and employees must contribute under the Federal Insurance Contributions Act (FICA).

B. MEDICARE
A health insurance program administered by the Social Security Administration for people sixty-five years of age and older and for some under sixty-five who are disabled.

C. PRIVATE RETIREMENT PLANS
The Employee Retirement Income Security Act of 1974 (ERISA) empowers the Labor Management Services Administration of the Department of Labor to oversee those who operate private pension funds.

  1. Vesting
  Generally, employee contributions to pension plans vest immediately; employee rights to employer contributions vest after five years.

  2. Investing
  Pension-fund managers must be cautious in investing and refrain from investing more than 10 percent of the fund in securities of the employer.

D. UNEMPLOYMENT COMPENSATION
The Federal Unemployment Tax Act of 1935 created a state system that provides unemployment compensation to eligible individuals.

V. COBRA AND OTHER EMPLOYMENT LAWS

A. COBRA
The Consolidated Omnibus Budget Reconciliation Act (COBRA) of 1985 prohibits the elimination of a worker's medical, optical, or dental insurance on the termination of most workers' employment.

B. FAMILY AND MEDICAL LEAVE ACT OF 1993 (FMLA)
Employers with fifty or more employees must provide employees with up to twelve weeks of family or medical leave during any twelve-month period, continue health-care coverage during the leave, and guarantee employment in the same, or a comparable, position when the employee returns to work.

C. FAIR LABOR STANDARDS ACT OF 1938 (FLSA)

1. Child Labor
Children under fourteen years can deliver newspapers, work for their parents, and work in entertainment and agriculture. Children fourteen and older cannot work in hazardous occupations.

2. Overtime Pay
Employees who work more than forty hours per week must be paid no less than one and a half times their regular pay for all hours over forty.

3. Minimum Wage
A specified amount ($4.25 per hour as of April 1, 1991) must be paid to employees in covered industries. Wages include the reasonable cost to furnish employees with board, lodging, and other facilities.

D. THE IMMIGRATION ACT OF 1990
Employers recruiting workers from other countries must (1) complete a certification process, (2) satisfy the Department of Labor that there is a shortage of qualified U.S. workers capable of performing the work, and (3) show that bringing aliens into this country will not adversely affect the existing labor market in that area.

STUDY TIP ☞ <u>The Basis for a Law</u>

To study this chapter, you might start from a personal perspective. Undoubtedly, you have had a job. What was your chief concern? The money, the accomplishment, the respect or friendliness of your co-workers, your employer's praise? If your chief concern was the money, you may also have been concerned that it keep coming, that there may be some security in the job. Thus, when considering the material in this chapter, you may want to ask why there isn't more protection against termina tion of employment at will.

TRUE-FALSE QUESTIONS (Answers at the Back of the Book)

____ 1. Employers can agree with unions not to handle, use, or deal in non-union-produced goods.

____ 2. Federal constitutional limitations do not always restrict private employers from testing their employees for drugs.

____ 3. Most employment contracts are considered to be "at will," which means that employers can fire employees for good, bad, or no cause, but employees cannot resign without good cause.

____ 4. Federal and state governments participate in insurance programs designed to protect employees and their families by covering the financial impact of retirement, disability, death, and hospitalization, but employers are not required to establish health insurance or pension plans.

____ 5. Children fourteen and older can work in hazardous occupations.

____ 6. Employees who work more than forty hours per week must be paid no less than one and a half times their regular pay for all hours over forty.

FILL-IN QUESTIONS (Answers at the Back of the Book)

Under the employment-at-will doctrine, _____ (either/ neither) party may terminate an employment relationship at any time and for any reason _____ (unless/ even if) a contract provides to the contrary. An employee who is fired in violation of a federal or state statute _____ (may/ may not) bring an action for wrongful discharge. _____ (Some/ No) courts have held that an implied contract exists between an employer and an employee. _____ (All/ A few states) have held that all employment contracts contain an implied covenant of good faith. An employer _____ (may/ may not) fire a worker for reasons that violate a public policy of the jurisdiction.

MULTIPLE-CHOICE QUESTIONS (Answers at the Back of the Book)

____ 1. With a few exceptions, only employers investigating losses due to theft may, without violating employees' rights of privacy, use

   a. polygraph tests.
   b. drug tests, unless proscribed in a collective bargaining agreement.
   c. electronic monitoring of employees, as long as employees are informed that they may be monitored.
   d. all of the above.

____ 2. Under the Immigration Act of 1990, employers recruiting workers from other countries must show that

   a. there is a shortage of qualified U.S. workers to perform the work.
   b. bringing aliens into the country will not adversely affect the existing labor market in that area.
   c. both a and b.
   d. none of the above.

____ 3. The two-part test for determining whether an injured employee can receive workers' compensation is

   a. the injury must have been accidental, and it must have arisen out of a preexisting disease or physical condition.

   b. the injury must have been intentional, and it must have arisen out of a preexisting disease or physical condition.

   c. the injury must have been accidental, and it must have arisen out of or in the course of employment.

   d. the injury must have been intentional, and it must have arisen out of or in the course of employment.

____ 4. COBRA

   a. bars the elimination of heath insurance on the termination of most workers' employment.

   b. provides for elimination of heath insurance on the termination of most workers' employment.

   c. provides for continuation of health insurance for up to twelve weeks of a worker's family or medical leave during any twelve-month period.

   d. specifies a minimum wage of $4.25 per hour.

____ 5. FMLA

   a. bars the elimination of heath insurance on the termination of most workers' employment.

   b. provides for elimination of heath insurance on the termination of most workers' employment.

   c. provides for continuation of health insurance for up to twelve weeks of a worker's family or medical leave during any twelve-month period.

   d. specifies a minimum wage of $4.25 per hour.

____ 6. Which of the following is TRUE?

   a. The Occupational Safety and Health Act establishes procedures for compensating employees injured on the job.

   b. The Old Age, Survivors, and Disability Insurance Act requires that businesses with one or more employees and affecting commerce be maintained free from recognized hazards.

   c. The Employee Retirement Income Security Act requires employers to pay into a fund that compensates unemployed individuals.

   d. The Fair Labor Standards Act includes child labor restrictions, and maximum hour and minimum wage provisions.

SHORT ESSAY QUESTIONS

1. Discuss the employment-at-will doctrine and its exceptions.

2. Discuss the protection that employees have from the financial impact of retirement, disability, death, hospitalization, and unemployment.

ISSUE SPOTTERS (Answers at the Back of the Book)

1. Falls Bottled Water Company's employees' handbook states that employees will be discharged only for good cause and promises that no employee will be discharged

without being given at least two warnings. One afternoon, Werner, a Falls supervisor, says to Hinton, "I don't like your looks. You're fired. Get out." Can Falls be held liable for breach of contract, based on the statements in the handbook?

2.   Workers' compensation laws establish a procedure for compensating workers who are injured on the job. Instead of suing, the worker files a claim with the appropriate state agency. Does the worker have to prove that the injury was caused by the employer's negligence?

3.   The Datadisc Company suffers a series of thefts of company equipment. Can Datadisc lawfully order its employees to take lie-detector tests? Can Datadisc lawfully discharge those employees who refuse to take the tests?

4.   In the previous problem, imagine that Datadisc employees agree to take the lie-detector tests. The tests are inconclusive, however, and the thefts of company equipment continue. Can Datadisc lawfully order its employees to undergo drug testing? Can Datadisc lawfully fire those employees who refuse to submit to the testing?

5.   In what ways are individuals provided with income protection on the termination of their employment or on retirement?

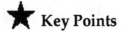 **Key Points**

The **key points** in this chapter include:

1. Title VII's prohibitions against discrimination.

2. What constitutes illegal sexual harassment.

3. Coverage under the Age Discrimination in Employment Act.

4. What the Americans with Disabilities Act provides.

5. The defenses against charges of employment discrimination.

Chapter 21:
Employment Discrimination

WHAT THIS CHAPTER IS ABOUT

The law restricts employers and unions from discriminating against workers on the basis of race, color, religion, national origin, gender, age, or handicap. A class of persons defined by one or more of these criteria is known as a protected class. This chapter outlines these laws.

CHAPTER OUTLINE

I. TITLE VII OF THE CIVIL RIGHTS ACT OF 1964

Prohibits employment discrimination against employees, applicants, and union members on the basis of race, color, national origin, religion, and gender.

A. TO WHOM TITLE VII APPLIES

Employers with fifteen or more employees, labor unions with fifteen or more members, labor unions that operate hiring halls (to which members go regularly to be rationed jobs as they become available), employment agencies, and federal, state, and local agencies.

B. THE EQUAL EMPLOYMENT OPPORTUNITY COMMISSION (EEOC)

1. Powers

Issues guidelines for interpreting the law and brings lawsuits against organizations that violate the law.

2. Procedure

(1) A victim files a claim with the EEOC; (2) the EEOC investigates and seeks a voluntary settlement; (3) if no settlement is reached, the EEOC may sue the employer; (4) if the EEOC chooses not to sue, the victim may file a lawsuit.

C. DISCRIMINATION BASED ON RACE, COLOR, NATIONAL ORIGIN, AND RELIGION
Employers cannot effectively discriminate against employees on the basis of race, color, national origin, or religion (unless there is a substantial, demonstrable relationship between the trait and the job, etc.).

D. DISCRIMINATION BASED ON GENDER
Employers cannot discriminate against employees on the basis of gender (unless the gender of the applicant can be proved essential to the job, etc.).

1. **Pregnancy Discrimination Act of 1978**
Employees affected by pregnancy or related conditions must be treated the same as other persons not so affected but similar in ability to work.

2. **Sexual Harassment**

   a. **Types of Harassment**
   (1) *Quid pro quo* harassment: when promotions, etc., are doled out on the basis of sexual favors; (2) hostile-environment harassment: when an employee is subjected to offensive sexual comments, etc. Proof of serious psychological injury to the victim not required.

   b. **Employers' Liability**
   When anyone (employee or nonemployee) harasses an employee, if the employer knew, or should have known, and failed to take immediate corrective action.

   c. **Standard for Determining Whether Conduct Violates Title VII**

      1) **The Traditional "Reasonable Person" Standard**
      If a reasonable person in the circumstances of the victim would have responded similarly, the response is reasonable.

      2) **"Reasonable Woman" and "Reasonable Man" Standards**
      Some courts hold that sexual harassment should be viewed from a "reasonable woman" or "reasonable man" perspective.

      3) **EEOC Guidelines and the Supreme Court**
      EEOC guidelines use the "reasonable person" standard but add that the victim's race, color, religion, gender, national origin, age, or disability must also be considered. The Supreme Court has held that to be liable, conduct must be abusive both objectively and subjectively.

E. INTENTIONAL AND UNINTENTIONAL DISCRIMINATION
Title VII prohibits both intentional and unintentional discrimination.

1. **Disparate-Treatment Discrimination**
Intentional discrimination by an employer against an employee.

   a. *Prima Facie* **Case**
   A plaintiff must show that (1) he or she is a member of a protected class, (2) he or she applied and was qualified for the job in question, (3) he or she was rejected by the employer, and (4) the employer continued to seek applicants for the position or filled the position with a person not in a protected class.

b. **Employer's Side of the Case**
The employer must articulate a legal reason for not hiring the plaintiff. To prevail, the plaintiff must show that the employer's reason is a pretext and that discriminatory intent motivated the decision.

2. **Disparate-Impact Discrimination**

a. **Types of Disparate-Impact Discrimination**
As a result of a job requirement or hiring practice, (1) an employer's work force does not reflect the percentage of members of protected classes that characterizes qualified individuals in the local labor market, or (2) members of a protected class are excluded from the employer's work force at a substantially higher rate than nonmembers.

b. *Prima Facie* **Case**
A person must show a connection between the requirement or practice and the disparity; no evidence of discriminatory intent is necessary.

F. **REMEDIES UNDER TITLE VII AND THE CIVIL RIGHTS ACT OF 1991**
Reinstatement, back pay, retroactive promotions, damages (compensatory damages only in cases of intentional discrimination).

1. **Punitive Damages**
May be recovered against a private employer only if the employer acted with malice or reckless indifference to an individual's rights.

2. **Limitations**
The sum of compensatory and punitive damages is limited to specific amounts against specific employers (from $50,000 against employers with one hundred or fewer employees to $300,000 against employers with more than five hundred employees).

II. DISCRIMINATION BASED ON AGE

A. **THE AGE DISCRIMINATION IN EMPLOYMENT ACT (ADEA) OF 1967**
Prohibits employment discrimination on the basis of age (including mandatory retirement), by employers with twenty or more employees, against individuals forty years of age or older.

B. **APPLICABLE PRINCIPLES**
Similar to Title VII (protects against intentional and unintentional discrimination; requires the establishment of a *prima facie* case, with the burden shifting from employee to employer and back; etc.).

III. DISCRIMINATION BASED ON DISABILITY

A. **THE AMERICANS WITH DISABILITIES ACT (ADA) OF 1990**
An employer cannot refuse to hire a person who is qualified but disabled.

1. **What is a Disability?**
"(1) [A] physical or mental impairment that substantially limits one or more of the major life activities of such individuals; (2) a record of such impairment; or (3) being regarded as having such an impairment." Includes AIDS, morbid obesity, etc.; not homosexuality or kleptomania.

2. **Reasonable Accommodations**

For a disabled person, an employer may have to make reasonable accommodations (establish more flexible working hours, create new job assignments, create or improve training materials and procedures).

a. **Undue Hardship**

Employers do not have to make accommodations that will cause "undue hardship" (impose a "significant difficulty or expense").

b. **Other Limits**

If a disabled employee can perform the essentials of his or her job without accommodation, no violation of the ADA has occurred.

3. **Preemployment Physicals**

Employers cannot (1) ask an applicant about the nature or extent of any known disability or (2) require a disabled person to take a preemployment physical (unless all applicants do). Disqualification must be from problems that render a person unable to perform the job for which he or she would be hired.

4. **Dangerous Workers**

An employer need not hire disabled workers who would pose a "direct threat to the health or safety" of co-workers or to themselves.

5. **Procedures, Remedies, and Penalties**

A claim may be commenced only after the plaintiff has pursued it through the EEOC. Remedies include reinstatement, back pay, a limited amount of compensatory and punitive damages (for intentional discrimination), and certain other forms of relief. Repeat violators may be ordered to pay fines of up to $100,000.

B. **REHABILITATION ACT OF 1973**

Includes essentially the same provisions as the ADA.

1. **Who Is Subject to the Rehabilitation Act**

Applies to federal employers; employers who receive federal aid (such as airports) or operate federal programs; and employers with federal service, supply, or construction contracts of $2,500 or more.

2. **Relief**

Relief against federal employers includes all remedies available to federal employees under Title VII. Relief against recipients of federal aid and those who operate federal programs includes back pay, but not compensatory or punitive damages, and recipients may also have their financial assistance withdrawn. Relief against federal contractors includes reinstatement or hiring and back pay; sanctions include the loss of government contracts.

C. **STATE LAWS**

Violations of the ADA may violate state laws prohibiting discrimination based on disability. Many state laws provide for increased damages.

IV. **AFFIRMATIVE ACTION PROGRAMS**

Attempt to "make up" for past patterns of discrimination by giving members of protected classes preferential treatment in hiring or promotion. Generally upheld if designed to correct existing imbalances in a work force and as long as employers consider factors in addition to race or gender.

V.   DEFENSES TO CLAIMS OF EMPLOYMENT DISCRIMINATION

A. BUSINESS NECESSITY

An employer may defend against a claim of discrimination by asserting that a practice that has a discriminatory effect is a business necessity.

B. *BONA FIDE* OCCUPATIONAL QUALIFICATION (BFOQ)

Another defense applies when discrimination against a protected class is essential to a job—that is, when a particular trait is a BFOQ. Generally restricted to cases in which gender is essential. Race can never be a BFOQ.

C. SENIORITY SYSTEMS

An employer with a history of discrimination may have no members of protected classes in upper-level positions. If no present intent to discriminate is shown, and promotions, etc., are distributed according to a fair seniority system, the employer has a good defense.

D. AFTER-ACQUIRED EVIDENCE

An employer who discovers, after discharging an employee, that the worker engaged in misconduct in applying for the job or while on the job may use that misconduct as a defense.

VI.   STATE LAWS PROHIBITING DISCRIMINATION

Most states have statutes that prohibit the kinds of discrimination prohibited under federal legislation. State statutes also often protect individuals, such as homosexuals, who are not protected under Title VII.

STUDY TIP 👉 Why?

After you have some familiarity with the law in an area, you may want to go beyond rote memorization of the principles to consider the societal basis of some of the doctrine. The material in this chapter is suited to consideration from a larger perspective. For example, you may ask about the reasons behind laws against discrimination—are the laws necessary? If so, why? If you don't think so, why not? Should society even be concerned with fairness in employment relationships? Why?

TRUE-FALSE QUESTIONS (Answers at the Back of the Book)

____ 1. Generally, affirmative action programs in which employers consider only race when making employment decisions are upheld as long as the programs are designed to correct imbalances in a work force.

____ 2. In a sexual harassment case, an employer cannot be liable if an employee did the harassing.

____ 3. Women affected by pregnancy must be treated for all employment-related purposes the same as other persons not so affected but similar in ability to work.

____ 4. Employment discrimination against persons with a physical or mental impairment that substantially limits "one or more major life activities" is prohibited. Impairments include blindness, cancer, AIDS, and learning disabilities.

____ 5. Discrimination complaints being brought under federal law must be filed with the Equal Opportunity Employment Commission.

____ 6. The Equal Employment Opportunity Commission cannot file a suit in federal court in its own name against those who it believes have violated civil rights laws.

FILL-IN QUESTIONS (Answers at the Back of the Book)

Compliance with the civil rights laws is monitored by the Equal Employment Opportunity Commission (EEOC), which _____ (can/ cannot) issue guidelines to interpret the law _____ (and/ but) can sue organizations that violate it. A victim files a claim with the EEOC, which investigates and _____ (sues/ may sue if conciliation between the parties does not occur). If the EEOC does not sue, the victim may sue. On proof of discrimination, a victim may be awarded _____ _____ (reinstatement and back pay/ reinstatement, back pay, and retroactive promotions). An injunction may _____ (also/ not) be granted.

MULTIPLE-CHOICE QUESTIONS (Answers at the Back of the Book)

____ 1. The first step in resolving a dispute involving alleged employment discrimination on the basis of race, color, national origin, religion, or sex is for the person who believes he or she is a victim of discrimination to

a. file a lawsuit.
b. attempt to resolve the problem with the employer.
c. contact a state or federal agency to see whether a claim is justified.
d. ask the Equal Opportunity Employment Commission to issue a guideline.

____ 2. Tad is a supervisor for the Quintana Roo Clothing Company. Meredith is an employee supervised by Tad. Tad reviews each employee's work with the employee once a month in private. In Meredith's fourth year of employment, during a monthly review, Tad begins making comments and touching Meredith in a way that Meredith perceives as sexually offensive. Meredith says nothing to the company, but suffers such anxiety that she quits less than a year later. If Meredith sues Quintana Roo, she will

a. win, because Tad's conduct constituted sexual harassment.
b. win, because Quintana Roo failed to take corrective action.
c. lose, because Meredith overreacted—a few comments and a little touching never hurt anyone.
d. lose, because Meredith said nothing to Quintana Roo.

_____ **3.** Uniontown Lumber Company requires all employees over forty-five years old to take and pass a physical test that is not imposed on younger employees. If an employee does not pass the test, he or she is discharged. Uniontown can avoid liability under the Age Discrimination in Employment Act only if the company

a. changes the requirement to have all employees over forty take the test.
b. changes the requirement to condition only promotion, not employment, on the test.
c. can show a legitimate business reason for the test.
d. has between twenty and thirty employees.

_____ **4.** Nacheko Paperworks requires that all its secretaries be able to type. Nacheko's secretarial pool is 10 percent minority. The population in the local labor market is 30 percent minority. Whitney, a member of a minority, applies to Nacheko for a secretarial job. Whitney cannot type but tells the company that she is willing to learn. When Nacheko does not hire her, she sues. She will

a. win, because Nacheko's work force does not reflect the same percentage of members of a protected class that characterizes qualified individuals in the local labor market.
b. win, because Whitney indicated that she was willing to learn, and an employer has an obligation to hire and train unqualified minority employees.
c. lose, because in this case being a member of the majority is a BFOQ.
d. lose, because Nacheko has a business necessity defense.

_____ **5.** Laszlo, who is hearing-impaired, applies for a position with the Snake River Fuel Company. Laszlo is well-qualified but is refused the job because, he is told, "We can't afford to accommodate you with an interpreter." If Laszlo sues Snake River, Laszlo will

a. win, if the court finds that Snake River has installed ramps for other disabled persons.
b. win, if the court finds that, under the circumstances, the interpreter would be a "reasonable accommodation."
c. lose, if the court finds that, under the circumstances, it is not an undue hardship for Laszlo to be refused the position.
d. lose, if the court finds that Laszlo could do the job only with the assistance of an interpreter.

_____ **6.** Title VII of the Civil Rights Act of 1964 prohibits

a. selecting or promoting employees on the basis of race or color.
b. making distinctions according to the race of a person's spouse, friends, or other contacts.
c. showing a preference for members of one minority over members of another.
d. all of the above

_____ **7.** Civil rights laws have helped

a. create opportunities for some persons who would not have had them otherwise.
b. change popular attitudes.
c. make possible recent economic gains by minorities and women.
d. all of the above.

SHORT ESSAY QUESTIONS

1. Compare and contrast disparate-treatment and disparate-impact discrimination and Title VII's response to each in the context of employment.

2. Discuss what the Americans with Disabilities Act requires of employers.

ISSUE SPOTTERS (Answers at the Back of the Book)

1. Lee, who is a member of a minority, graduates from college with a technical degree. Lee learns of a job opening at Kessel Technical Company for which he is well-qualified. He applies for the job but is rejected. Kessel continues to seek applicants for the position. If Kessel eventually fills the position with a person who is not a member of a minority, can Lee make out a case against Kessel for discrimination?

2. Garret is a supervisor for Subs & Suds, a fast-food restaurant. Joli is an employee supervised by Garret. When Subs & Suds announces that sales are down and the work force will have to be "downsized," Garret calls Joli into the office and tells her that if she grants him sexual favors, she will not be laid off. Is this sexual harassment?

3. The Americans with Disabilities Act prohibits employment discrimination against disabled persons. Who are "disabled persons"?

4. The state of New York enacts a statute prohibiting all women from working in public safety occupations at night. The statute provides that its intent is to protect women from the dangers of certain night-time occupations. Rosa, a police officer who prefers the night shift, sues the state when she is transferred onto the day shift. The state argues that because the statute does not discriminate against women on the basis of race, color, religion, or national origin, but applies to all women equally, it is not illegal. What might the court rule?

5. Cal, a light-skinned African American, works for Nash Security Company. Cal believes that his supervisor Anita, a dark-skinned African American, discriminated against him in awarding a promotion. Could Cal file a suit against Nash, alleging discrimination on the basis of color?

 Key Points

The **key points** in this chapter include:

1. The process behind union elections and collective bargaining.

2. What strikes are legal and what strikes are illegal.

3. Unfair employer labor practices.

4. Unfair union labor practices.

5. The rights of nonunion employees

Chapter 22:
Labor Law

WHAT THIS CHAPTER IS ABOUT

This chapter outlines labor law and legal recognition of the right to form unions, the process of unionizing a company, the process of collective bargaining, and labor practices that are considered fair and unfair under federal law.

CHAPTER OUTLINE

I. **FEDERAL LABOR LAW**

    A. **NORRIS-LAGUARDIA ACT OF 1932**
    Restricts federal courts' power to issue injunctions against unions engaged in peaceful strikes, picketing, and boycotts.

    B. **NATIONAL LABOR RELATIONS ACT OF 1935 (NLRA)**
    Established the right of employees to bargain collectively and to strike; prescribed unfair employer practices; created the NLRB to oversee union elections, prevent employers from engaging in unfair practices, investigate employers in response to employee charges of unfair labor practices, issue cease-and-desist orders.

    C. **LABOR-MANAGEMENT RELATIONS ACT OF 1947 (TAFT-HARTLEY ACT)**
    Prohibits unions from refusing to bargain with employers, engaging in certain types of picketing, featherbedding, and other unfair union practices. Expressly preserves union shops, but allows states to pass right-to-work laws, which make it illegal to require union membership for employment.

D. LABOR-MANAGEMENT REPORTING AND DISCLOSURE ACT OF 1959

1. **Internal Union Business**
Requires regular elections of union officers, under secret ballot; prohibits ex-convicts and Communists from holding union office; makes union officials accountable for union property; allows members to participate in union meetings, nominate officers, vote in proceedings.

2. **Hot-Cargo Agreements**
Outlawed certain hot-cargo agreements (in which employers voluntarily agreed with unions not to handle, use, or deal in non-union-produced goods of other employers).

II. THE DECISION TO FORM OR TO SELECT A UNION

A. WORKERS SIGN AUTHORIZATION CARDS
A majority of the relevant workers must sign authorization cards, which state that the workers wnat a certain union to represent the workforce.

B. THE EMPLOYER IS ASKED TO RECOGNIZE THE UNION
If the employer refuses, unionizers must present authorization cards from at least 30 percent of the workers to be represented to the NLRB regional office with a petition for an election.

C. THE NLRB DETERMINES THE APPROPRIATE BARGAINING UNIT
This requires a mutuality of interest among the workers to be represented. Mutuality of interest requires—

1. **Similarity of Jobs**
Similar levels of skill, wages, benefits, working conditions.

2. **Geographic Proximity**
It may be a problem if the workers are at many different sites.

3. **No Management Employees**
Members of management cannot be part of a union.

III. UNION ELECTION
If no union has been certified within the past twelve months to represent the workers, the NLRB orders an election to determine employee choice regarding union representation. The NLRB supervises the election.

A. UNION ELECTION CAMPAIGN

1. **Employer Limits**
Employers may limit the campaign activities of union supporters (such as where on company property and when campaigning may occur).

2. **Restrictions on Employer Limits**
An employer may prohibit *all* solicitation during work time or in certain places but may not prohibit *only* union solicitation. Workers also have a right to a reasonable opportunity to campaign (nonworking areas on the employer's property during nonworking time).

B. MANAGEMENT ELECTION CAMPAIGN

1. Employer Advantages
Employers may campaign on company property on company time without giving union supporters an opportunity for rebuttal.

2. Restrictions on Employer Advantages
If the employer commits an unfair labor practice, the NLRB may invalidate an election (order a new election; direct the employer to recognize the union).

a. No Threats
An employer may not make threats of reprisals if employees vote to unionize. Employers may not question individual workers about their positions on unionization.

b. No Last-minute Speeches
An employer cannot make an election speech on company time to assembled workers within twenty-four hours of an election, unless employees attend voluntarily on their own time.

c. No Surveillance
An employer may not undertake certain types of surveillance of workers or even create the impression of surveilling workers.

C. DECERTIFICATION ELECTION

1. May Be Sought by Employees
Through a petition to the NLRB, with a showing of 30 percent employee support and no certification within the past year.

2. No Decertification for One Year after Certification
During this period, it is presumed that the union enjoys majority support; after this period, the presumption is rebuttable.

D. ELECTION RESULTS
If a fair election is held and the union wins, the NLRB will certify the union as the exclusive bargaining representative of the workers polled.

IV. COLLECTIVE BARGAINING
The central legal right of a union is to serve as the sole representative of the group of workers in bargaining with the employer over the workers' rights.

A. SUBJECTS OF BARGAINING

1. Appropriate Subjects

a. Terms of Employment
Wages, hours of work, safety rules, insurance coverage, pension and other employee benefits plans, procedures for employee discipline, and procedures for employee grievances against the company.

b. Decision to Relocate a Plant
An employer must bargain over a relocation if it does not involve a basic change in the nature of the operation (with exceptions).

2. **Illegal Subjects**
   Featherbedding (hiring unnecessary excess workers); closed shop (requiring union membership as a condition of employment).

3. **Possible Subjects**
   Management may choose to bargain over decisions otherwise within its discretion (such as severance pay or rights of transfer to other plants in the event of plant shut-down) to obtain concessions on other subjects.

B. **No Unilateral Changes during Bargaining**
   Management may not make unilateral changes in important working conditions, such as wages or hours of employment, unless bargaining reaches an impasse or in cases of business necessity.

C. **GOOD FAITH BARGAINING**

1. **Bad Faith Bargaining Is an Unfair Labor Practice**
   Includes refusing to meet with union representatives; excessive delaying tactics; insisting on unreasonable contract terms; engaging in a campaign to undermine the union; constantly shifting positions on disputed terms; sending bargainers who lack authority to commit to a contract.

2. **Options If a Party Refuses to Bargain in Good Faith**
   The NLRB can order a party to bargain in good faith. The other party may be excused from bargaining.

V.   STRIKES

A. **THE RIGHT TO STRIKE**
   Guaranteed by the NLRA, within limits, and strike activities, such as picketing, are protected by the First Amendment. Nonworkers have a right to participate in picketing. Workers can also refuse to cross a picket line of fellow workers who are engaged in a lawful strike.

B. **ILLEGAL STRIKES**
   Violent strikes (including the threat of violence); massed picketing; sitdown strikes; wildcat strikes; hot-cargo agreements; strikes that contravene no-strike clauses in previous collective bargaining agreements.

1. **Common Situs Picketing**
   Picketing cannot be directed against a secondary employer.

2. **Strikes That Threaten National Health or Safety**
   These strikes are not illegal, but to encourage their settlement, the president of the United States can obtain an injunction to last for eighty days, during which the government can work to produce a settlement.

C. **REPLACING OR REHIRING STRIKERS**

1. **Replacement Workers**
   An employer may hire substitute workers to replace strikers.

2. **Economic Strikes**
   Strikers have no right to return to their jobs, but former strikers must be given preference to any vacancies and also retain their seniority rights.

3. **Unfair Labor Practice Strikes**
   Employer unfair labor practice strike—strikers must be given their jobs.
   Union unfair labor practice strike— strikers need not be rehired.

VI.   LOCKOUTS

An employer can shut down to prevent employees from working, but may not use a lockout to break a union and pressure employees into decertification.

VII.   EMPLOYER UNFAIR LABOR PRACTICES

A.   REFUSAL TO RECOGNIZE UNION AND NEGOTIATE

B.   INTERFERENCE IN UNION ACTIVITIES
An employer may not interfere with, restrain, or coerce employees in the exercise of their rights to form a union and bargain collectively.

C.   DOMINATION OF UNIONS
The NLRA forbids company unions and other forms of employer domination of workers' unions.

D.   DISCRIMINATION AGAINST UNION EMPLOYEES
Employers cannot discriminate against union workers (in layoffs, hiring, or closing a union plant).

VIII.   UNION UNFAIR LABOR PRACTICES

A.   SECONDARY BOYCOTTS

B.   DISCRIMINATION AGAINST NONUNION WORKERS
A union cannot threaten an employee with violence, use economic coercion, picket, or otherwise discriminate (or influence an employer to do so) against workers because they refuse to join a union.

C.   FEATHERBEDDING

D.   REFUSAL TO BARGAIN IN GOOD FAITH WITH EMPLOYER

E.   EXCESSIVE FEES OR DUES
A nonunion employee subject to a union shop clause who must pay dues cannot be required to contribute to causes or to lobby politicians.

IX.   RIGHTS OF NONUNION EMPLOYEES

A.   CONCERTED ACTIVITY
Activity must be taken by employees for their mutual aid regarding wages, hours, or terms and conditions of employment. An action by a single employee may be protected, if it is taken for the benefit of other employees and the employee discussed it with other approving workers.

B.   SAFETY
An employee can walk off the job if he or she has a good faith belief that working conditions are abnormally dangerous.

C.   EMPLOYEE COMMITTEES
The central problem with employee committees is that they may become the functional equivalent of a union that is dominated by management. Thus, these committees cannot perform union functions.

STUDY TIP ☞ Marking Your Text

Marking in your text—and in this outline—will improve your understanding and remembering of the subject matter. Common methods include underlining important words and concepts, and highlighting with a colored felt-tip marker. Because marking requires a closer reading of the material to decide what to mark, it helps you to organize the material for yourself and to retain it for the exam.

TRUE-FALSE QUESTIONS (Answers at the Back of the Book)

____ 1. A factor in determining the mutuality of interest among workers to be represented by a bargaining unit is the similarity of jobs of the workers to be unionized.

____ 2. The central legal right of management is to serve as the representative of workers in bargaining with the union over the rights of employees.

____ 3. An employer may use a lockout if there is some economic justification for it.

____ 4. Most secondary boycotts are illegal, but employers can agree with unions not to handle, use, or deal in non-union-produced goods.

____ 5. When workers must be laid off, an employer cannot consider union participation as a criterion for deciding whom to fire.

____ 6. The NLRA protects concerted action on the part of certified unions only.

FILL-IN QUESTIONS (Answers at the Back of the Book)

1.   Peaceful strikes, picketing, and boycotts are protected under the _____ _____ (National Labor Relations/ Norris-LaGuardia) Act, which also restricts federal courts in enjoining unions engaged in peaceful strikes.

2.   Employees' rights to organize, to engage in collective bargaining through elected representatives, and to engage in concerted activities for those and other purposes were established in the _____ (National Labor Relations/ Norris-LaGuardia) Act.

3.   Requiring union membership as a condition of employment is proscribed by the Labor-Management _____ (Relations/ Reporting and Disclosure) Act. The act also _____ (allows/ prohibits) requiring workers to join the union after a certain time on the job. The act also _____ (allows/ proscribes) laws making it illegal to require union membership for continued employment.

MULTIPLE-CHOICE QUESTIONS (Answers at the Back of the Book)

____ 1. Chester is an employee of Heinie Products, Inc. Chester and other employees contact various unions and designate Amalgamated Machinists Union as their bargaining representative. When Heinie learns that its employees are unionizing, Heinie refuses to bargain with Amalgamated and fires Chester for "choosing the wrong side." If Chester complains to the NLRB, Heinie may be found to have violated

a. the Norris-LaGuardia Act.
b. the National Labor Relations Act.
c. the Labor-Management Relations Act.
d. the Labor-Management Reporting and Disclosure Act.

____ 2. Which of the following is NOT an employer unfair labor practice?

a. Refusing to give union workers pay for time spent on union activities
b. Preventing union support of an employee with a grievance against the employer
c. Making threats that interfere with employees' decision to join a union
d. Asking employees to declare openly their views on a union

____ 3. Cement Workers of America (CWA) represents employees of Ratner Concrete Company. During collective bargaining, CWA demands that Ratner decrease deductibles under Ratner's health insurance plan, improve the safety rules in all company operations, keep its plant in Crescent City open for at least five years, and provide a new procedure for employee grievances against the company. Which of these demands can Ratner refuse to bargain over?

a. Decreasing deductibles under Ratner's health insurance plan
b. Improving the safety rules in company operations
c. Keeping the plant in Crescent City open
d. Providing a new procedure for employee greivances

____ 4. Union of Metalcraft Employees (UME) represents employees of Ames Hard Metal Company. When bargaining reaches an impasse, UME calls a strike. Striking workers set up a twenty-four hour picket line around Ames's plant. UME sends nonworkers to participate in the picketing. On the first day of the strike, to show solidarity, strikers form a massed barrier to deny nonunion workers access to the plant. Which of these is NOT lawful?

a. A twenty-four hour picket line around Ames's plant
b. Nonworkers' participation in the picketing
c. Strikers' denying nonunion workers access to the plant
d. Both b and c

____ 5. The NLRB schedules an election for Tree Clock Company production employees to vote on whether to be represented by the American Production Workers Union (APWU). During the brief campaign, Tree may NOT

a. campaign among workers against the union.
b. give a speech against the union within twenty-hours of the election.
c. restrict union solicitation to nonwork areas on company property during nonworking time.
d. threaten employees with the loss of their jobs if APWU wins the election.

___   6. International Assembly Workers Union (IAWU) represents employees of Botel Assembly Company. When bargaining reaches an impasse, IAWU calls a strike. During the strike, Botel hires replacement workers. After the strike, Botel refuses to reemploy former strikers, unless they agree to forfeit their seniority. If IAWU sues Botel, IAWU will

   a. win, because former strikers must be given preferential rights over replacement workers and must retain their seniority.
   b. win, because former strikers must be given preferential rights to new vacancies and must retain their seniority.
   c. lose, because former strikers have no preferential rights over replacement workers or to new vacancies, regardless of seniority.
   d. lose, because calling a strike when bargaining is at an impasse is illegal.

SHORT ESSAY QUESTIONS

1. Discuss some of the legislation concerning labor unions and collective bargaining.

2. Discuss those types of strikes that are illegal.

ISSUE SPOTTERS (Answers at the Back of the Book)

1. Rosita is not a member of a union. Rosita applies for work with Sankuru Company. Sankuru tells Rosita that it requires union membership as a condition of employment. Rosita applies for work with Scilly Manufacturing Corporation. Scilly does not require union membership as a condition of employment but requires employees to join the union after six months on the job. Are either of these conditions illegal? Would it make any difference if Rosita, Sankuru, and Scilly were in a right-to-work state?

2. There are certain subjects that an employer must bargain over in response to employees' demands. The National Labor Relations Act requires that employers bargain with workers over wages, hours of work, and other terms and conditions of employment. What are examples of "other terms and conditions of employment"?

3. National Paper Workers (NPW) represents employees of White Paper Company. In negotiations with White, to obtain higher wages for the employees, NPW agrees not to strike for the term of the collective bargaining agreement. If NPW calls a strike during the period of the contract, can White obtain an injunction against the strike based on the no-strike clause?

4. Beth is an employee of Silver Skis Company. Beth is a vocal union advocate. Silver fires Beth, on grounds that she did not work the exact hours reported on her time card—although Silver has never discharged an employee for this reason. If Beth complains, can Silver be required to prove that it did not have a discriminatory motive in discharging Beth?

5. Baum Bakery has five nonunion employees. The employees discuss working conditions with Baum, who refuses to make any changes. The employees decide that one of them should engage in a walkout protest. When the employee walks out, with the acknowledged assent of the others, Baum fires him. Has Baum committed an unfair labor practice?

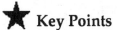 **Key Points**

The **key points** in this chapter include:

1. What is and what is not unfair and deceptive advertising.

2. Federal laws that deal with information on labels and packages.

3. Regulation of different types of sales.

4. Regulation of credit in consumer transactions.

5. Federal health and safety laws.

Chapter 23:
Consumer Protection

WHAT THIS CHAPTER IS ABOUT

Federal and state laws protect consumers from unfair trade practices, unsafe products, discriminatory or unreasonable credit requirements, and other problems related to consumer transactions. This chapter focuses on federal consumer law.

CHAPTER OUTLINE

I. ADVERTISING
The Federal Trade Commission Act of 1914 created the Federal Trade Commission (FTC) to prevent unfair and deceptive trade practices.

A. UNFAIR AND DECEPTIVE ADVERTISING
Advertising is deemed deceptive if a consumer would be misled by it.

1. **Practices That Are Deceptive**
Scientifically untrue claims; misleading price claims; bait-and-switch ads (when a seller refuses to show an advertised item, etc.).

2. **Practice That May Be Deceptive**
A celebrity endorsement, if the celebrity does not use the product.

3. **Practices That Are Not Deceptive**
Puffing (vague generalities, obvious exaggeration).

B. FTC ACTIONS AGAINST DECEPTIVE ADVERTISING
If the FTC believes that an ad is unfair or deceptive, it sends a formal complaint to the advertiser, who may agree to settle. If not, the FTC can hold a hearing (see Chapter 6) and issue a cease-and-desist order or require counteradvertising (to inform the public of misinformation).

C. TELEMARKETING AND FAX ADVERTISING

1. **Telephone Consumer Protection Act (TCPA) of 1991**

   Prohibits (1) phone solicitation using an automatic dialing system or a prerecorded voice and (2) transmission of ads via fax without the recipient's permission. Consumers can recover actual losses or $500 for each violation, whichever is greater. If a defendant willfully or knowingly violated the act, a court can award treble damages.

2. **State Laws**

   Most states also have laws regulating phone solicitation.

II. LABELING AND PACKAGING

A. FAIR PACKAGING AND LABELING ACT OF 1966

Requires that product labels identify the product; net quantity of contents; quantity of servings, if the number of servings is stated; manufacturer; packager or distributor. More can be required (such as fat content).

B. OTHER FEDERAL LAWS

Fur Products Labeling Act of 1951, Wool Products Labeling Act of 1939, Flammable Fabrics Act of 1953, Smokeless Tobacco Health Education Act of 1986.

III. SALES

Federal agencies that regulate sales include the FTC and the Federal Reserve Board of Governors, which governs credit provisions in sales contracts. Many states have laws governing home sales.

A. DOOR-TO-DOOR SALES

States' "cooling-off" laws permit a buyer to rescind a door-to-door purchase within a certain time. The FTC has a three-day period. If state law is more favorable, it governs. The FTC requires a seller to notify a buyer of the right to cancel (if the sale is in Spanish, notice must be in Spanish).

B. TELEPHONE AND MAIL-ORDER SALES

Consumers are partly protected by federal laws prohibiting mail fraud and by state law that parallels federal law.

1. **FTC "Mail or Telephone Order Merchandise Rule" of 1993**

   For goods bought via phone lines or through the mail, merchants must ship orders within the time promised in their ads, notify consumers when orders cannot be shipped on time, and issue a refund within a specified time if a consumer cancels an order.

2. **Postal Reorganization Act of 1970**

   Unsolicited merchandise sent by the mail may be retained, used, discarded, or disposed of, without obligation to the sender.

C. REAL ESTATE SALES

1. **Interstate Land Sales Full Disclosure Act of 1968**

   A seller or lessor of one hundred or more lots of unimproved land, if the sale or lease is part of a common promotion, must file a statement with the Department of Housing and Urban Development (HUD), which must approve before the land can be offered for sale or lease.

2. **Real Estate Settlement Procedures Act (RESPA), as Revised in 1976**
A lender must—

a. Within three business days after a person applies for a mortgage (1) send a booklet prepared by HUD that explains settlement procedures, describes costs, and outlines legal rights, and (2) give an estimate of most of the settlement costs.
b. Identify individuals or firms that the applicant is required to use for legal or other services, including title search and insurance.
c. If the loan is approved, provide a truth-in-lending statement that shows the annual percentage rate on the mortgage loan.

IV.   CREDIT PROTECTION

A. TRUTH-IN-LENDING ACT (TILA) OF 1968
Title I of the Consumer Credit Protection Act (CCPA), administered by the Federal Reserve Board, requires the disclosure of credit terms to debtors.

1. **To Whom TILA Applies**
Creditors who, in the ordinary course of business, lend money or sell goods on credit to consumers, or arrange for credit for consumers.

2. **Regulation Z**
Applies in any transaction involving an installment sales contract in which payment is to be made in more than four installments.

   a. **Disclosure Requirements**
   A lender must disclose all material facts (annual percentage rate of interest, finance charges, etc.) clearly and conspicuously.

   b. **Three-Day Rescission Period**
   If a lender takes a security interest in a consumer's principal dwelling, the consumer can rescind the transaction within three days. In some cases, the three days can extend to three years.

   c. **Remedies and Penalties**
   A creditor may be liable for twice the amount of the finance charge (but no more than $1,000), plus attorneys' fees. Criminal penalties include up to a $5,000 fine and one year in jail.

3. **Consumer Leasing Act of 1988**
Those who lease or arrange to lease consumer goods in the ordinary course of their business, if the goods are priced at $25,000 or less and the lease term exceeds four months, must disclose all material terms (finance charges, dates of payments, etc.) clearly and conspicuously.

4. **Fair Credit Billing Act of 1974**

   a. **Disputes over Products Bought with a Credit Card**
   If a good faith effort to resolve a dispute with a seller is unsuccessful, the buyer can withhold payment. The credit-card issuer must then intervene and attempt to settle the dispute.

   b. **Disputes over Credit-Card Bills**
   If a debtor believes there is an error, he or she may suspend payment (within sixty days of receipt of the bill). The credit-card company must resolve the dispute within ninety days.

5. **Other Provisions of TILA**
   Liability of a cardholder is $50 per card for unauthorized charges made before the issuer is notified that the card is lost. An issuer cannot bill a consumer for unauthorized charges if a card was improperly issued.

B. **EQUAL CREDIT OPPORTUNITY ACT OF 1974**
   Prohibits (1) the denial of credit on the basis of race, religion, national origin, color, sex, marital status, or age and (2) credit discrimination on the basis of whether an individual receives certain forms of income.

C. **FAIR CREDIT REPORTING ACT (FCRA) OF 1970**

1. **What the FCRA Provides**
   Consumer credit reporting agencies may issue credit reports only for certain purposes (extension of credit, etc.); a consumer who is denied credit, or is charged more than others would be, on the basis of a report must be notified of the fact and of the agency that issued the report.

2. **Consumers Can Have Inaccurate Information Deleted**
   If a consumer discovers that the report contains inaccurate information, the agency must delete it within a reasonable period of time.

D. **FAIR DEBT COLLECTION PRACTICES ACT (FDCPA) OF 1977**
   Applies only to debt-collection agencies that, usually for a percentage of the amount owed, attempt to collect debts on behalf of someone else.

1. **What the FDCPA Prohibits**

   a. Contacting the debtor at the debtor's place of employment if the employer objects.
   b. Contacting the debtor during inconvenient times or at any time if the debtor is represented by an attorney.
   c. Contacting third parties other than the debtor's parents, spouse, or financial advisor about payment unless a court agrees.
   d. Using harassment, or false and misleading information.
   e. Contacting the debtor any time after the debtor refuses to pay the debt, except to advise the debtor of further action to be taken.

2. **What the FDCPA Requires**
   Collection agencies must give a debtor notice that he or she has thirty days to dispute the debt and request written verification of it.

3. **Remedies**
   A debt collector may be liable for actual damages, plus additional damages not to exceed $1,000 and attorneys' fees.

V. **CONSUMER HEALTH AND SAFETY**

A. **FEDERAL FOOD, DRUG, AND COSMETIC ACT (FFDCA) OF 1938**
   Sets food standards, safe levels of food additives, classifications of food and food advertising; regulates medical devices. Drugs must be shown to be effective and safe. Enforced by the Food and Drug Administration (FDA).

B. **CONSUMER PRODUCT SAFETY ACT OF 1972**
   Includes a scheme for the regulation of consumer products and consumer safety under the Consumer Product Safety Commission (CPSC). The CPSC—

1. Conducts research on product safety.
2. Sets standards for consumer products and bans the manufacture and sale of a product that is potentially hazardous to consumers.
3. Removes from the market any products imminently hazardous and requires manufacturers to report on any products already sold or intended for sale if the products have proved to be hazardous.
4. Administers other product safety legislation.

VI.   STATE CONSUMER PROTECTION LAWS

State laws (typically directed at deceptive trade practices) may provide more protection for consumers than do federal laws. (See Chapter 11 on the Uniform Commercial Code). The Uniform Consumer Credit Code (UCCC) includes sections on truth in lending, fine-print clauses, and so on, but has been adopted in part in only a few states.

STUDY TIP ☞   IPAC

If your test includes an essay question in the form of a hypothetical, you may find the following format to be useful in answering the question: Introduction, Principle, Application, Conclusion. Begin your answer with a short introduction, identifying what the question is about. Next, state the general principle that applies to the situation, and discuss how it applies to the facts. If you argue both sides to an issue, argue one side first, then argue the other side. Finally, come to a conclusion.

TRUE-FALSE QUESTIONS (Answers at the Back of the Book)

____   1. Advertising will be deemed deceptive if a consumer would be misled by the advertising claim.

____   2. In general, labels must be accurate—they must use words as those words are understood by the ordinary consumer.

____   3. In both real estate and non-real estate transactions, consumers have a right to rescind their contracts even though a creditor has made all required disclosures.

____   4. The TILA applies only to creditors who, in the ordinary course of business, lend money or either sell on credit or arrange for the extension of credit to debtors who are natural persons.

____   5. The TILA provides that a creditor who violates the act may be liable for twice the amount of a finance charge, up to $1,000, plus attorneys' fees, as well as a $5,000 fine and up to one year in jail. The TILA also provides for contract rescission.

____ 6. Under the Fair Credit Reporting Act, consumers can correct any misinformation that leads to a denial of credit, employment, or insurance, but they cannot receive information about the source of the misinformation or about anyone who was given the misinformation.

FILL-IN QUESTIONS (Answers at the Back of the Book)

The Truth-in-Lending Act contains provisions regarding credit cards. One provision limits the liability of the cardholder to _____ ($50/ $500) per card for unauthorized charges made _____ (after/ before) the credit card issuer is notified that the card has been lost. Another provision _____ (allows/ prohibits) a credit card company _____ (from billing/ to bill) a consumer for any unauthorized charges _____ (even if/ if) the credit card was improperly issued by the company.

MULTIPLE-CHOICE QUESTIONS (Answers at the Back of the Book)

____ 1. The Kelley Company advertises its cereal, "Fiber Rich," as a product that reduces cholesterol. Finding no scientific evidence that Fiber Rich reduces cholesterol, the FTC holds a hearing and ultimately issues a cease-and-desist order. If the FTC believes that the order will not be enough to correct the impression held by the public that Fiber Rich can lower cholesterol, which of the following would be the most appropriate?

   a. Civil penalties
   b. Affirmative advertising
   c. Corrective advertising
   d. Multiple product orders

____ 2. Which of the following is NOT information required on product labels under the Fair Packaging and Labeling Act?

   a. The identity of the product, the net quantity of the contents, and the quantity of servings if that number is stated
   b. Warnings about the health hazards associated with the use of smokeless tobacco similar to those contained on ordinary tobacco product packages
   c. The identity of the manufacturer and the packager or distributor
   d. Nutrition details, including how much and what type of fat a product contains

____ 3. Marlena is bilingual. Byron comes to Marlena's home and, after a twenty-minute presentation in English, sells her a vacuum cleaner. Before leaving, he hands her a piece of paper that contains in English a notice of the right to cancel a sale within three days. Marlena's state provides a cooling-off period of three days. Four days later, Marlena tells Byron that she is rescinding the sale. If Byron sues to enforce the sale, Byron will

   a. win, because Marlena waited too long before attempting to rescind the sale.
   b. win, because the notice was in English only, which is all that's required.
   c. lose, because the notice should have been written in two languages.
   d. lose, because the state and federal cooling-off periods run consecutively.

____   4. Which of the following is TRUE?

a. The Interstate Land Sales Disclosure Act primarily concerns disclosures that mortgage lenders must make.
b. The Interstate Land Sales Disclosure Act requires that a lender refer a borrower to certain individuals for legal and other services related to home-buying.
c. The Real Estate Settlement Procedures Act primarily concerns HUD's oversight of sales by sellers of one hundred or more lots of unimproved real estate.
d. The Real Estate Settlement Procedures Act requires that a booklet prepared by HUD be sent within three business days to a person who applies for a mortgage.

____   5. Regulation Z requires disclosure of certain information in certain credit transactions. This information includes:

a. The specific dollar amount being financed, the annual percentage rate of interest, and any financing charges, premiums or points
b. The number, amounts, and due dates of payments and any penalties imposed on delinquent payments or prepayment
c. Both a and b
d. None of the above

____   6. Herbie takes out two student loans from First Bank. After one year of college, Herbie quits school and goes to work. He does not make payments on the loans as he agreed when he borrowed the money. The bank agrees with Mighty Collection Agency that if Mighty collects the debt, it can keep a percentage of whatever amount is collected. To collect the money from Herbie, Mighty can

a. contact Herbie at his place of employment, even if his employer objects.
b. contact Herbie at unusual or inconvenient times or any time if he retains an attorney.
c. contact third parties, including Herbie's parents, unless ordered otherwise by a court.
d. contact Herbie at any time to advise him of further action that Mighty will take.

____   7. The Heidi Doll Company begins marketing a new doll. The doll's clothes and hair are highly flammable, and some of the doll accessories are small enough to choke a little child. The Consumer Product Safety Commission (CPSC) believes that the doll is imminently hazardous and orders it removed from toy store shelves. If Heidi sues the CPSC, Heidi will

a. lose, because the CPSC has sufficiently broad authority to remove from store shelves any product that it believes is imminently hazardous.
b. lose, because the CPSC can remove any product, regardless of whether the agency believes that it is imminently hazardous.
c. win, because the CPSC exceeded its authority under the Consumer Product Safety Act—the CPSC can ban toys, but it cannot order them removed from stores.
d. win, because the CPSC has no authority to ban or remove any product.

SHORT ESSAY QUESTIONS

1. Discuss some of the more common deceptive advertising techniques and the ways in which the FTC may deal with such conduct.

2. Discuss the primary provisions of the Truth-In-Lending Act.

ISSUE SPOTTERS (Answers at the Back of the Book)

1. Schemp Appliance Company advertises GEM televisions sets at a very low price. Schemp keeps only a few of the GEM sets in stock and tells its salespersons to switch consumers attracted by the advertised price to more expensive, big-screen Melman sets. Schemp tells its sales staff that if all else fails, refuse to show the GEM sets, and if a consumer insists on buying one, do not promise delivery within a reasonable time. Has Schemp violated any law?

2. Estes Candy Company wants to sell its candy bars in a normal-sized package labeled "Gigantic Size." Gayland Fabrics Corporation wants to advertise its sweaters as having "That Wool Feel," but does not want to specify on labels that the sweaters are 100 percent polyester. Continental Tobacco Company wants to sell its cigarettes without any of several warnings about the health hazards associated with smoking. What stops these firms from marketing their products as they would like?

3. Munn Motors sells used cars with a label on each car that states that the car is being sold "as is," that Munn makes no other promises, and that service contracts are available at an additional charge. Is there anything else that Munn should include?

4. Erin buys a portable compact disc player from Aptheker Electric. Erin purchases it with her credit card. When the player proves defective, Erin asks Aptheker to repair or replace it, but Aptheker refuses. What can Erin do?

5. Suter Pharmaceuticals, Inc., believes it has developed a new drug that will be effective in the treatment of some AIDS patients. Although the drug has had only limited laboratory testing, Suter wants to make the drug widely available as soon as possible. Before Suter markets its drug, what must Suter show the Food and Drug Administration?

 Key Points

The **key points** in this chapter include:

1. Ccommon law actions available against polluters.

2. The National Environmental Policy Act and complementary laws.

3. Federal regulation of air and water pollution.

4. Federal laws relating to toxic chemicals.

5. Federal regulation of radiation.

Chapter 24:
Environmental Law

WHAT THIS CHAPTER IS ABOUT

This chapter covers environmental law, which is the law that relates to environmental protection—common law actions and federal statutes and regulations.

CHAPTER OUTLINE

I. COMMON LAW ACTIONS

A. NUISANCE
Persons cannot use their property in a way that unreasonably interferes with others' rights to use or enjoy their own property. An injured party may be awarded damages or an injunction.

B. NEGLIGENCE AND STRICT LIABILITY
A business that fails to use reasonable care may be liable to a party whose injury was foreseeable. Businesses that engage in ultrahazardous activities are strictly liable for whatever injuries the activities cause.

II. FEDERAL REGULATION

A. NATIONAL ENVIRONMENTAL POLICY ACT (NEPA) OF 1969
Requires that all federal agencies consider environmental factors when making significant decisions.

1. **When an Environmental Impact Statement Must Be Prepared**
   Whenever a major federal action significantly affects the quality of the environment. An action qualifies as *major* if it involves a substantial commitment of resources (monetary or otherwise). An action is *federal* if a federal agency has the power to control it.

2. **What an EIS Must Analyze**
   (1) The impact on the environment that the action will have, (2) any adverse effects to the environment and alternative actions that might be taken, and (3) irreversible effects the action might generate.

3. **When an Agency Decides that an EIS Is Unnecessary**
   It must issue a statement supporting this conclusion.

B. **COMPLEMENTARY FEDERAL LAWS**
   Other federal laws that require the consideration of environmental values in agency decision making include the Fish and Wildlife Coordination Act of 1958 and the Endangered Species Act of 1973.

C. **ENVIRONMENTAL PROTECTION AGENCY (EPA)**
   Coordinates federal environmental responsibilities and administers most federal environmental policies and statutes.

III. **AIR POLLUTION**
   The Clean Air Act of 1963 (and amendments) is the basis for regulation.

A. **MOBILE SOURCES**
   Regulations governing air pollution from automobiles and other mobile sources specify standards and time schedules. For example, under the 1990 amendments to the Clean Air Act—

1. **New Automobiles' Exhaust**
   Manufacturers must cut emission of nitrogen oxide by 60 percent and emission of other pollutants by 35 percent by 1998. Another set of emission controls may be ordered after the year 2000.

2. **Commuters' Pollution**
   An employer (with over one hundred employees in a major metropolitan area) must support programs to increase the number of commuting employee passengers per vehicle by 25 percent by 1999.

3. **Gasoline**
   Service stations must sell gasoline with a higher oxygen content (in forty-one cities that have carbon monoxide pollution in the winter). Beginning in 1995, service stations must sell even cleaner burning gasoline in Los Angeles and eight other polluted urban areas.

B. **STATIONARY SOURCES**
   The EPA sets air quality standards for stationary sources (such as industrial plants), and the states formulate plans to achieve them. For example, under the 1990 amendments to the Clean Air Act—

1. **110 of the Oldest Coal-burning Power Plants in the United States**
   Must cut emissions by 40 percent by the year 2001 to reduce acid rain.

2. **Utilities**
   Granted "credits" to emit certain amounts of sulfur dioxide, and those that emit less can sell their credits to other polluters.

3. **Major New Sources**
   Must use the maximum achievable control technology (MACT) to reduce emissions from the combustion of fossil fuels (coal and oil).

4. **Other Factories and Businesses**
Production of chlorofluorocarbons, carbon tetrachloride, and methyl chloroform (linked to depleting the ozone layer) must stop by 2002. Industrial emissions of 189 specific hazardous air pollutants must be reduced by 90 percent by 2000 (through the best available technology).

C. **PENALTIES**
Civil penalties of up to $25,000 per day, or an amount equal to a violator's economic benefits from noncompliance. Criminal fines are possible.

IV. WATER POLLUTION

A. **NAVIGABLE WATERS**
Coastal and freshwater wetlands, and intrastate lakes and streams used by interstate travelers and industries. The Clean Water Act of 1972 (amended the Federal Water Pollution Control Act (FWPCA) of 1948) provided—

1. **Goals**
(1) Make waters safe for swimming, (2) protect fish and wildlife, (3) eliminate the discharge of pollutants into the water.

2. **Limits on Discharges Based on Best Available Technology**
Time schedules (extended by amendment in 1977 and by the Water Quality Act of 1987) limit discharges of pollutants.

3. **Permits**
Municipal and industrial polluters must obtain permits before discharging wastes into navigable waters. Filling or dredging wetlands requires a permit from the Army Corps of Engineers.

4. **Penalties and Remedies**
Civil penalties from $10,000 per day (up to $25,000 per violation) to $25,000 per day. Criminal penalties from fines of $2,500 per day to $1 million total and one to fifteen years' imprisonment. Injunctions, damages, and clean-up costs can be imposed.

B. **DRINKING WATER**
The Safe Drinking Water Act of 1974 requires the EPA to set maximum levels for pollutants in public water systems. System operators must come as close as possible to the standards by using the best available technology.

C. **OCEAN DUMPING**
The Marine Protection, Research, and Sanctuaries Act of 1972—

1. **Radiological Waste and Other Materials**
Dumping of radiological, chemical, and biological warfare agents, and high-level radioactive waste is prohibited. Transporting and dumping other materials (with exceptions) requires a permit.

2. **Penalties**
Civil penalties of not more than $50,000 or revocation or suspension of a permit. Criminal penalties of up to a $50,000 fine, imprisonment for not more than a year, or both. Injunctions can be imposed.

V. TOXIC CHEMICALS

A. **PESTICIDES AND HERBICIDES**
The Federal Insecticide, Fungicide, and Rodenticide Act (FIFRA) of 1947—

1. **Registration, Certification, and Use**
   Pesticides and herbicides must be (1) registered before they can be sold, (2) certified and used only for approved applications, and (3) used in limited quantities when applied to food crops.

2. **Labels**
   Labels must include directions for the use of a pesticide or herbicide, warnings to protect human health and the environment, a statement of treatment in the case of poisoning, and a list of the ingredients.

3. **Penalties**
   For registrants and producers: suspension or cancellation of registration, up to a $50,000 fine, imprisonment up to one year. For commercial dealers: up to a $25,000 fine, imprisonment up to one year. For farmers and other private users: a $1,000 fine, imprisonment up to thirty days.

B. TOXIC SUBSTANCES
Under the Toxic Substances Control Act of 1976, for substances that potentially pose an imminent hazard or an unreasonable risk of injury to health or the environment, the EPA may require special labeling, set production quotas, or limit or prohibit the use of a substance.

C. HAZARDOUS WASTES

1. **Resource Conservation and Recovery Act (RCRA) of 1976**
   Under RCRA, the EPA determines which forms of solid waste are hazardous, and sets requirements for disposal, storage, and treatment. Penalties are based on the seriousness of a violation and the probability of harm (penalties may be doubled for repeat offenders).

2. **Comprehensive Environmental Response, Compensation, and Liability Act (CERCLA) of 1980 (Superfund)**
   Regulates the clean-up of leaking hazardous waste disposal sites. If a release or a threatened release occurs, the EPA can clean up the site and recover the cost from any potentially responsible party.

   a. **Potentially Responsible Parties**
      (1) The person who generated the wastes disposed of at the site, (2) the person who transported the wastes to the site, (3) the person who owned or operated the site at the time of the disposal, or (4) the current owner or operator.

      1) **Parent Company**
         May be liable as an "operator" for clean-up costs for a spill by its subsidiary, based on the relationship between the two firms.

      2) **Officers and Shareholders**
         May be liable, based on their control of their corporations.

      3) **Trustees**
         A trustee who is the record owner of a contaminated site is an "owner" under Superfund and may be liable for clean-up costs.

      4) **Lenders**
         A lender who participates in management of a borrower may qualify as an "owner or operator." A lender who can influence a borrower's decision regarding hazardous waste may be liable.

b. **Joint and Several Liability**
One party can be charged with the entire cost (which that party may be able to recoup in a contribution action against others).

VI.   RADIATION

A. Nuclear Power Plants
Regulated almost exclusively by the federal government under the Atomic Energy Act of 1954. The Nuclear Regulatory Commission (NRC) prepares an EIS for each proposed nuclear plant, which the NRC also licenses.

B. Radioactive Waste
Low-level waste generated by private facilities is the responsibility of each state under the Low Level Radioactive Waste Policy Act of 1980. The NRC regulates the use and disposal of most other nuclear materials.

VII. STATE AND LOCAL REGULATION
States regulate the environment through zoning or more direct regulation. City, county, and other local governments control some aspects through zoning laws, waste removal and disposal regulations, aesthetic ordinances, and so on.

STUDY TIP 🖙 <u>Administering Environmental Laws</u>

At the federal level, environmental law is inseparable from administrative law. The primary regulatory statutes are administered by agencies. What that means is that the regulation of business conduct under environmental laws is subject to administrative law procedures and principles. You may find it helpful when studying either this chapter or Chapter 6, or both, to consider the material in tandem.

TRUE-FALSE QUESTIONS (Answers at the Back of the Book)

____ 1. Common law doctrines that were applied against polluters centuries ago no longer apply.

____ 2. States may restrict discharge of chemicals into the water or air, regulate disposal of toxic wastes, and regulate disposal of other wastes.

____ 3. Local governments can control some aspects of the environment through zoning laws.

____ 4. A party who violates the Clean Air Act may realize economic benefits from noncompliance because there is no provision for assessing a penalty equal to those benefits.

____   **5.**   The Environmental Protection Agency sets maximum levels for pollutants in public water systems.

____   **6.**   The private nuclear power plant industry is regulated almost exclusively by the federal government.

FILL-IN QUESTIONS (Answers at the Back of the Book)

The National Environmental Policy Act requires _____ (federal/ state and local) agencies to prepare environmental impact statements (EIS) when major _____ (federal/ state and local) actions significantly affect the quality of the environment. An EIS analyzes (1) the _____ _____ (environmental impact that an action will have/ environment's impact on a project), (2) any adverse effects to the _____ (environment/ project) and alternative courses of action, and (3) irreversible effects that _____ (an action might cause to the environment/ the environment might cause to the project). If an agency decides that an EIS is unnecessary, it must issue a statement announcing that decision _____ (and reasons/ but it need not provide reasons) supporting the conclusion.

MULTIPLE-CHOICE QUESTIONS (Answers at the Back of the Book)

____   **1.**   Oestle Corporation transports radioactive waste materials from Plutonium, Inc., to Oestle's storage facility near Clermount. In an accident, a truckload of Plutonium waste spills into the yards of a Clermount neighborhood, and residents develop a number of allegedly radiation-related diseases. The residents sue Oestle, but they are unable to prove a failure on the part of Oestle to exercise reasonable care. The residents will

a.   win, because businesses that engage in ultrahazardous activities are strictly liable for any harm.
b.   win, because obviously someone was negligent, and it was not the residents.
c.   lose, because they are unable to prove Oestle failed to use reasonable care.
d.   lose, because the relation between radiation and specific diseases is too hard to prove.

____   **2.**   Which of the following actions requires an EIS?

a.   New York state's conversion of a mental hospital to a prison hospital.
b.   The Department of the Interior's approval of coal mining operations in several northwestern states.
c.   The Department of the Interior's approval of minor landscaping around a federal courthouse in St. Louis.
d.   The Department of Defense's elimination of civilian jobs at an Air Force base in Florida.

____   **3.**   The Clean Air Act provides the basis for the EPA's regulation of air pollution from mobile sources and stationary sources. Those regulations set

a.   standards for emissions from cars and other mobile sources but not timetables for compliance with those standards.
b.   uniform standards for mobile source emissions in all urban areas.
c.   different standards that apply to different stationary sources.
d.   a single level of ambient standards for pollution from stationary sources.

____   4. The Clean Water Act provides the basis for the EPA's regulation of water pollution.   Which of the following is TRUE about the act or the regulations?

a. The act establishes a goal of eliminating contamination of drinking water from all underground sources.
b. The act establishes a permit system under which polluters must apply after discharging wastes.
c. The regulations specify limits for discharges of types of pollutants.
d. The regulations specify generally that any available technology be installed to attain limits on discharges of types of pollutants.

____   5. The Faraday Viera Company operates a hazardous waste storage and treatment facility.   Petrochemico, Inc., transports to Viera's facility hazardous waste in unlabeled containers.   Viera buries the containers without determining their contents.   If the containers leak, and the Environmental Protection Agency investigates, Viera could be found to have violated

a. the Federal Insecticide, Fungicide, and Rodenticide Act.
b. the Resource Conservation and Recovery Act.
c. the Comprehensive Environmental Response, Compensation, and Liability Act.
d. both b and c.

____   6. In the previous question, Petrochemico could be found to have violated

a. the Federal Insecticide, Fungicide, and Rodenticide Act.
b. the Resource Conservation and Recovery Act.
c. the Comprehensive Environmental Response, Compensation, and Liability Act.
d. both b and c.

____   7. Three States Power Company operates a nuclear power plant on the Sherry River.   Over a period of several years, the plant releases radioactive steam into the atmosphere, dumps radioactive coolant into the river, and buries radioactive rods in a ditch on the property.   If the state sues, Three States might be found to have violated

a. the Clean Air Act and the Clean Water Act.
b. the Resource Conservation and Recovery Act.
c. the Comprehensive Environmental Response, Compensation, and Liability Act.
d. any of the above.

SHORT ESSAY QUESTIONS

1.   Discuss what the National Environmental Policy Act and its complementary laws require.

2.   Identify and discuss federal laws regulating toxic chemicals.

ISSUE SPOTTERS (Answers at the Back of the Book)

1. Oppen Company's plant belches smoke and fumes. Oppen's operation includes a short railway system, and trucks enter and exit the grounds continuously. Constant vibrations from the trains and trucks rattle a nearby residential neighborhood. If the residents sue Oppen, on what grounds might the court refuse to enjoin the operation?

2. In 1970, the Environmental Protection Agency (EPA) was established to administer most federal environmental policies and statutes. What are some other federal agencies that have authority to regulate specific environmental matters?

3. Spartina City lies on the shore of a bay that empties into the Atlantic Ocean. White's Trash Company removes garbage from the dumpsters behind Spartina's local businesses. Further inland, the Green Park Corporation collects radioactive waste from the local utility's nuclear power plant. On the other side of the bay, Fort McFarland Military Base stores chemical warfare agents for disposal. Can White, Green Park, or Fort McFarland dump their waste in the ocean?

4. The Redgeway Chemical Corporation generates hazardous wastes from its operations. Central States Trucking Company transports those wastes to I. J. Osakwe, Inc., which owns a hazardous waste disposal site. Osakwe sells the property to Uno Corporation. If the site is inspected, and a clean-up is ordered, who can be held liable for the cost?

5. The National Paint Company manufactures luminescent paint that includes a radioactive substance in its ingredients. National buries the waste generated from its manufacturing operations on its property. The Cutter Investment Company buys the property and sells it to the Royal Palm Manufacturing, Inc. Royal Palm is ordered to clean up the waste. On what common law theory might Royal Palm successfully sue National?

 **Key Points**

The **key points** in this chapter include:

1. Basic interests in real property ownership.

2. The priorities of competing claims under recording statutes.

3. Forms of private land-use control.

4. Forms of public land-use control.

Chapter 25:
Land-Use Control and Real Property

WHAT THIS CHAPTER IS ABOUT

This chapter covers the nature of real property and the nature of ownership rights in real property. The chapter also outlines the right of the government to take private land for public use, zoning laws, and other restrictions on ownership, including easements and profits.

CHAPTER OUTLINE

I. THE NATURE OF REAL PROPERTY

Real property consists of land and the buildings, plants, and trees that it contains. Real property is immovable.

A. LAND

Includes the soil on the surface of the earth, natural products or artificial structures attached to it, the water on or under it, and the air space above.

B. AIR SPACE AND SUBSURFACE RIGHTS

Limitations on air rights or subsurface rights normally have to be indicated on the document transferring title at the time of purchase.

1. Air Rights

Flights over private land do not normally violate the property owners' rights (unless they interfere with the enjoyment and use of the land).

2. Subsurface Rights

Ownership of the surface can be separated from ownership of the subsurface. In excavating, if a subsurface owner causes the land to subside, he or she may be liable to the owner of the surface.

C. **PLANT LIFE AND VEGETATION**
A sale of land with growing crops on it includes the crops, unless otherwise agreed. When crops are sold by themselves, they are considered personal property (and governed by the Uniform Commercial Code [UCC 2–107(2)]).

D. **FIXTURES**
Personal property so closely associated with certain real property that it is viewed as part of it (such as plumbing in a building). Fixtures are included in a sale of land if the contract does not provide otherwise.

1. **Factors in Determining Whether an Item is a Fixture**
The intent of the parties, whether the item can be removed without damaging the real property, and whether the item is sufficiently adapted so as to have become a part of the real property.

2. **Trade Fixtures**
Installed for a commercial purpose by a tenant, whose property it remains, unless removal would irreparably damage the real property.

II. OWNERSHIP INTERESTS IN REAL PROPERTY

A. **FEE SIMPLE**

1. **Fee Simple Absolute**
A fee simple owner has the most rights possible—to give the property away, sell it, transfer it by will, use it for virtually any purpose, and possess it to the exclusion of all the world—potentially forever.

2. **Fee Simple Defeasible**
Conditional ownership. If the condition is not met, the land reverts to the original owner. A conveyance of a fee simple defeasible usually includes the words as long as, until, while, or during ("to A, as long as the property is used for a school").

B. **LIFE ESTATE**
Lasts for the life of a specified individual ("to A for his life"). A life tenant can use the land (but cannot commit waste), mortgage the life estate, and create liens, easements, and leases (but not longer than the life defining the estate).

C. **FUTURE INTERESTS**
Residuary interest that an owner retains to retake possession if condition of the fee simple defeasible is not met or when the life estate ends.

1. **Reversions and Remainders**
If the owner retains ownership of a future interest, it is a reversionary interest. If the owner transfers rights in a future interest to another, it is a remainder ("to A for life, then to B").

2. **Executory Interest**
An interest that does not take effect immediately on the expiration of another interest ("to A for life and one year after A's death to B").

D. **LEASEHOLD ESTATES**
Created when an owner or landlord conveys the right to possess and use property to a tenant for a certain period of time.

1. **Tenancy for Years**
   Created by contract (which can sometimes be oral) by which property is leased for a specific period (a month, a year, a period of years). At the end of the period, the lease ends (without notice). If the tenant dies during the lease, the lease interest passes to the tenant's heirs.

2. **Periodic Tenancy**
   Created by a lease specifying only that rent is to be paid at certain intervals. Can arise if a landlord allows a tenant for years to hold over. Automatically renews unless terminated (on one period's notice).

3. **Tenancy at Will**
   A tenancy for as long as the landlord and tenant agree. Exists when a tenant for years retains possession after termination with the landlord's consent before payment of the next rent (when it becomes a periodic tenancy). Terminates on the death of either party.

4. **Tenancy at Sufferance**
   Possession of land without right (without the owner's permission).

E. CONCURRENT OWNERSHIP

1. **Tenancy in Common**
   Each of two or more persons owns an undivided portion of the property. The portions need not be equal. On death, a tenant's interest passes to his or her heirs. Most states presume that a co-tenancy is a tenancy in common unless there is a clear intention to establish a joint tenancy.

2. **Joint Tenancy**
   Each of two or more persons owns an undivided interest in the property; a deceased joint tenant's interest passes to the surviving joint tenant or tenants. Can be terminated at any time before a joint tenant's death by gift, by sale, or by partition (divided into equal parts).

3. **Tenancy by the Entirety**
   Created by a transfer of real property to a husband and wife; neither spouse can transfer separately his or her interest during his or her life. In some states, this tenancy has been effectively abolished. A divorce, either spouse's death, or mutual agreement will terminate this tenancy.

4. **Community Property**
   Each spouse owns an undivided half interest in property acquired by either spouse during their marriage (except property acquired by gift or inheritance). Recognized in only some states, on divorce the property is divided equally in a few states and at a court's discretion in others.

III. PRIVATE CONTROL OF LAND USE

A. NONPOSSESSORY INTERESTS

1. **Easements and Profits**
   Easement: the right of a person to make limited use of another person's land without taking anything from the property. **Profit**: the right to go onto another's land and take away a part or product of the land.

   a. **Creation of an Easement or Profit**
      By deed, will, contract, implication, necessity, or prescription.

b. **Effect of a Sale of Property**
The benefit of an easement or profit goes with the land. The burden goes with the land only if the new owner recognizes it, or knew or should have known of it.

c. **Termination of an Easement or Profit**
Terminates when deeded back to the owner of the land that is burdened; its owner becomes the owner of the property burdened; or it is abandoned with the intent to relinquish the right to it.

2. **Licenses**
The revocable right of a person to come onto another person's land.

B. **COVENANTS RUNNING WITH THE LAND**
A covenant runs with the land (the original parties and their successors are entitled to its benefit or burdened with its obligation) if—

1. It is created in a written agreement (usually the document that conveys the land).
2. The parties intend that it run with the land (the agreement states that all the promisor's "successors, heirs, or assigns" will be bound).
3. The covenant touches and concerns the land (limits on the burdened land must have some connection to the land).
4. The original parties are in privity of estate when the covenant is created.

C. **EQUITABLE SERVITUDES**
Similar to covenants running with the land. The most significant difference is that privity of estate is not required to enforce an equitable servitude.

IV.   PUBLIC CONTROL OF LAND USE

A. **POLICE POWER**
A state can regulate uses of land within its jurisdiction.

1. **General Plans**
Land-use laws typically follow a local government general plan, which may be supplemented by special, area, or community plans.

2. **Zoning Laws**
Divide an area into districts to which land-use regulations apply.

a. **Types of Restrictions**
Use restrictions—kind of use (commercial, residential). Structural restrictions —engineering features and architectural design.

b. **Variances**
An owner can obtain a variance if (1) it is impossible to realize a reasonable return on the land as zoned, (2) the ordinance adversely affects only the owner (not all owners), (3) granting a variance will not substantially alter the essential character of the zoned area.

3. **Other Regulations**
Subdivision regulations—local requirements for dedication of land for schools, etc. Growth-management ordinances—limit building permits.

4. **Limits on the State's Power**

Regulation cannot be (1) confiscatory (or the owner must be paid just compensation); (2) arbitrary or unreasonable (taking without due process under the Fourteenth Amendment); or (3) discriminatory, under the Fourteenth Amendment.

B. **EMINENT DOMAIN**

The government can take private property for public use. To obtain title, a condemnation proceeding is brought. The Fifth Amendment requires that just compensation be paid for a taking; thus, in a separate proceeding a court determines the land's fair value (usually market value) to pay the owner.

STUDY TIP 👉 <u>The Art of Studying</u>

To have a good grasp of unfamiliar material, it is usually not sufficient to simply read through it. The material must be read, reread, understood, and in some cases memorized. This is as true in the case of property law (which is the oldest body of Anglo-American law) as it is in the case of other topics. Of course, once you master the art of studying, you can use it in a variety of circumstances in aspects of life that may have little to do with school—studying the issues to participate in the political process, for example.

TRUE-FALSE QUESTIONS (Answers at the Back of the Book)

_____ 1. Real property consists of, in part, land and buildings and the gas, water, and other utility services connected to the buildings.

_____ 2. A fee simple absolute is potentially infinite in duration and can be disposed of by deed or by will.

_____ 3. The owner of a life estate has the same rights as a fee simple owner.

_____ 4. The difference between an easement and a profit is that an easement allows a person to use land and take something from it, while a profit allows a person only to use land.

_____ 5. A periodic tenancy is created by an express contract by which property is leased for a specified period of time, such as a month, a year, or a period of years.

_____ 6. Under the Fifth Amendment, private property may be taken for public use without just compensation under the government's power of eminent domain.

_____ 7. A landowner whose land has been limited by a zoning ordinance to a particular use can obtain a variance by showing that his or her alternative use of the land would substantially alter the essential character of the zoned area.

FILL-IN QUESTIONS (Answers at the Back of the Book)

1. An owner in fee simple absolute who conveys the estate to another in fee simple defeasible retains _____ (a possibility of reverter/ an executory interest). If the conditions of the conveyance are not met, the _____ _____ (next designated heir/ original owner) takes ownership of the estate.

2. An owner in fee simple who conveys the estate to another as a life estate retains a _____ (remainder/ reversion). When a life estate is conveyed, the grantor has not disposed of the interest in the land remaining after the grantee's life, and thus, the grantor retains a _____ (remainder/ reversion) that will become possessory on the grantee's death.

3. These future interests exist in the present in the sense that the owner can transfer the future interest. When an owner transfers a future interest, the interest in the property held by the buyer or receiver is known as either _____- _____ (a possibility of reverter/ an executory interest) or a _____ (remainder/ reversion).

MULTIPLE-CHOICE QUESTIONS (Answers at the Back of the Book)

____ **1.** Sigourney owns an acre of land on the Bee River. The federal government dams the Bee, and a lake forms behind the dam, covering Sigourney's acre. If Sigourney sues the government for compensation, Sigourney will

a. win, because, under the Fifth Amendment, the federal government cannot take property for public use without just compensation.
b. win, because, under tort law, property cannot be taken for any reason without just compensation.
c. lose, because, under the Fifth Amendment, only state governments cannot take property for public use without just compensation.
d. lose, because the Fourteenth Amendment requires compensation for temporary takings only.

____ **2.** Path Development Corporation wants to renovate a warehouse near downtown Bay City to include shops, restaurants, and a theatre. Connected by a skyway to the warehouse, Path wants to build an apartment tower. Before starting construction, to determine local policy concerning growth and what contribution Path must make to the infrastructure, Path should consult

a. Bay City's general development plan.
b. Bay City's specific downtown area plan.
c. local zoning ordinances.
d. all of the above.

____ **3.** RD Corporation wants to develop a suburban tract, subdividing the parcel into smaller plots for single-family homes. As the parcel is developed, the area will need streets, sewers, new schools, and other public facilities. Formation of the subdivision and these facilities are the responsibility of

a. RD.
b. the same local agency that oversees the zoning process.
c. RD and the same local agency that oversees the zoning process.
d. the state.

____ 4. Jay, Inc., buys a tract to develop into a corporate complex. After construction begins, the county commission zones most of the surrounding area, which has not been developed, for a nature preserve and zones Jay's tract one-quarter commercial, three-quarters nature preserve. If Jay sues the county, Jay will

   a. win, because the surrounding area has been zoned nature preserve, and there is no rational basis for also imposing the classification on Jay's property.
   b. win, because the county has effectively confiscated Jay's property without compensation.
   c. lose, because the surrounding area has been zoned nature preserve, and there is no rational basis for not also imposing the classification on Jay's property.
   d. lose, because the county can effectively confiscate Jay's land without compensation.

____ 5. Most zoning laws provide means by which a property owner may be granted a variance from the ordinance if

   a. an owner finds it impossible to realize a reasonable return on the land as zoned.
   b. the adverse effect of the ordinance is particular to the person seeking the variance and not of similar effect on other owners within the zone.
   c. granting a variance will not substantially alter the character of the zone.
   d. all of the above.

____ 6. Elle's estate, Fauna, is next to Rich's estate, Flora. Rich grants to Elle the privilege of crossing Flora to get to Fauna. Rich sells Flora to Elle. Later, Elle sells Fauna to Calvin. Which of the following is TRUE?

   a. A revival of the profit across Flora is included in the price of Fauna.
   b. An easement across Flora to Fauna may be created anew.
   c. There is no easement across Flora to Fauna unless Elle acknowledges one.
   d. A license to cross Flora is included in the price of Fauna.

SHORT ESSAY QUESTIONS

1. Discuss and compare the principal features of the four forms of concurrent property ownership: tenancies in common, joint tenancies, tenancies by the entirety and community property.

2. Describe the nature of the power of eminent domain, the process by which private property is condemned for a public purpose and the way in which it differs from a restriction on land use.

ISSUE SPOTTERS (Answers at the Back of the Book)

1. Egon owns an office building in fee simple—that is, Egon is free to do with the property whatever he wants. Egon can give the building away, sell it, or transfer it by will. Egon can also transfer only some of the rights that he holds, in which case the transferee acquires less than absolute ownership of the building. If Egon transfers temporary possession of the building to the Schelling Corporation, can Schelling transfer only some of the rights that it holds to the Hegel Company?

2. Naomi owns a half acre of land that fronts on Lake Sacajawea. Ruth owns the half acre behind Naomi's land. No road borders Naomi's land, but Ruth's driveway runs between a road and Naomi's property, so Naomi uses Ruth's driveway. If Naomi sells her land to Dee, can Naomi also convey the right-of-way across Ruth's property to Dee?

3. Roxane leases office space in Alvin's building for a one-year term. At the end of the period specified in the lease, the lease ends without notice, and possession of the office space returns to Alvin. If Roxane dies during the period of the lease, what happens to the leased property?

4. A state can regulate land-use through zoning laws. For example, Ote City can designate certain areas within its limits for industrial, commercial, residential, and mixed uses. Ty owns a small plot in a mixed-use area in Ote. Can Ote limit only Ty's plot to residential use?

4. Roberta's house is on an acre of land in an area that allows houses on half-acres. Roberta proposes to divide her property and build a new house on the other half-acre. Although the proposed structure complies with all zoning requirements, Roberta must obtain a residential building permit from the local authorities. On what grounds, unrelated to Roberta, can the authorities refuse to grant the permit?

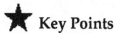 **Key Points**

The **key points** in this chapter include:

1. The Sherman Act and the activities that it proscribes.

2. The Clayton Act and the activities that it proscribes.

3. The agencies and others responsible for enforcing antitrust laws.

4. Exemptions to antitrust enforcement.

Chapter 26: Antitrust and Monopoly

WHAT THIS CHAPTER IS ABOUT

This chapter outlines the background, exemptions, and enforcement of the major antitrust statutes—the Sherman Act, the Clayton Act, and the Federal Trade Commission Act. Monopoly is covered in some detail. Keep in mind that the basis of the antitrust laws is a desire to foster competition (to result in lower prices and so on).

CHAPTER OUTLINE

I.   **PUBLIC POLICY AND THE ORIGINS OF ANTITRUST LAW**

A. **MARKET POWER**
Extent to which a firm can ignore competitors in setting its prices or can in some way limit competition.

B. **RESTRAINTS OF TRADE**
Agreements between suppliers in a market to limit output. Agreements between business firms that reduce competition are against public policy (except covenants-not-to-compete in the sale of a business).

C. **FEDERAL LEGISLATION**
When monopolies increased in the late nineteenth century, Congress felt that the common law (under which an agreement to limit competition is unenforceable but cannot be challenged by one who is not a party to it) was not sufficient to protect against anticompetitive conduct.

II. **MAJOR FEDERAL ANTITRUST LAWS**
Antitrust laws seek to promote competitive business conduct and limit the anticompetitive use of market power.

A. SHERMAN ACT OF 1890
Prohibits—

1. **Restraints of Trade [Section 1]**
Requires two or more persons; focus is on agreements (written or oral) that are restrictive (see Chapter 27).

2. **Monopolies [Section 2]**
Applies to individuals and to several people; concerns the structure of a monopoly in the marketplace; focus is on the misuse of monopoly power (see below).

B. CLAYTON ACT OF 1914
Aimed at practices not covered by the Sherman Act. Violations are subject to civil, not criminal, penalties. Conduct is illegal if it substantially tends to lessen competition or create monopoly power—

1. **Price Discrimination [Section 2]**
Seller charges different prices to competitive buyers for identical goods (see Chapter 27).

2. **Exclusionary Practices [Section 3]**
Exclusive-dealing contracts and tying arrangements (see Chapter 27).

3. **Corporate Mergers [Section 7]**
A person or firm cannot hold stock or assets in another firm if the effect may be to substantially lessen competition (see Chapter 27).

4. **Interlocking Directorates [Section 8]**
No person may be a director in two or more corporations at the same time if either firm has capital, surplus, or undivided profits of more than $12,092,000 or if a firm's competitive sales are $1,209,000 or more.

C. FEDERAL TRADE COMMISSION ACT OF 1914
Section 5 condemns all forms of anticompetitive behavior that are not covered under other federal antitrust laws.

III. ENFORCEMENT OF ANTITRUST LAWS

A. DEPARTMENT OF JUSTICE (DOJ)
Prosecutes violations of the Sherman Act as criminal or civil violations. Violations of the Clayton Act are not crimes; the DOJ can enforce it only through civil proceedings. Remedies include divestiture and dissolution.

B. FEDERAL TRADE COMMISSION (FTC)
Enforces the Clayton Act; has sole authority to enforce the Federal Trade Commission Act; issues administrative orders; can seek court sanctions.

C. PRIVATE PARTIES

1. **Damages**
Can sue for treble damages and attorneys' fees under the Clayton Act if injured by a violation of any federal antitrust law (except the FTC Act).

2. **Injunctions**
May seek an injunction to prevent antitrust violations if the violation injured business activities protected by the antitrust laws.

IV.   EXEMPTIONS FROM ANTITRUST LAWS

A. LABOR ACTIVITIES

B. AGRICULTURAL ASSOCIATIONS AND FISHERIES
Except exclusionary practices or restraints of trade against competitors.

C. INSURANCE COMPANIES
Exempt in most cases when state regulation exists.

D. U.S. EXPORTERS
May cooperate to compete with similar foreign associations (if it does not restrain trade in the United States or injure other U.S. exporters).

E. PROFESSIONAL BASEBALL

F. OIL MARKETING
States set quotas on oil to be marketed in interstate commerce.

G. OTHER EXEMPTIONS

1. Activities approved by the president in furtherance of defense.
2. Cooperative research among small business firms.
3. Research or production of a product, process, or service by joint ventures consisting of competitors.
4. State actions, when the state policy is clearly articulated and the policy is actively supervised by the state.
5. Activities of regulated industries when federal commissions, boards, or agencies have primary regulatory authority.
6. Joint efforts by businesspersons to obtain legislative, judicial, or executive action. (Exception: an action is not protected if "no reasonable [person] could reasonably expect success on the merits" and it is an attempt to make anticompetitive use of government processes.)

V.   MONOPOLIES
May violate Section 2 of the Sherman Act.

A. MONOPOLIZATION
Requires two elements: (1) the possession of monopoly power in the relevant market and (2) the willful acquisition or maintenance of that power.

1. Monopoly Power
Sufficient market power to control prices and exclude competition.

a. Market-Share Test
A firm has monopoly power if its share of the relevant market is 70 percent or more.

b. The Relevant Market Has Two Elements—

1) Relevant Product Market
All products with identical attributes and those that are sufficient substitutes for each other.

2) Relevant Geographical Market
If competitors sell in only a limited area, the geographical market is limited to that area.

2. **Intent Requirement**

If a firm has market power as a result of a purposeful act to acquire or maintain that power through anticompetitive means, it is a violation. Intent may be inferred from evidence that the firm had monopoly power and engaged in anticompetitive behavior.

B. **PREDATORY PRICING**

Selling substantially below costs of production to drive competitors from the market (prices can then be raised to high levels) is not a violation if firm is (1) attempting to gain access to established market and (2) unlikely to obtain monopoly profits in the future.

C. **ATTEMPTS TO MONOPOLIZE**

An action must (1) be intended to exclude competitors and garner monopoly power and (2) have a dangerous probability of success.

STUDY TIP 👉 <u>Economics and Antitrust</u>

A simple understanding of economics can make it easier to understand antitrust law. Some professors take a strong economic approach to the subject. They emphasize the economic theory behind antitrust theory and antitrust law. There is a difference between what economic analysis suggests the law should be and what the law is, however. Thus, some professors also offer economic criticisms of antitrust law.

TRUE-FALSE QUESTIONS (Answers at the Back of the Book)

____ 1. Antitrust law is that body of statutes and principles that regulate business conduct so as to promote the forms of competition that benefit society.

____ 2. A firm that can substantially ignore competitors in setting a price for its product or can limit competition in its market has considerable market power.

____ 3. In determining whether a given firm is a monopoly, size in relation to the market is what matters because monopoly involves power to affect prices and output.

____ 4. To constitute the offense of attempted monopolization of a market, a challenged action must be specifically intended to exclude competitors and garner monopoly power.

___ **5.** Under the Clayton Act, no person can be a director in two or more corporations at the same time unless elimination of competition among the corporation would violate any of the antitrust laws.

___ **6.** The only remedy that the Department of Justice can ask a court to impose for an antitrust violation is divestiture.

FILL-IN QUESTIONS (Answers at the Back of the Book)

Restraint of trade and monopoly power are fundamental concepts in antitrust law. _____ (Monopoly power/ Restraint of trade) is any agreement between firms that has the effect of reducing competition in the marketplace. The most direct way of thinking of _____ (monopoly power/ restraint of trade) is that the _____ (monopolist/ restrainer of trade) has the ability to ignore the effect of raising its product price on the ability of competitors to enter its particular product market. Extreme market power is an example of _____ (monopoly power/ restraint of trade). _____ (Monopoly power/ Restraint of trade) is simply an extreme amount of market power. Any firm that is not entirely constrained by the potential response of a rival in deciding what price to charge for its product has some degree of market power. Whether such power is of a magnitude to warrant calling it _____ (monopoly power/ a restraint of trade) is one of the most difficult tasks encountered in the application of antitrust law.

MULTIPLE-CHOICE QUESTIONS (Answers at the Back of the Book)

___ **1.** Concern over the trust problem led to enactment of the all of the following EXCEPT

a. the Sherman Act.
b. the Clayton Act.
c. the Railway Labor Act.
d. the Federal Trade Commission Act.

___ **2.** Head Company controls 80 percent of the market for lamps in the southern part of North Carolina. Head is sued for monopolizing the lamp market. It would NOT be an argument in Head's favor for Head to contend that

a. the relevant product market includes other furniture accessories.
b. the relevant geographical market includes all North and South Carolina.
c. Head's market share is a result of a combination of business acumen, the development of a superior lamp, and historical circumstances.
d. Head has monopoly power, but it was acquired willfully.

3. Which of the following is required to establish a violation of the Clayton Act's price discrimination provision?

a. A seller charging different buyers different prices for identical goods
b. No more than one buyer buying different kinds of goods
c. Different production and transportation costs
d. No more than one price at a level no less than that charged by competitors

_____ 4. Pine Video Corporation and Family Rentals, Inc., are two of the hundreds of competitors in the market for video tape rentals. Pine is a regional chain. Family is a national chain with a market share of 6 percent. In Pine's region, Family reduces its prices. Despite the price-cutting, Pine loses no customers. If Pine sues Family, on grounds of attempted monopolization under Section 2 of the Sherman Act, Pine will

a. win, because Family apparently possesses no market power.
b. win, because Family apparently possesses market power.
c. lose, because Family apparently possesses no market power.
d. lose, because Family apparently possesses market power.

_____ 5. A private party wishing to sue under the Sherman Act must prove a violation under an antitrust law that

a. directly caused or was a substantial factor in causing an injury to the party.
b. affected business activities of the party that were protected by the antitrust laws.
c. also violated Section 5 of the Federal Trade Commission Act..
d. both a and b.

_____ 6. Which of the following is exempt from antitrust enforcement?

a. Efforts by businesspersons to obtain government action, even if illegitimate means are employed
b. Exporters cooperating to compete with similar foreign associations.
c. Professional sports
d. Research by consortiums of competitors to cooperate in the development of new automobile technology

SHORT ESSAY QUESTIONS

1. Discuss the concept of price discrimination as it is featured in the Clayton Act.

2. Discuss the ways in which the federal government and private litigants enforce the antitrust laws.

ISSUE SPOTTERS (Answers at the Back of the Book)

1. Prendo Company develops a new series of computer and video games that incorporate lasers. The series has wide appeal. Prendo begins to earn profits that are on a level with the appeal of the games and that eclipse those of its rivals. For a time, Prendo is the only seller in the computer-video-laser game market. What is this kind of market called?

2. The Dexx Artificial Sweetener Company develops new methods that cut costs and increase output, ultimately hurting Dexx's competitors. When Dexx is sued for monopolizing its market, the firm contends that it has no monopoly power because the relevant market includes artificial sweetener and sugar. What will the court say?

3. The Clayton Act prohibits four distinct forms of business behavior that are considered to reduce competition or lead to monopoly power—price discrimination (charging

different buyers different prices for identical goods), exclusionary practices, corporate mergers, and interlocking directorates. The behavior is illegal only under a certain general condition, however. What is that condition?

4.   Federal agencies that enforce federal antitrust laws include the Department of Justice and the Federal Trade Commission. Private parties may also sue under the laws. In recent years, more than 90 percent of all antitrust actions have been brought by private parties. Why?

5.   Labor unions are exempt from the application of the antitrust laws. Unions can organize and bargain collectively without violating the antitrust laws, and strikes and other labor activities are not considered violations. How can a union lose its exemption?

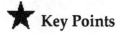 **Key Points**

The **key points** in this chapter include:

1. Restraints of trade that constitute *per se* violations of antitrust laws.

2. Restraints subject to a rule-of-reason analysis.

3. The applications of a "soft *per se* rule" to various anticompetitive activities.

4. Classifications of activities subject to antitrust law.

Chapter 27:
Antitrust and Restraints of Trade

WHAT THIS CHAPTER IS ABOUT

This chapter outlines the aspect of antitrust at which most of the statutes have been directed: anticompetitive agreements between rival firms to fix prices, restrict output, divide markets, exclude other competitors, or otherwise limit competition. The focus of this chapter is on concerted behavior.

CHAPTER OUTLINE

I. OVERVIEW OF RESTRAINTS OF TRADE

A. *PER SE* VIOLATIONS
Agreements that are blatantly anticompetitive are illegal *per se*..

B. RULE OF REASON
A court considers the purpose of an agreement, the power of the parties, the effect of the action on trade, and in some cases, whether there are less restrictive alternatives to achieve the same goals. If the competitive benefits outweigh the anticompetitive effects, the agreement is held lawful.

C. SOFT *PER SE* **RULE**
In some cases, the United States Supreme Court has stated that it is applying a *per se* rule, but the Court's analysis suggests that it is weighing benefits against harms under a rule of reason.

II. HORIZONTAL RESTRAINTS
Agreements that restrain competition between rivals in the same market.

A. PRICE FIXING
Any agreement among competitors to fix prices is a *per se* violation.

B. HORIZONTAL MARKET DIVISION

An agreement between competitors to divide up territories or customers is a *per se* violation.

C. TRADE ASSOCIATIONS

Businesses within the same industry or profession organized to pursue common interests (exchange information, set industry standards, etc.). The rule of reason is applied.

D. GROUP BOYCOTTS

An agreement by two or more sellers to refuse to deal with a particular person or firm is a *per se* violation, if it is intended to eliminate competition or prevent entry into a given market.

E. JOINT VENTURES

An undertaking by two or more individuals or firms for a specific purpose. If it does not involve price fixing or market divisions, the agreement will be analyzed under the rule of reason.

III. VERTICAL RESTRAINTS

A restraint of trade that results from an agreement between firms at different levels in the manufacturing and distribution process. (Backward integration moves down the chain of production toward a supplier; forward integration moves up toward the consumer market.)

A. TERRITORIAL OR CUSTOMER RESTRICTIONS

An agreement between a manufacturer and a distributor or retailer to restrict sales to certain area or customers. Judged under a rule of reason.

B. RESALE PRICE MAINTENANCE AGREEMENT

An agreement between a manufacturer and a distributor or retailer in which the manufacturer specifies what retail prices of its products. Normally considered a *per se* violation.

C. REFUSALS TO DEAL

A firm is free to deal, or not, unilaterally, with whomever it wishes.

D. PRICE DISCRIMINATION

If a seller charges different prices to competitive buyers for identical goods.

1. Elements

(1) The seller must be engaged in interstate commerce, (2) the effect of the price discrimination must be to substantially lessen competition or create a competitive injury, and (3) a seller's pricing policies must include a reasonable prospect of the seller's recouping its losses.

2. Exception

When a lower price is charged temporarily and in good faith to meet another seller's equally low price to the buyer's competitor.

E. EXCLUSIONARY PRACTICES

1. Exclusive-Dealing Contracts

A contract under which a seller forbids the buyer to buy products from the seller's competitors. Prohibited if the effect is "to substantially lessen competition or tend to create a monopoly."

2. **Tying Arrangements**

When a seller conditions the sale of a product on the buyer's agreement to buy another product produced or distributed by the same seller. Legality depends on the agreement's purpose and its likely effect on competition in the relevant markets. Subject to the "soft" *per se* rule.

F. MERGERS

A person or firm cannot hold stock or assets in another firm if the effect may be to substantially lessen competition.

1. **Horizontal Mergers**

Merger between firms that compete with each other in the same market. If it creates an entity with more than a small percentage market share, it is presumed illegal. Factors include market concentration.

   a. **Market Concentration—FTC/DOJ Guidelines**

   Herfindahl-Hirschman Index (HHI), computed by adding the squares of each of the percentage market shares of firms in the relevant market.

   1) **Pre-merger HHI Between 1,000 and 1,800**

   The industry is moderately concentrated, and the merger will be challenged only if it increases the HHI by 100 points or more.

   2) **Pre-merger HHI Greater than 1,800**

   The market is highly concentrated; if a merger produces an increase in the HHI between 50 and 100 points, it raises concerns; more than 100 points, it is likely to enhance market power.

   b. **Other Factors**

   The relevant market's history of tending toward concentration, ease of entry into that market, economic efficiency, financial condition of the merging firms, nature and price of the products, and so on.

2. **Vertical Mergers**

When a company at one stage of production acquires a company at a higher or lower stage of production. Legality depends on market concentration, barriers to entry into that market, and the parties' intent.

3. **Conglomerate Mergers**

   a. **Market-extension Merger**

   When a firm seeks to sell its product in a new market by merging with a firm already established in that market.

   b. **Product-extension Merger**

   When a firm seeks to add a closely related product to its existing line by merging with a firm already producing that product.

   c. **Diversification Merger**

   When a firm merges with another firm that offers a product or service wholly unrelated to the first firm's existing activities.

STUDY TIP 🖙 <u>Results</u>

In reading and studying cases, particularly those that involve complex circumstances—such as the cases in this chapter and Chapter 26—you may find it helpful to keep in mind that generally a case can have only one of three results:

1. The plaintiff proves his or her side of the case and wins;

2. The plaintiff fails to prove his or her side of the case and loses; or

3. The defendant proves his or her side of the case, and the plaintiff loses.

TRUE-FALSE QUESTIONS (Answers at the Back of the Book)

____ **1.** If an agreement is deemed a *per se* violation of Section 1 of the Sherman Act, a court analyzes its legality under what is referred to as a rule of reason.

____ **2.** The line between *per se* violations of Section 1 of the Sherman Act and agreements judged under a rule of reason is well-defined.

____ **3.** A contractual agreement between a manufacturer and an independent retailer, conditioning the retailer's future supply of the manufacturer's product on its willingness to resell only at a price set by the manufacturer is a form of horizontal restraint.

____ **4.** The essence of price fixing is the restriction of output by eliminating price competition in which firms seek to sell more by charging less than their rivals.

____ **5.** A vertical restraint is any agreement that in some way restrains competition between rival firms competing in the same market.

____ **6.** Exclusive dealing occurs when sellers charge different buyers different prices for identical goods.

____ **7.** Price discrimination occurs when a seller forbids a buyer from buying products from the seller's competitors.

FILL-IN QUESTIONS (Answers at the Back of the Book)

1. Prices may be controlled by a _____ (horizontal/ vertical) market division—an agreement to divide a market among competitors. _____ (Horizontal/ Vertical) relationships occur at the same level of operations. The division _____ (may/ must) be geographical _____ (and/ or) by class of customer. Each firm is free not only from price competition but from competition regarding quality, customer service, and anything else. Currently, _____ (horizontal/ vertical) market divisions are considered to be *per se* violations of the Sherman Act.

2.   Another set of restraints involves those imposed by a seller on a buyer, or vice versa, in what is termed a _____ (horizontal/ vertical) relationship. _____ (Horizontal/ Vertical) relationships encompass the entire chain of production. A single firm that carries out two or more of the different functional phases in the chain is a _____ (horizontally/ vertically) integrated firm. Marketing decisions within a _____ (horizontally/ vertically) inte-grated firm are not subject to attack under Section 1, although the legality of certain other classes of restraints are judged under a rule of reason and others are deemed *per se* violations.

MULTIPLE-CHOICE QUESTIONS (Answers at the Back of the Book)

_____   1.   Montezuma Sound, Inc., sells its brand-name products directly to franchised retailers. Montezuma limits or increases the number of franchisees in a given area, depending on how well or poorly its existing franchisees do. Azteca Stereo wants to increase the number of its stores, but Montezuma says no. If Azteca sues Montezuma, Azteca will

a. win, because Montezuma's restriction on its dealers is a *per se* violation of Section 1 of the Sherman Act.

b. win, because, as judged under a rule of reason, Montezuma's restriction on its dealers undercuts intrabrand competition.

c. lose, because Montezuma's restriction on its dealers is not a *per se* violation of Section 1 of the Sherman Act.

d. lose, because, as judged under a rule of reason, Montezuma's restriction on its dealers promotes interbrand competition.

_____   2.   Manufacturers of digital audio tape (DAT) players form the DAT Manufacturers Association (DATMA). DATMA confers a seal of "quality approval" on all DAT players manufactured by members who abide by cer-tain market-allocation restrictions. DATMA urges wholesalers and retail-ers not to buy non-approved DAT players, which generally are made by firms that enter the market after DATMA is formed. DATMA refuses to deal with any wholesaler or retailer who carries any non-approved prod-uct. If Sunn Company, a manufacturer of a nonapproved product, sues DATMA, Sunn will

a. win, because DATMA's boycott is a *per se* violation of Section 1 of the Sherman Act.

b. win, because, as judged under a rule of reason, DATMA's boycott undercuts efficiency in the operation of the market.

c. lose, because DATMA's boycott is not a *per se* violation of Section 1 of the Sherman Act.

d. lose, because, as judged under a rule of reason, DATMA's boycott promotes efficiency in the operation of the market.

_____   3.   If a joint venture does not involve price-fixing or market divisions, it will be analyzed under the rule of reason. Whether a venture is upheld may de-pend on any of the following factors EXCEPT

a. the purposes of the venture.

b. the venture's effect on intrabrand competition.

c. the potential benefits relative to the likely harms.

d. whether there are less restrictive alternatives to achieve the same goals.

    4. The Clayton Act prohibits price discrimination. All of the following are violations EXCEPT

  a. different cash discounts to different buyers for identical goods.
  b. varied delivery terms of identical goods to different buyers in similar locations.
  c. different prices for identical goods sold in high volume under different market conditions.
  d. both a and b.

    5. Nibble, Inc., manufactures toys. Toyz, Inc., is authorized to sell Nibble toys, but does so at prices below Nibble's suggested retail prices. Cecil's Toy Company, another Nibble dealer, complains to Nibble about Toyz's prices. Nibble agrees to terminate Toyz's dealership. The agreement between Nibble and Cecil is

  a. a *per se* violation of Section 1 of the Sherman Act, because Nibble agreed to terminate Toys R You's dealership.
  b. a *per se* violation of Section 1 of the Sherman Act, because it includes no provision for setting prices to be charged by Cecil.
  c. not a *per se* violation of Section 1 of the Sherman Act, because it includes no provision for setting prices to be charged by Cecil.
  d. not a *per se* violation of Section 1 of the Sherman Act, because Nibble did not agree to continue Cecil's dealership.

    6. Corso Corporation conditions the sale of Corso's high-speed supercomputer to New Mexico Research Corporation on New Mexico's agreeing to purchase all supercomputer accessories from Corso. Corso is the only party in the market selling the supercomputer. New Mexico's purchase of the software and other accessories from Corso makes New Mexico's purchase of accessories from other sellers unnecessary. If Corso is sued for violation of the Clayton Act, Corso will

  a. lose, if the court finds that Corso has sufficient market power in both products' markets to coerce the purchase of the supercomputer and affect a substantial amount of commerce in the accessories' market.
  b. lose, if the court finds that Corso has sufficient market power to affect a substantial amount of commerce in the accessories' market.
  c. win, if the court finds that Corso's restriction on its buyers is not a *per se* violation of Section 1 of the Sherman Act.
  d. win, if the court finds that, as judged under a rule of reason, Corso's restriction on its buyers promotes interbrand competition.

    7. Southwest Bauxite Miners Association is a group of independent bauxite mining companies. When demand for bauxite falls due to a recession, and new deposits of ore are discovered, the price threatens to drop. Aluminum Producers Association (APA), a group of major aluminum refining companies, agree to buy Southwest's excess supply and to refine and sell it according to a certain schedule that will increase the price of aluminum. Which of the following is FALSE?

  a. The APA agreement is a price-fixing agreement.
  b. The APA agreement is a horizontal restraint on trade.
  c. The APA agreement is a horizontal market division.
  d. The APA agreement is a *per se* violation of Section 1 of the Sherman Act.

SHORT ESSAY QUESTIONS

1. Discuss how Section 1 of the Sherman Act deals with horizontal restraints (price fixing, horizontal market divisions, trade associations, group boycotts and joint ventures).

2. Discuss how the Clayton Act deals with exclusive dealing contracts and tying arrangements.

ISSUE SPOTTERS (Answers at the Back of the Book)

1. Sufy Corporation manufactures digital audio tape (DAT) players. Sufy agrees with other DAT manufacturers that each firm that begins selling DAT players to dealers in remote communities in which the players have not been available will thereby have the exclusive right to sell in that area. Why are agreements such as this treated as *per se* violations of Section 1 of the Sherman Act?

2. The National Brickmakers Association (NBA) promotes the common interests of firms and individuals in the brick industry. The NBA provides for the exchange of information among its members, the setting of industry standards, and the pooling of resources to represent the members' interests to various governmental bodies. Four of the NBA's member firms control most of the market sales. How might these firms use the NBA to facilitate anticompetitive activities?

3. Boyd Bicycle Corporation conditions sales of its bicycles to retailers on the dealers' reselling the bikes only at prices that Boyd allows. Valley Bike Company, a dealer, sues Boyd on the ground that this condition violates antitrust law because it is anticompetitive. What might Boyd argue in favor of its resale price condition?

4. Moe's Toys, Inc., charges Larry a lower price than Moe charges Curly for the toys. The difference cannot be justified by differences in production or transportation costs. Larry could buy toys from ShepCo at a lower price than Moe charges Curly, and Moe has lowered his price to Larry to undersell ShepCo. Curly sues Moe, on grounds of price discrimination. What might Moe's best argument be in defense of his pricing?

5. Peca Cola Corporation does not allow its buyers—retail grocery stores, restaurants, and entertainment concessions, including theaters, auditoriums, and arenas—to purchase products from Peca's competitors. Peca's customers make up almost half of the market. Peca's four largest competitors use similar exclusive dealing contracts with their customers. Together, the five dealers control 85 percent of the market. Their respective market shares changed little over time. If the government sues Peca for "substantially lessening competition or tending to create a monopoly," could the court agree?

 Key Points

The **key points** in this chapter include:

1. The definition of a security under the Securities Act of 1933.

2. Securities exempt from registration.

3. Transactions in which securities are exempt from registration.

4. The regulation of insider trading under Section 10(b) of the Securities Exchange Act of 1934 and SEC Rule 10b-5.

5. Insider profits under Section 16(b) of the Securities Exchange Act of 1934.

Chapter 28:
Securities Regulation

WHAT THIS CHAPTER IS ABOUT

Corporations are financed through stocks and bonds—securities. The general purpose of securities laws is to provide sufficient, accurate information to investors to enable them to make informed buying and selling decisions about securities. This chapter provides an outline of federal securities laws.

CHAPTER OUTLINE

I. **CORPORATE FINANCING**

A. **BONDS**
Issued as evidence of funds that a firm borrows from investors. Bond indenture specifies the terms. A trustee ensures the terms are met.

B. **STOCKS**
(1) Need not be paid back, (2) stockholders receive dividends only when voted by the directors, (3) stockholders are the last investors to be paid on dissolution, and (4) stockholders vote for management and on major issues.

1. **Common Stock**
Provides an interest with regard to (1) control, (2) earning capacity, and (3) net assets. Includes voting rights (one vote per share), which apply to election of the board and changes in the ownership structure.

2. **Preferred Stock**
Priority over common stock to dividends and to payment on dissolution of the corporation. May or may not include the right to vote.

II.   SECURITIES ACT OF 1933

Requires that all essential information concerning the issuance (sales) of new securities be disclosed to investors.

A.   WHAT A SECURITY IS

1.   Courts' Interpretation of the Securities Act

A security exists in any transaction in which a person (1) invests (2) in a common enterprise (3) reasonably expecting profits (4) derived primarily or substantially from others' managerial or entrepreneurial efforts. In other words, a security is an *investment*.

2.   Examples

Stocks, bonds, investment contracts in condominiums, franchises, limited partnerships, and oil or gas or other mineral rights.

B.   REGISTRATION STATEMENT

Before offering securities for sale, issuing corporations must (1) file a registration statement with the Securities and Exchange Commission (SEC) and (2) provide investors with a prospectus that describes the security being sold, the issuing corporation, and the investment or risk.

1.   What a Registration Statement Must Include

a.   Description of the significant provisions of the security and how the registrant intends to use the proceeds of the sale.
b.   Description of the registrant's properties and business.
c.   Description of the management of the registrant; its security holdings; its remuneration and other benefits, including pensions and stock options; and any interests of directors or officers in any material transactions with the corporation.
d.   Financial statement certified by an independent public accountant.
e.   Description of pending lawsuits.

2.   Twenty-Day Waiting Period after Registration

Securities cannot be sold for twenty days (oral offers can be made).

3.   Advertising

During the waiting period, very limited written advertising is allowed. After the period, all written advertising is prohibited, except a tombstone ad, which simply tells how to obtain a prospectus.

4.   Liability and Penalties

Liability exists if a registration statement or prospectus contains material false statements or omissions. Potentially liable parties: anyone who signed the statement. Penalties: damages, fines, imprisonment.

C.   EXEMPT SECURITIES

Securities that can be sold (and resold) without being registered include—

1.   Small Offerings under Regulation A

An issuer's offer of up to $5 million in securities in any twelve-month period (including up to $1.5 million in nonissuer resales). The issuer must file with the SEC a notice of the issue and an offering circular (also provided to investors before the sale). A company can "test the waters" (determine potential interest) before preparing the circular.

2. Other Exempt Securities

a. All bank securities sold prior to July 27, 1933.

b. Commercial paper if maturity does not exceed nine months.

c. Securities of charitable organizations.

d. Securities resulting from a reorganization issued in exchange for the issuer's existing securities and certificates issued by trustees, receivers, or debtors in possession in bankruptcy (see Chapter 16).

e. Securities issued exclusively in exchange for the issuer's existing securities, provided no commission is paid (such as stock splits).

f. Securities issued to finance the acquisition of railroad equipment.

g. Any insurance, endowment, or annuity contract issued by a state-regulated insurance company.

h. Government-issued securities.

i. Securities issued by banks, savings and loan associations, farmers' cooperatives, and similar institutions.

D. EXEMPT TRANSACTIONS

The following apply only to the transaction in which the securities are issued (except for issues under Rule 504). A resale may be made only after registration (unless the resale qualifies as an exempt transaction).

1. Regulation D—Limited Offers

Offers that involve a small amount of money or are not made publicly.

a. Rule 504—Small Offerings

Noninvestment company offerings up to $1 million in a twelve-month period.

b. Rule 504a—Blank-Check Company Offerings

Offerings up to $500,000 in any one year by companies with no specific business plans are exempt if (1) no general solicitation or advertising is used; (2) the SEC is notified of the sales; and (3) precaution is taken against nonexempt, unregistered resales.

c. Rule 505—Small Offerings

Private, noninvestment company offerings up to $5 million in a twelve-month period if (1) no general solicitation or advertising is used; (2) the SEC is notified of the sales; (3) precaution is taken against nonexempt, unregistered resales; and (4) there are no more than thirty-five unaccredited investors. If the sale involves any unaccredited investors, all investors must be given material information about the company, its business, and the securities.

d. Rule 506—Private Offerings

Rule 506 has essentially the same requirements as Rule 505, except (1) there is no limit on the amount of the offering and (2) the issuer must believe that each unaccredited investor has sufficient knowledge or experience to evaluate the investment.

2. Rule 147—Intrastate Issues

Offerings in the state in which the issuer is organized and doing business are exempt if—

a. 80 percent of the issuer's assets are in the state of issue.

b. 80 percent of the issuer's revenue is from business in the state.

c. 80 percent of the net income from the issue is used in the state.

d. For nine months after the sale, no resale is made to a nonresident.

3. **Section 4(6)—Offers to Accredited Investors Only**
   An offer up to $5 million is exempt if (1) no general solicitation or advertising is used; (2) the SEC is notified of the sales; (3) precaution is taken against nonexempt, unregistered resales; and (4) there are no unaccredited investors.

4. **Rule 144 and Rule 144A—Resales**
   Resales of restricted securities acquired under Rule 504a, Rule 505, Rule 506, or Section 4(6) trigger the registration requirements for everyone, unless the party selling them complies with Rule 144 or Rule 144A.

   a. **Rule 144—Limited Resales**
      Securities may be resold without registration if (1) there is adequate current public information about the issuer (under the Securities Exchange Act of 1934); (2) the person selling the securities has owned them for at least two years; (3) they are sold in certain limited amounts in unsolicited brokers' transactions; and (4) the SEC is given notice of the resale.

      1) **Exception for Affiliates**
         An affiliate controls, is controlled by, or is in common control with the issuer. Subject to the same requirements, except that an affiliate need not have owned the securities for two years.

      2) **Exception for Nonaffiliates**
         Any person (except an affiliate) who has owned the securities for at least three years is subject to none of these requirements.

   b. **Rule 144A—Qualified Institutional Buyers**
      Securities may be resold if (1) the buyer is a qualified institutional buyer (an institution that owns and invests at least $100 million in securities), and (2) the seller tells the buyer that the seller is relying on the exemption under Rule 144A.

   c. **Issuers and Underwriters Cannot Qualify for these Exemptions**

II.   SECURITIES EXCHANGE ACT OF 1934
Regulates the markets in which securities are traded by requiring disclosure by Section 12 companies (corporations with securities on the exchanges) and firms with assets in excess of $5 million and five hundred or more shareholders.

A. **INSIDER TRADING—SECTION 10(b) AND SEC RULE 10b-5**
   Section 10(b) proscribes the use of "any manipulative or deceptive device or contrivance in contravention of such rules and regulations as the [SEC] may prescribe." Rule 10b-5 prohibits the commission of fraud in connection with the purchase or sale of any security (registered or unregistered).

   1. **What Triggers Liability**
      Any material omission or misrepresentation of material facts in connection with the purchase or sale of any security.

   2. **Who Can Be Liable**
      Those who take advantage of inside information when they know that it is unavailable to the person with whom they are dealing.

a. Insiders

Officers, directors, majority shareholders, and persons having access to or receiving information of a nonpublic nature on which trading is based (accountants, attorneys).

b. Outsiders

1) Tipper/Tippee Theory

One who acquires inside information as a result of an insider's breach of fiduciary duty to the firm whose shares are traded can be liable, if he or she knows or should know of the breach.

2) Misappropriation Theory

One who wrongfully obtains inside information and trades on it to his or her gain can be liable, if a duty to the lawful possessor of information was violated and harm to another results.

B. INSIDER REPORTING AND TRADING—SECTION 16(b)

Officers, directors, and shareholders owning 10 percent of the securities registered under Section 12 are required to file reports with the SEC concerning their ownership and trading of the securities.

1. Corporation Is Entitled to All Profits

A firm can recapture *all* profits realized by an insider on *any* purchase and sale or sale and purchase of its stock in any six-month period.

2. Applicability of Section 16(b)

Applies to stock, warrants, options, securities convertible into stock.

C. INSIDER-TRADING SANCTIONS

1. Insider Trading Sanctions Act of 1984

The SEC can bring suit in federal court against anyone violating or aiding in a violation of the 1934 act or SEC rules. Penalties may include triple the profits gained or the loss avoided by the guilty party.

2. Insider Trading and Securities Fraud Enforcement Act of 1988

a. Provisions

Enlarged the class of persons who may be subject to civil liability for insider-trading violations, increased criminal penalties, and gave the SEC authority to (1) reward persons providing information leading to the prosecution of violators and (2) make rules specifically to prevent insider trading.

b. Penalties

Maximum jail term is ten years; fines up to $1 million for individuals and to $2.5 million for partnerships and corporations.

D. PROXY STATEMENTS—SECTION 14(A)

Regulates the solicitation of proxies from shareholders of Section 12 companies. Whoever solicits a proxy must disclose, in the proxy statement, all of the pertinent facts. Penalties include injunctions to prevent a vote from being taken, and damages.

III. REGULATION OF INVESTMENT COMPANIES

Investment companies and mutual funds are regulated by the Investment Company Act of 1940, the Investment Company Act Amendments of 1970, and the Securities Act Amendments of 1975.

A. WHAT AN INVESTMENT COMPANY IS

Any entity that (1) "is * * * engaged primarily * * * in the business of investing, reinvesting, or trading in securities" or (2) is engaged in such business and more than 40 percent of the company's assets consist of investment securities. (Does not include banks and other financial firms).

B. WHAT AN INVESTMENT COMPANY MUST DO

Register with the SEC by filing a notification of registration and, each year, file reports with the SEC. All securities must be in the custody of a bank or stock-exchange member.

C. WHAT AN INVESTMENT COMPANY CANNOT DO

No dividends may be paid from any source other than accumulated, undistributed net income. There are restrictions on investment activities.

IV. STATE SECURITIES LAWS

All states regulate the offer and sale of securities within individual state borders. Exemptions from federal law are not exemptions from state laws, which have their own exemptions.

STUDY TIP 👉 <u>Imagine Yourself in the Classsroom</u>

Budget your study time and stick to the budget. Each hour is an essential step in attaining your academic goals. Create a place for your studying where you will not be disturbed. As you study, imagine yourself in the classroom—this will help you to keep your learning focused.

TRUE-FALSE QUESTIONS (Answers at the Back of the Book)

_____ 1. Generally, under the Securities Act of 1933, if a security does not qualify for an exemption, it must be registered before it is offered to the public through any facility of interstate commerce.

_____ 2. During the waiting period after registration before a sale can occur, the registrant can issue a prospectus to investors.

_____ 3. Securities issued by charitable organizations, banks, and farmers' cooperatives are normally exempt from the SEC registration requirements.

____ 4. Securities resulting from a corporate reorganization issued for exchange with the issuer's existing security holders are not exempt from the SEC registration requirements.

____ 5. The Securities Act of 1933 is concerned primarily with the resale of securities, and the Securities Exchange Act of 1934 is concerned primarily with disclosure on the issuance of securities.

____ 6. Exemptions under the Securities Exchange Act of 1934 include the solicitation of proxies from shareholders by managers of Section 12 companies who request authority to vote on behalf of the shareholders on certain issues.

FILL-IN QUESTIONS (Answers at the Back of the Book)

The SEC can award "bounty" payments to persons providing information leading to the _____ (conviction/ prosecution) of insider-trading violations. Civil penalties include _____ (double/ triple) the profits gained or the loss avoided. Criminal penalties include maximum jail terms of _____ (five/ ten) years, and fines of $___ (1/ 2.5) million for individuals and $___ (1/ 2.5) million for partnerships and corporations.

MULTIPLE-CHOICE QUESTIONS (Answers at the Back of the Book)

____ 1. Ed is an officer of Elk Corporation. Ed learns that Elk has developed a new process for its products. Ed believes that when the process is announced, Elk stock's price will increase. Ed tells Fab, Ed's attorney, who tells Gert, Fab's accountant. Ed, Fab, and Gert each buy Elk stock through a national exchange without telling the sellers of the new process. When the process is announced, the price increases, and Ed, Fab, and Gert each sell their stock. Which of them could be subject to liability under Rule 10b-5?

   a. All of them
   b. Ed and Fab only
   c. Ed only
   d. None of them

____ 2. Which of the following is exempt from the registration requirements?

   a. Superior, Inc., is a private, noninvestment company. In one year, Superior advertises a $300,000 offering.
   b. Erie, Inc., is a noninvestment company. In one year, Erie advertises two $1.75 million offerings. Buying the issues are sixty accredited investors and twenty unaccredited investors. Erie notifies the SEC of the sales, takes precaution against nonexempt, unregistered resales, and gives information about itself, its business, and the securities to unaccredited investors only.
   c. Huron, Inc., makes a $5.5 million private offering to twenty accredited investors and less than thirty unaccredited investors. Huron advertises the offering, notifies the SEC, and takes precaution against nonexempt, unregistered resales. Huron believes that each unaccredited investor is sophisticated enough to evaluate the investment. Huron gives material information about itself, its business, and the securities to all investors.
   d. Ontario, Inc., in one year, advertises two $2.25 million offerings. Buying the issues are twelve accredited investors. Ontario notifies the SEC of the sales and takes precaution against nonexempt, unregistered resales.

____ 3. Hi is an officer of Lo Corporation. In June, Hi learns that market tests indicate Lo's new product will sell very well. Hi buys 1,000 shares of Lo stock. In July, the product is released, and sales exceed expectations. In September, as part of Lo's downsizing, Hi is laid off. In October, Hi sells his Lo stock, realizing a profit. If Lo sues Hi under Section 16(b), Lo will

    a. win, because Hi was a Lo officer who bought and sold Lo stock within a six-month period.
    b. win, because Hi used inside information in connection with the purchase and sale of Lo stock.
    c. lose, because Hi was not a Lo officer when he realized the stock profit.
    d. lose, because Hi did not use inside information in connection with the purchase and sale of Lo stock.

____ 4. A registration statement must include which of the following?

    a. A description of the security, its relationship to the registrant's other securities, and how the registrant intends to use the proceeds
    b. A description of the registrant's properties, management—including interests in any material transactions with the firm—and pending lawsuits
    c. All of the above, plus a certified financial statement
    d. None of the above, except a certified financial statement

____ 5. Which of the following is NOT an element of the definition of a security?

    a. An investment
    b. A common enterprise
    c. A reasonable expectation of profits
    d. An expectation that the profits will be derived entirely from the managerial or entrepreneurial efforts of the investor

SHORT ESSAY QUESTIONS

1. Describe the process by which a company sells securities to the public.

2. How do the securities laws regulate insider trading?

ISSUE SPOTTERS (Answers at the Back of the Book)

1. What agency investigates securities fraud and regulates the activities of investment brokers? What agency supervises the activities of mutual funds? What agency recommends the prosecution of those who violate securities laws?

2. When a corporation wishes to issue certain securities, it must provide sufficient information for an unsophisticated investor to evaluate the financial risk involved. Specifically, the law imposes liability for making a false statement or omission that is "material." What sort of information would an investor consider material?

3. Mel is a vice president of Flax, Inc. Mel knows that a Flax engineer has just discovered a new lode of platinum, an element essential to Flax operations. Mel believes that when the news is made public the price of Flax's stock will increase. Can Mel take advantage of his inside information to buy and sell Flax stock?

4.   The Securities Act of 1933, the Securities Exchange Act of 1934, and other securities regulation is federal law. Mott Assembly Corporation incorporated in Ohio, does business exclusively in Ohio, and offers its securities for sale only in Ohio. Are there state securities laws to regulate the sale of securities within individual state borders?

5.   What is the most important action a firm takes before selling its shares to the public?

Chapter 1

Answers

True-False Questions

1. T
2. F. The positivist law school of jurisprudence adheres to the belief that there can be no higher law that a nation's positive law (the law created by a particular society at a particular point in time). The belief that law should reflect universal moral and ethical principles that are part of human nature is adhered to by the natural law school of jurisprudence.
3. T
4. T
5. T
6. F. Each state's constitution is supreme within each state's borders, so long as it does not conflict with the U.S. Constitution.
7. F. The National Conference of Commissioners on Uniform State Laws drafted the Uniform Commercial Code and proposed it for adoption by the states.
8. T
9. T
10. T
11. F. The reference means that the statute may be found in Section 2627 in Title 26 of the United States Code.
12. F. When more than one judge or justice decides a case, and the decision is not unanimous, those who do not agree with the majority may express their views in concurring or dissenting opinions.

Fill-in Questions

with similar facts; precedent; permits a predictable

Multiple-Choice Questions

1. C. Legal realists believe that judges are influenced by the beliefs and attitudes unique to their individual personalities, that the application of precedent should be tempered by each case's specific circumstances, and that extra-legal sources should be considered in making decisions.
2. D. The use of precedent—the doctrine of *stare decisis*—permits a predictable, quick, and fair resolution of cases. If the application of the law was unpredictable, there would be no consistent rules to follow and no stability. Retroactivity is not a feature of

stare decisis; in fact, retroactivity conflicts with the principle of certainty (for example, if statutes making crimes of activities that previously were no crimes were given retroactive effect, action known to be rightful at the time it was taken would be punished).

3. D. When determining which rules and policies to apply in a given case, and in applying them, a judge may examine any of these sources. Which of these is chosen and receives the greatest emphasis will depend on the nature of the case and the judge hearing it.

4. C. In addition to case law, when making decisions, courts may consider other sources of law, including, in particular cases, the U.S. Constitution, state constitutions, and administrative agency rules and regulations. The National Conference of Commissioners on Uniform State Laws and other organizations propose uniform codes and model laws and urge their adoption, but their enactment is a legislative matter. Until they are enacted, they are only proposals.

5. C. Civil law concerns the duties that exist between persons or between citizens and their governments, excluding crimes. Criminal law is concerned with wrongs, classified as crimes, committed against the public as a whole. A tort is a breach of a private duty. A tort is not a crime, but gives rise to a remedy in a civil action.

6. A. Equity and law do provide different remedies—injunctions and specific performance, for example, are equitable remedies, and damages is a remedy at law. A jury in an action in equity serves only in an advisory capacity. Most states no longer maintain separate courts of law and equity.

7. C. State appellate court opinions may appear in state-published, consecutively numbered volumes titled *Reports* and in regional units of West Publishing Company's *National Reporter System*.

8. A. In a citation, "N.E.2d" is an abbreviation for West's regional reporter, *North Eastern Reporter, Second Series*. The numbers are volume and page references. Title and section references are included in statutory citations.

9. D. In the title of a case (*Abel v. Cain*, for instance) in a trial court, Abel would be the plaintiff (the person who filed the suit) and Cain the defendant. Some appellate courts place the name of the party appealing a decision first, so that this same case on appeal may be called *Cain v. Abel*.

10. A. When more than one judge or justice decides a case, a judge or justice who does not agree with the majority may write a dissenting opinion. A judge or justice who concurs with the judgment, but for different reasons than those given in the majority opinion may write a concurring opinion. The parties do not write opinions for the court.

11. D. In this form of legal reasoning, a judge applies a general principal to the facts of a case and draws a conclusion.

12. A. In reasoning by analogy, a judge compares the facts in one case to the facts in another case and to the extent that the facts are similar, applies the same rule. If the facts are distinguishable, different rules may apply.

Issue Spotters

1. Yes. A judge can decide that a precedent is incorrect. There may have been changes in technology, for example, or business practices, or society's attitudes.

2. No. The U.S. Constitution is the supreme law of the land. A law in violation of the Constitution will be declared unconstitutional.

3. In volume 26 of the *Wisconsin Reports, Second Series*, on page 683, or in volume 133 of the *North Western Reporter, Second Series*, on page 267.

4. No. If this were the title of a case in a trial court, Jones would be the plaintiff (the person who filed the suit) and Smith the defendant. Some appellate courts place the name of the party appealing a decision first, so that this same case on appeal may be called *Smith v. Jones*.

5. When there is not a unanimous opinion, a majority opinion is written, outlining the views of the majority of the judges or justices. A judge or justice who wants to emphasize a point that was not emphasized in the unanimous or majority opinion may write a concurring opinion. A dissenting opinion may be written by a judge or justice who does not agree with the majority.

Chapter 2

True-False Questions

1. T

2. F. Compliance with the law does not always equate with ethical behavior. The law reflects and codifies many of society's ethical values, but it does not codify all ethical requirements. An action might be legal but unethical.

3. F. Duty-based ethics derive from religious sources. Religious ethical standards are absolute: It is not the consequences of an act that determine how ethical the act is; it is the nature of the act itself. Telling a lie would be unethical whether or not anyone is helped by it.

4. F. According to utilitarianism, it is the consequences of an act that determine how ethical the act is. Applying this theory requires determining who will be affected by an action, assessing the positive and negatives effects of alternatives, and choosing the alternative that will provide the greatest benefit for the most people. Utilitarianism is premised on acting so as to do the greatest good for the greatest number of people.

5. T

6. F. In situations involving trade-offs, the balance that must be struck is rarely all "good." The choice is often between equally good alternatives—benefiting many versus harming a few, for example.

7. T

8. F. A manufacturer is strictly, not absolutely, liable for harm caused by its products. A consumer's injury caused by the consumer's misuse of a product may raise an ethical issue, but it is normally unlikely to create liability in the manufacturer.

9. T

10. F. Conduct that would have been considered acceptable twenty years ago may not be considered acceptable today. A sense of what is ethical varies from individual to individual and from group to group, and these ethics vary over time. Most of the major ethical issues confronting businesses today were of little public concern at the turn of the century.

Fill-in Questions

proper behavior; appropriate conduct; create or amend a law; more effectively represents

Multiple-Choice Questions

1. A. Business ethics focuses on the application of moral principles in a business context. Business ethics is a subset of ethics that relates specifically to what constitutes right and wrong in situations that arise in business.

2. A. Ethical reasoning relating to business has traditionally been characterized by two fundamental approaches—duty-based ethics and utilitarianism. Duty-based ethics derive from religious sources.

3. C. Religious ethical standards are absolute—it is the nature of an act that determines how ethical the act is, not its consequences—but this absoluteness is tempered by the Golden Rule, which mandates compassion.

4. B. Utilitarianism is premised on acting so as to do the greatest good for the greatest number of people.

5. B. Utilitarianism requires determining who will be affected by an action, assessing the positive and negatives effects of alternatives, and choosing the alternative that will provide the greatest benefit for the most people. This approach has been criticized as tending to reduce the welfare of human beings to plus and minus signs on a cost-benefit worksheet.

6. A. In situations involving trade-offs, a balance that must be struck is rarely all good. Marketing a product that is beneficial to most consumers but harmful to some would result in a Type I error. Not selling the product would result in a Type II error.

7. D. A corporate employer who responds to what the employer sees as a moral obligation to correct for past discrimination by adjusting pay differences raises an ethical conflict between employer and employee and between corporation and shareholder. Increasing the pay of some employees may reduce profits and the ability of the employer to give pay increases to other employees. Lower profits will also decrease dividends to shareholders.

8. B. Mega Corporation's policy provided a safe workplace, but it violated an ethical and legal duty to provide equal employment opportunity, because distinctions based on sex must relate to the ability to perform a job, and pregnant women can perform as well as anyone else. This hypothetical is nearly identical to the situation in *United Automobile Workers v. Johnson Controls, Inc.*, (Case 2.1).

9. C. Despite the seemingly insoluble dilemma, a decision must be made. Only through a reasoned consideration of the factors can an intelligent trade-off be made.

10. D. Recognizing the nature of the trade-off between these factors is the first step in the ethical decision-making process.

11. A. Striking this balance can be difficult. What is required is well-defined ethical standards and a willingness to apply them.

Issue Spotters

1. Under a duty-based ethical standard, it is not the consequences of an act that determine how ethical the act is; it is the nature of the act itself. Stealing would be unethical regardless of whether the fruits of the crime are given to the poor. In contrast, utilitarianism is premised on acting so as to do the greatest good for the greatest number of people. It is the consequences of an act that determine how ethical the act is.

2. From a utilitarian perspective, the plant will likely be closed, because closing it would benefit the greatest number of persons—future and other current employees, as well as shareholders.

3. When a corporate executive has to decide whether to market a product that would be beneficial to most consumers but that might have undesirable side effects for a small percentage of users, the trade-off is the benefit to the many versus the harm to the few.

4. When Acme Corporation decides to respond to what Acme sees as a moral obligation to correct for past discrimination by adjusting pay differences among its employees, an ethical conflict is raised between Acme and its employees and between Acme and its shareholders.

5. When a product is not defectively made, and warnings concerning its use are adequate, the manufacturer is not liable under the law for injuries resulting from the product's misuse. From an ethical perspective, it is difficult to see how a consumer's unforeseeable product misuse would give rise to a manufacturer's liability.

Chapter 3

True-False Questions

1. F. Pleadings consist of a complaint and an answer, not a motion to dismiss.
2. F. In ruling on a motion for summary judgment, a court can consider evidence outside the pleadings, such as answers to interrogatories.
3. T
4. F. A defendant can file an answer that includes an affirmative defense. The defendant can also file a motion to dismiss or an answer that includes a counterclaim. A defendant will be held in default if he or she fails to file any response to a complaint.
5. F. The process that involves gaining a look at and access to materials and documents in the hands of an opposing party prior to trial is the discovery process.
6. T
7. F. The plaintiff in a civil case must prove a case by a preponderance of the evidence (the claim is more likely to be true than the defendant's). Some claims (such as fraud) must be proved by clear and convincing evidence (the truth of the claim is highly probable).

Fill-in Questions

to dismiss; for judgment on the pleadings; summary judgment

Multiple-Choice Questions

1. D. A complaint contains a statement alleging jurisdictional facts, a statement of facts entitling the complainant to relief, and a statement asking for a specific remedy.
2. B. A motion to dismiss for failure to state a claim on which relief can be granted alleges that according to the law, even if the facts in the complaint are true, the defendant is not liable.
3. D. Discovery saves time by preserving evidence, narrowing the issues, preventing surprises at trial, and avoiding a trial altogether in some cases.
4. A. Once a jury is chosen, a trial begins with the parties' opening statements, after which the plaintiff calls and examines the first witness. The defendant cross-examines the same witness, and there is an opportunity for redirect and recross-examinations of other witnesses. The defendant then presents his or her case. The plaintiff can refute the defendant's case in a rebuttal, and the defendant can meet that evidence in a rejoinder. Afterwards, the parties present their closing arguments, and the jury retires to consider a verdict.
5. C. After the verdict, the losing party can move for a new trial or for a judgment notwithstanding the verdict. If these motions are denied, he or she can appeal.
6. D. Settling for less than you are owed may be wise in terms of future expenses, time waiting, time lost, and frustration.
7. B If Denny's motion to dismiss is granted, the case is at an end. If the motion is denied, Denny must

file an answer or a default judgment will be entered against him.

8. A. An important part of the discovery process, a deposition is sworn testimony. Interrogatories are a series of written questions for which written answers are prepared and signed under oath by the plaintiff or defendant. A request for admissions is a written request to an opposing party for an admission of the truth of matters relating to the trial. A pretrial conference involves the plaintiff, defendant, and judge.

9. A. After the plaintiff calls and questions the first witness on direct examination, the defendant questions the witness on cross-examination. The plaintiff may then question the witness again (redirect examination), and the defendant may follow (recross-examination). Then the plaintiff's other witnesses are called, and finally the defendant presents his or her side of the case.

Issue Spotters

1. First, Jan should consult an attorney. The attorney will help Jan to consider the merits and the costs of a possible lawsuit and other alternatives. If Jan wishes to proceed with the suit, the next steps will include serving Dean with a complaint and summons.

2. Jan needs to make use of the discovery process to see her opponent's relevant papers and obtain answers to her questions. The papers may be released in response to a request for documents. The questions may be answered in response to interrogatories.

3. Dean could file a motion for a directed verdict. This motion asks the judge to direct a verdict for Dean on the ground that Jan presented no evidence that would justify granting Jan relief. The judge grants the motion if there is insufficient evidence to raise an issue of fact.

4. This is not necessarily the end of their case. Either a plaintiff or a defendant, or both, can appeal a judgment to a higher court. An appellate court can affirm, reverse, or remand a case, or take any of these actions in combination. To appeal successfully, it is best to appeal on the basis of an error of law, because appellate courts do not usually reverse on findings of fact.

5. Jan can ask the court to order a sheriff to seize property owned by Dean and hold it until Dean pays the judgment. If Dean fails to pay, the property can be sold at a public auction and the proceeds given to Jan, or the property can be transferred to Jan in lieu of payment.

Chapter 4

True-False Questions

1. F. The major difference between negotiation and mediation is that mediation involves the presence of a third party—a mediator—who assists the parties in reaching an agreement.
2. F. When a dispute arises, the parties may agree to submit it to arbitration, or in some instances, a court may order arbitration.
3. T
4. T
5. F. In court-annexed arbitration, either party may reject an award, and the case will go to trial, with the court reconsidering all evidence and legal questions as though no arbitration occurred.
6. T

Fill-in Questions

Negotiation; Mediation; a mediator; Arbitration; an arbitrator

Multiple-Choice Questions

1. B. A mediator does not decide a controversy, there is no deadline, and there are no sanctions that the parties have not agreed to.
2. A. Arbitration is the settling of a dispute by an impartial third party who renders a legally binding decision. The amount of money involved is immaterial, and the dispute need not arise from a written agreement.
3. C. A court may compel compliance with an award, but a court will not alter an award—a court will not look at the merits of a dispute, the sufficiency of the evidence, or the arbitrator's reasoning.
4. A. If an award does not completely resolve a controversy, it may be set aside.
5. C. In most states, court-annexed arbitration is available only when a party demands a jury trial, a dispute does not involve title to real estate, and a court's equity powers are not involved.
6. B. The basic difference between a traditional trial and a summary jury trial is that in the latter the verdict is only advisory.

Issue Spotters

1.   Society cannot (and should not) rely exclusively on the courts to resolve disputes, because other means may be less expensive, faster, more sensitive to the parties' underlying concerns, and more responsive to underlying problems.

2.   Unlike litigation, negotiation involves no third parties.

3.   Under the U.S. Constitution, federal law is pre-eminent. Thus, federal policy favoring arbitration can override state law favoring litigation.

4.   The rules are likely to be less restrictive, because the arbitrator is an expert in the subject matter involved and there is less fear that she will be swayed by improper evidence.

5.   Yes. Submission of the dispute is mandatory, but compliance with a decision is voluntary.

Chapter 5

True-False Questions

1.   F. The relationship between the federal government and the state governments is a partnership—neither is superior to the other except within the particular area of authority granted to it under the Constitution.

2.   F. The rights secured by the Constitution are not absolute. The government gives constitutional principles their form and substance. The United States Supreme Court gives meaning to, and determines the boundaries of, these rights.

3.   T

4.   T

5.   F. In the supremacy clause, the Constitution provides that the Constitution, laws, and treaties of the United States are the supreme law of the land. When there is a direct conflict between a federal law and a state law, the state law is held to be invalid, even if concurrent federal and state powers are involved.

6.   T

7.   T

8.   F. Generally, a warrant is required to enter business premises to conduct a search—although no warrant is required for seizures of spoiled or contaminated food or to search a business in a highly regulated industry. The standard of probable cause is not the same as in nonbusiness contexts, however. A general and neutral enforcement plan will justify issuance of a warrant.

9.   T

Fill-in Questions

states; states; state; state; validity

Multiple-Choice Questions

1.   D. When conflicts arise regarding the question of whether the federal or state government should be exercising power in a particular area, the Supreme Court resolves them by deciding which governmental system is empowered to act under the Constitution.

2.   B. The first ten amendments to the Constitution, known as the Bill of Rights, embody protections against various types of interference by the federal government. Through the Fourteenth Amendment, most of these guarantees have been held to apply at the state level as well.

3.   C. Congress determines the jurisdiction of the federal courts, but the president can veto congressional legislation, and the Supreme Court has the power to hold acts of the other branches of the federal government unconstitutional.

4.   D. The Fifth Amendment privilege against self-incrimination is available only to natural persons, and a corporation is not a natural person.

5.   A. Commercial speech that is neither related to illegal activities nor misleading may not be restricted unless a state has a substantial interest that cannot be achieved by less restrictive means.

6.   D. Under the establishment and free exercise clauses, the government must accommodate all religions but be hostile toward none—that is, government action must be neutral toward religion.

7.   D. Substantive due process is protected by two clauses in the Constitution: The due process clause of the Fourteenth Amendment applies to state and local governments, and the due process clause of the Fifth Amendment applies to the federal government.

8.   C. Equal protection means that the government must treat similarly situated individuals in a similar manner. This is guaranteed by two clauses in the Constitution: The equal protection clause of the Fourteenth Amendment applies to state and local governments, and the due process clause of the Fifth Amendment is interpreted to guarantee equal protection by the federal government.

Issue Spotters

1.   Yes. Under the commerce clause, according to the Supreme Court, Congress has the power to regulate any activity—interstate or intrastate—that affects interstate commerce.

2.   No. Even if commercial speech is not related to illegal activities nor misleading, it may be restricted if a state has a substantial interest that cannot be achieved by less restrictive means. In this case, the interest in energy conservation is substantial, but it could be achieved by less restrictive means.

3.   No. The First Amendment requires that the government not prohibit the free exercise of religious practices. But an individual's religious beliefs are not considered to excuse him or her from compliance with an otherwise valid law. That would inhibit the government's ability to enforce prohibitions of socially harmful conduct.

4.   No. The law would be unconstitutional on substantive due process grounds, because it abridges freedom of speech. The law would be unconstitutional on procedural due process grounds, because it imposes a penalty without giving an accused a chance to defend his or her actions.

5.   No. The tax would violate equal protection if the only reason that could be asserted for it was to protect local businesses from out-of-state competition.

Chapter 6

True-False Questions

1.   T
2.   F. Complaints may be brought by agencies, private citizens, or organizations, but are prosecuted by agencies.
3.   F. All four types of agency rulemaking procedures can result in binding rules; all four procedures offer the public an opportunity to object to a proposed rule.
4.   F. Either side may appeal, usually to a federal circuit court or a federal district court, or the agency commission may review the case, but if there is no appeal, the initial order becomes final.
5.   T
6.   T

Fill-in Questions

informal; general statement of basis and purpose; *Federal Register*; in writing; must; *Federal Register*; thirty

Multiple-Choice Questions

1.   B.   The Government-in-the-Sunshine Act requires "every portion of every meeting of an agency" that is headed by a "collegial body" to be open to "public observation."
2.   D.   Information may be provided through either of these methods.
3.   A.   Notice-and-comment rulemaking, or informal rulemaking—which is the most common—includes notice, opportunity for comment, and a general statement of basis and purpose.
4.   C.   The president's veto is a method by which agency authority can be checked. The checks noted in the other choices are Congress's.
5.   B.   A party must exhaust all other means of resolving a controversy with an agency. Otherwise, the APA presumes the reviewability of an action, a party must have standing, and courts do not issue advisory opinions.
6.   D.   An agency's basic functions are rulemaking, enforcement, and adjudication, supplemented by broad investigative powers.

Issue Spotters

1.   Administrative law is intended to inhibit agency arbitrariness and overreaching by courts' review of agency actions and by the political control of Congress and the executive branch. Another limitation is the Administrative Procedure Act (APA). Constitutional restraints also apply.

2.   A legislative rule must not violate the Constitution, involve an impermissible grant of legislative authority, or exceed the power conferred on the agency by its enabling statute.

3.   Under the APA, the ALJ is separated from the investigative and prosecutorial staff, as are the members of the agency's commission. *Ex parte* communication between the ALJ and a party to a proceeding is prohibited. An ALJ is exempt from agency discipline except on a showing of good cause.

4.   A court will make an independent finding if required by statute; inadequate fact-finding proceed-

ings were used; or new facts are raised in a proceeding to enforce a nonadjudicatory action.

5. The Freedom of Information Act requires the federal government to reveal certain "records" to "any person" on request.

Chapter 7

True-False Questions

1. T

2. F. Some countries reject any role for women professionals. Equal employment opportunity is a fundamental policy in the United States, however.

3. T

4. F. Legal systems in all nations can be generally divided into *common* law and civil law systems.

5. T

6. F. Some contract law has been internationalized through the CISG, but parties contracting internationally can agree to apply other law to their contract disputes.

7. F. Under the employment-at-will doctrine, employers are free to hire and fire employees "at will"—that is, for any reason or no reason at all.

8. F. Business firms depend largely on local legal protection of intellectual property rights.

9. T

Fill-in Questions

Council of Ministers; A commission; Council; commission; an elected assembly; Council; commission; binding; European Court of Justice

Multiple-Choice Questions

1. B. When business is international, ethical considerations become international and may include political issues. In taking a stand on political issues, a business should be sensitive to the economic and cultural differences between nations.

2. A. Nations that have federal systems divide governmental powers between national and provincial governments. Nations with centralized governments have unitary systems, with no independent local governments.

3. A. In the United States and in India, the courts can declare a law illegal if it violates their constitution. Courts do not have this power in Great Britain.

Only a special constitutional council invalidates laws in France. In Germany, only a special court has this power.

4. D. Although increasingly influenced by statutory law, common law systems are based on judicial decisions and precedent. Despite this general frame of reference, common law courts in different nations have developed different principles.

5. D. Civil law systems are based on statutory law. In a civil law system, courts are permitted to interpret the code and apply the rules, but they are not to develop their own body of law.

6. B. In many countries, however, judges are actively involved in trials, such as by questioning witnesses. In the United States, besides a less participatory role at trial, a federal judge is less likely to be influenced by politics, in part because he or she cannot be removed by impeachment except in extreme cases.

7. B. For example, mutual assent (offer and acceptance) is a common element for an enforceable contract. But the details of its application varies in different countries. In Germany, for instance, a written offer must be held open for a reasonable time, unless the offer states otherwise, and oral offers must be accepted immediately or they expire. In Mexico, if a time for acceptance is not stated in an offer, the offer is deemed to be held open for three days (plus whatever time is necessary for the mails).

8. D. Swiss and Turkish courts will reduce damages if an award would cause undue hardship to a negligent party. In Italy, a plaintiff must sue within five years of a tort's commission.

Issue Spotters

1. The Foreign Corrupt Practices Act of 1977 prohibits American firms from offering payments to foreign officials to secure favorable contracts. But payments to minor officials to, for example, facilitate paperwork are not prohibited.

2. Language differences can confound efforts to do business abroad in such instances as when, for example, advertising slogans are translated word-for-word. Such slogans may be nonsense in different languages. Body movements, gestures, and facial expressions also have different meanings. In the United States, for example, a nod of the head indicates "yes," while in Greece, the same gesture means "no." Colors and numbers are also associated with different meanings.

3. There is a European Court of Justice that can review each nation's court decisions on EU law. The European Court of Justice is the ultimate authority on EU law.

4. Most countries impose price controls of some kind or on at least some goods. Taiwan, for example, sets prices that are charged for some basic goods. India regulates the prices of raw materials and other goods and products. In Mexico, the president can impose price controls to correct for surpluses or shortages.

5. In some countries, employers may fire employees without notice only for such reasons as employee violence, imprisonment, excessive absenteeism, or lying on a job application. In other nations, a worker may be discharged only if he or she commits a criminal offense, loses a license or other employment qualification, or seriously breaches his or her duties. In some countries, to discharge an employee for cause, an employer must first submit the proposed discharge to mediators or a labor committee.

Chapter 8

True-False Questions

1. T
2. F. The act of state doctrine and the doctrine of sovereign immunity tend to immunize foreign nations from the jurisdiction of U.S. courts
3. F. The Foreign Sovereign Immunities Act sets forth the major exceptions to the immunity of foreign nations to U.S. jurisdiction.
4. T
5. T
6. T

Fill-in Questions

An expropriation; A confiscation; an expropriation; a confiscation

Multiple-Choice Questions

1. B. Foreign and domestic firms may be sued for violations of U.S. antitrust laws.
2. B. The Foreign Corrupt Practices Act prohibits any U.S. firm from bribing foreign officials to influence official acts.
3. A. Under certain conditions, the doctrine of sovereign immunity immunizes foreign nations from

the jurisdiction of U.S. courts. Under the Foreign Sovereign Immunities Act, a foreign state is not immune when the action is based on a commercial activity carried on in the United States by the foreign state.

4. C. The act of state doctrine is provides that the judicial branch of one country will not examine the validity of public acts committed by a recognized foreign government within its own territory.

5. C. Sources of international law include international customs that have evolved among nations in their relations with each other.

6. A. In the Civil Rights Act of 1991, Congress provided for the extraterritorial effect of Title VII (as already existed for the Age Discrimination in Employment Act of 1967 and the Americans with Disabilities Act of 1990).

Issue Spotters

1. To enforce international law, other countries or international organizations can try persuasive tactics, coercive actions (such as the severance of diplomatic relations and boycotts) and war.

2. Under Article II, Section 2, of the U.S. Constitution, the president has the power "by and with the Advice and Consent of the Senate, to make Treaties, provided two-thirds of the Senators present concur."

3. Under the principle of comity, the United States defers and gives effect to foreign laws and judicial decrees that are consistent with U.S. law and public policy.

4. Congress may set export quotas to inhibit exports. For instance, Congress may limit the export of technologically-advanced goods. To stimulate exports, Congress may use incentives and subsidies, such as tax benefits or credit guarantees.

5. Probably not. To be protected outside the United States, a product must be patented under the laws of the country in which the protection is sought.

Chapter 9

True-False Questions

1. T
2. T

3.   F. Ordinarily, courts will not evaluate the adequacy of consideration, unless it is so grossly inadequate as to "shock the conscience" of the court.
4.   F. An adult who enters into a contract with a minor cannot avoid contractual duties unless the minor opts to avoid the contract.
5.   F. To commit fraudulent misrepresentation, one party must intend to mislead another.
6.   F. An adhesion contract is written exclusively by one party and presented to the other party with no opportunity to negotiate.

Fill-in Questions

objective; objective; subjective; Objective; did; circumstances surrounding

Multiple-Choice Questions

1.   A. In general, ads are treated as invitations to negotiate, not offers.
2.   C. An offer must be communicated to the offeree, so that the offeree knows it. Ordinarily, one cannot agree to a bargain without knowing that it exists.
3.   D. To be enforced in court, a contract must call for the performance of a legal act. Selling an illegal product is not the performance of a legal act.
4.   A. A right to the payment of money is freely assignable, and an assignment need not be supported by consideration to be enforceable.
5.   D. Generally, a unilateral mistake does not give the mistaken party any right to relief. There are two exceptions. One of the exceptions is that the rule is not applied if the other party knew or should have known that a mistake was made.
6.   B. To avoid a contract on grounds of innocent misrepresentation, the misrepresentation must concern a material fact.

Issue Spotters

1.   Under the objective theory of contracts, if a reasonable person would have thought that Shorty accepted Buck's offer when Shorty signed and returned the letter, a contract was made, and Shorty is bound.
2.   No. Revocation of an offer may be implied by conduct inconsistent with the offer.
3.   Yes. Under the doctrine of detrimental reliance, or promissory estoppel, Manuela is entitled to $5,000 from Don when she graduates.

4.   No. When parties base their contract on a common assumption about a material fact that proves false, the transaction may be avoided if because of the mistake a different exchange of values occurs from the exchange of values that the parties contemplated.
5.   A condition is part of a contract. If a condition is not satisfied, the obligations of the parties are discharged. In other words, under this contract, if the money is not raised, neither Remy nor Brandt need to perform.

Chapter 10

True-False Questions

1.   T
2.   F. Complete performance occurs when performance is within the bounds of reasonable expectations. Substantial performance occurs when performance is slightly below reasonable expectations.
3.   F. When performance is not substantial, a breach is material—the nonbreaching party is excused from performing and can sue for damages caused by the breach. If a breach is not material, the nonbreaching party's duty to perform may be only suspended until the breach is remedied.
4.   T
5.   F. An innocent party is discharged when another party to the contract materially alters it without the innocent party's consent.
6.   T

Fill-in Questions

Rescission; Novation; Substitution of a new contract; An accord; accord

Multiple-Choice Questions

1.   C. Any breach entitles the nonbreaching party to sue for damages, but only a material breach discharges the nonbreaching party from the contract.
2.   D. Novation substitutes a new party for an original party by agreement of all the parties.
3.   B. An accord is an executory contract to perform an act to satisfy a contractual duty that has not been discharged. An accord suspends the original obligation. A satisfaction is the performance of the accord.

4.   D. The failure of CIB does not qualify to discharge or suspend Gil's duty.

5.   C. A failure to perform entitles the nonbreaching party to rescind, and the parties must make restitution by returning goods, property, or money conveyed. The bank's failure has no effect on Aziz's rights.

6.   B. Specific performance is granted to a buyer in a contract for the sale of land. The legal remedy is inadequate because every piece of land is considered unique.

Issue Spotters

1.   No. Aloha has substantially performed its duties under the contract. For the sake of justice and fairness, Ho will be held to his duty to pay, less damages for the deviation from the contract deadline.

2.   Contracts that are executory on both sides—contracts on which neither party has performed—can be rescinded solely by agreement. Contracts that are executed on one side—contracts on which one party has performed—can be rescinded only if the party who has performed receives consideration for the promise to call off the deal.

3.   Their deaths before fulfilling the contract discharge the contract and their estates' liability for their nonperformance.

4.   No. To recover consequential damages—damages that flow from the consequences of a breach but that are caused by circumstances beyond the contract—the breaching party must know, or have reason to know, that special circumstances will cause the nonbreaching party to suffer the additional loss.

5.   Yes. Contracts for the sale of goods rarely qualify for specific performance, because substantially identical goods can be bought in the market. If goods are unique, however, specific performance will be ordered.

Chapter 11

True-False Questions

1.   F. Unlike the common law rule that contract modification must be supported by new consideration, the UCC requires no consideration for an agreement modifying a contract.

2.   F. A writing will be sufficient if indicates that a contract was intended and—except for transactions between merchants—if it is signed by the party against whom enforcement is sought. Except for output and requirements contracts, a contract is not enforceable beyond the quantity of goods shown in the writing. Other terms can be proved by oral testimony or be supplied by the UCC's open term provisions.

3.   T

4.   T

5.   F. Ordinarily, specific performance is considered inappropriate if damages will place the buyer in the position that he or she would have been in if the seller had fully performed.

6.   F. This is the definition of an implied warranty. Representations concerning quality, condition, description, or performance potential of goods are express warranties.

Fill-in Questions

1.   conforming; and

2.   accepting; the contract; buyer; receipt; even if

Multiple-Choice Questions

1.   A. When goods are to be picked up by a buyer, if a seller is a nonmerchant, risk passes on the seller's tender of delivery, absent a contrary agreement.

2.   C. If a contract that involves a sale of identified goods does not specify a place of delivery, and the buyer is to pick up the goods, and the parties know when they contract that the goods are located somewhere other than at the seller's place of business, the location of the goods is the place for their delivery.

3.   D. If a buyer wrongfully cancels a contract or refuses to accept goods, a seller can sue for damages: the difference between the contract price and the market price (at the time and place of tender). If the market price is less than the contract price, damages include the seller's lost profits.

4.   C. The buyer must designate defects that are ascertainable by reasonable inspection, or those defects cannot be used to justify rejection or to establish breach if the seller could have cured them on being seasonably notified.

5.   C. If a bailee holds goods for a seller and the goods are delivered without being moved, risk passes when the buyer receives a negotiable document of title for the goods.

6.   B.   An implied warranty of merchantability arises in every sale of goods by a merchant who deals in goods of the kind. It makes no difference whether the merchant knew of or could have discovered a defect that makes a product unsafe.

Issue Spotters

1.   Yes. Under the UCC, if a merchant gives assurances in a signed writing that an offer will remain open, the offer is irrevocable.
2.   If Lois is right, Silk must pay and seek indemnification from Silk's insurance company. If Silk is right, Lois must seek indemnification from Lois's insurance company and may still have an obligation to deliver conforming goods to Silk.
3.   Yes. At common law and under the UCC, a seller is obligated to deliver goods in conformity with a contract in every detail. Because of the harshness of the rule, however, there are exceptions.
4.   In all three instances, Angelina can bring an action to recover the purchase price and incidental damages. Of course, Angelina must hold the goods for Lilian.
5.   Makoto should argue that Gindin breached an implied warranty of fitness for a particular purpose. An implied warranty of fitness for a particular purpose arises when a seller knows a particular purpose for which a buyer will use goods and that the buyer is relying on the seller's skill and judgment to select suitable goods.

Chapter 12

True-False Questions

1.   T
2.   T
3.   F. A reasonable apprehension or fear of immediate harmful or offensive contact is an essential element of assault.
4.   T
5.   F. A single indignity or annoyance is usually not enough to support an action for the intentional infliction of emotional distress, but repeated annoyances, coupled with threats, may be.
6.   F. Defamation may be committed orally, in writing, or in a form of communication that has the potentially harmful qualities characteristic of writing—pictures, signs, statues, and films.
7.   F. Edison's statement is seller's talk, or puffing. For fraud to occur, more than this must be involved.
8.   T
9.   T
10.   F. An individual with knowledge, skill, or intelligence superior to that of an ordinary person has a higher standard of care—his or her duty is that which is reasonable in light of those capabilities.
11.   T

Fill-in Questions

1.   negligence;
2.   defense of assumption of risk; assumption; assumption;
3.   negligence; contributory;
4.   negligence; comparative; negligence; negligent;
5.   failure to use reasonable care; had the last clear chance to avoid the accident and failed to do so

Multiple-Choice Questions

1.   C. A tort action is a civil action in which one person brings a suit of a personal nature against another.
2.   C. Feeble is guilty of assault—an intentional, unexcused act that creates in another person a reasonable apprehension of immediate harmful or offensive contact.
3.   A. To delay a customer suspected of shoplifting, a merchant must have probable cause (which requires more than a mere suspicion).
4.   B. Madonna is a public figure. To recover damages, a public figure must prove that a defamatory statement was made with actual malice—that is, with knowledge of its falsity or reckless disregard for the truth.
5.   C. A person may not be liable for defamatory statements if he or she enjoys a privilege. Absolute privilege exists in limited situations, including judicial proceedings.
6.   D. Acts that constitute intrusion into another's affairs or seclusion include invading someone's home, illegally searching someone's belongings, eavesdropping by wiretap, unauthorized scanning of a bank account, compulsory blood testing, and window peeping.
7.   D. Trespass to land occurs when a person, without permission, enters onto another's land, or remains

on the land. Harm to the land is not required. A trespasser can be removed by reasonable force.

8.   A. The basis of the tort of defamation is publication of a statement that holds an individual up to contempt, ridicule, or hatred. Publication means that statements are made to or within the hearing of persons other than the defamed party. Dictating a letter to a secretary constitutes publication; a secretary reading a letter constitutes publication.

9.   B. Failing to exercise reasonable care is potentially tortious conduct. Whether conduct is unreasonable depends on a number of factors, including how easily the injury could have been guarded against. Unless a retail firm has taken all reasonable precautions against potential injuries to its customers, it may be held to have breached its duty of care to those invitees.

10.   A. To satisfy the elements of a negligence cause of action, a breach of a duty of care must cause the harm. If an injury would not have occurred without the breach, there is causation in fact. Causation in fact can usually be determined by the but-for test: But for the wrongful act, the injury would not have occurred.

11.   D. Abnormally dangerous activities (1) involve potentially serious harm to persons or property, (2) involve a high degree of risk that cannot be completely guarded against by the exercise of reasonable care, and (3) are activities not commonly performed in the area.

12.   D. To be prepared to deal with potential legal problems, a retailer should do all of these and more: a retailer should properly train employees who will deal with shoplifters and, even for the most minor lawsuit, hire an attorney and be willing to settle out of court.

13.   C. One of the elements of negligence is causation. Causation has two parts: causation in fact and proximate cause. Causation in fact is a question in fact (a question of cause and effect). Proximate cause is a question not of fact but of law and policy.

Issue Spotters

1.   Yes. Adam is guilty of battery—an unexcused, harmful, or offensive physical contact intentionally performed. He is not guilty of assault, though.

2.   Yes. The tort that has been committed is false imprisonment—the intentional confinement or restraint of another person without justification.

3.   Yes. Trespass to personal property occurs when an individual unlawfully harms another's personal property or otherwise interferes with the owner's right to exclusive possession and enjoyment.

4.   The question is one of proximate cause. Proximate cause is a question not of fact but of law and policy for a court to decide: should a negligent actor's responsibility extend to consequences that could not have been anticipated?

5.   Yes. An owner of a domestic animal, such as Gary's vicious dog, is strictly liable for harm caused by the animal if the owner knew, or should have known, as Gary did, that the animal had a propensity to harm others.

Chapter 13

True-False Questions

1.   F. It is not required that the third party act in bad faith or with malice, but he or she must interfere for the purpose of advancing his or her economic interest.

2.   F. Defenses to wrongful interference torts include bona fide competitive behavior and other legal conduct.

3.   T

4.   T

5.   T

6.   T

7.   F. Crime requires the performance of a prohibited act. Most crimes require an act of commission, but some acts of omission are crimes, and attempting certain acts may also be crimes.

8.   F. This is the definition of robbery.

Fill-in Questions

federal; state; two; maintain; participate in; racketeering

Multiple-Choice Questions

1.   C. Under RICO, it is a federal crime to use income obtained from racketeering activity to maintain an interest in a business enterprise.

2.   C. RICO provides for both civil and criminal liability.

3. A. The distinction between competition and predatory behavior often depends on whether a business is attempting to attract customers in general or to solicit only customers who have shown an interest in a similar product of a specific competitor. The latter activity constitutes wrongful interference with a business relationship.

4. B. An individual's right to privacy includes the right to the exclusive use of his or her identity. The use of one person's name or likeness by another, without permission and for the benefit of the user, constitutes appropriation.

5. D. Defamation occurs when an individual makes a false statement that injures another's reputation. If the statement injures someone in a profession, business, or trade or adversely affects a business entity in its credit rating and other dealings, it constitutes defamation in a business context.

6. D. Larceny is the wrongful or fraudulent taking and carrying away by any person of the personal property of another. There is no distance requirement—three steps is enough.

7. B. Embezzlement is the fraudulent conversion of property or money owned by one person but entrusted to another.

Issue Spotters

1. No. Bona fide competitive behavior is a privileged interference even if it results in the breaking of a contract. The public policy that favors free competition in advertising outweighs any instability that competitive activity causes in contractual relations.

2. Yes. Passing on false information about a person's credit standing or business reputation that impairs the person's ability to obtain further credit is defamation and entitles the defamed person to damages.

3. The use of one person's name or likeness by another, without permission and for the benefit of the user, constitutes appropriation. A person's identity may be "public," but it is not public property. An individual's right to privacy includes the right to the exclusive use of his or her identity.

4. Yes. Forgery is the fraudulent making or altering of any writing that changes the legal liability of another. In some instances, authorization to sign another's name negates a charge of forgery regardless of fraud, but a purchaser of traveler's checks agrees to sign the checks himself or herself. 5. With respect to the gas station, Maxy has committed obtaining

goods by false pretenses. Maxy might also be charged with forgery, and most states have special statutes covering illegal use of credit cards.

Chapter 14

True-False Questions

1. F. An action based on negligence does not require privity of contract.

2. T

3. F. In an action based on strict liability, a plaintiff does not have to prove that there was a failure to exercise due care.

4. F. Under the crashworthiness doctrine, liability is imposed for defects in the design or construction of motor vehicles that increase the extent of injuries to passengers if an accident occurs—even when the defects do not cause the accident.

5. F. Strict liability for personal injuries caused by defective goods does extend to those who lease the goods.

6. T

Fill-in Questions

limitations; does not begin until; repose; repose; limitations

Multiple-Choice Questions

1. C. One who voluntarily chooses to use a product with a complete realization of the risks to which he or she exposes himself or herself normally voluntarily assumes those risks—regardless of how the realization was acquired.

2. B. Evergreen misrepresented the character of the contents of the bottle.

3. A. It is not public policy that a person is entitled to compensation from the manufacturer of the product (or anyone else) simply because the person is injured by the product.

4. B. A less dangerous alternative (than the unguarded opening) was economically feasible, but Silo failed to produce it.

5. C. Many products cannot be made entirely safe for all consumers, and any food or drug involves some risk, if only from over-consumption. "Unreasonably

dangerous" means dangerous to an extent beyond that which the ordinary consumer would expect.

6. A. All courts extend the strict liability of manufacturers and other sellers to injured bystanders. There is no imposition of a requirement of privity.

7. D. Assumption of risk is a defense in an action based on strict liability if the following elements are shown: (1) the plaintiff voluntarily engaged in the risk while realizing the potential danger, (2) the plaintiff knew and appreciated the risk created by the defect, and (3) the plaintiff's decision to undertake the known risk was unreasonable.

Issue Spotters

1. Empire is liable to Keith, Woody, Mick, and Charlie. A manufacturer is liable for its failure to exercise due care to any person who sustains an injury proximately caused by a negligently made (defective) product.

2. Yes. Under the doctrine of strict liability, persons may be held liable for the results of their acts regardless of their intentions or their exercise of reasonable care—that is, regardless of fault.

3. Yes. Suppliers are generally required to expect reasonably foreseeable misuses and to design products that are either safe when misused or marketed with some protective device.

4. Yes. Anchor may be held liable—the strict liability doctrine has been expanded to include suppliers of component parts.

5. Yes. Most courts will consider a plaintiff's negligence in apportioning liability, resulting in an application of the doctrine of comparative negligence in strict liability cases.

Chapter 15

True-False Questions

1. T
2. F. A copyright is granted automatically.
3. T
4. T
5. F. The same policies and restrictions that apply to trademarks apply to service, certification, and collective marks.

6. F. Unlike copyright and trademark protection, protection of trade secrets extends to ideas and their expression.

7. T
8. T
9. F. The right to privacy is protected under tort law and, to a certain extent, under the Constitution. Damages may be awarded for unauthorized intrusion into private records or unauthorized examination of a bank account.

Fill-in Questions

copyright; mask works; mask work; Copyright

Multiple-Choice Questions

1. A. A firm that makes, uses, or sells another's patented design, product, or process without the patent owner's permission commits patent infringement. It is not required that an invention be copied in its entirety.

2. D. Software products often do not meet the "novel" and "not obvious" requirements for a patent because much software simply automates procedures that can be performed manually. Also, the basis for a computer program is often a mathematical equation or formula, which is not patentable.

3. C. Only a compiler's selection and arrangement may have copyright protection. Raw facts may be copied at will.

4. D. In applying and interpreting the Computer Software Copyright Act of 1980, courts have extended protection to all the listed items except computer programs' "look and feel."

5. A. Registration is not necessary to obtain protection from trademark infringement.

6. C. Computer hardware is patentable.

7. B. Theft or unauthorized use of computer data and services does not fit within the common law definition of larceny, because larceny requires a physical taking and carrying away of property from another's possession.

8. B. Business processes and information that cannot be patented, copyrighted, or trademarked are protected against appropriation by others as trade secrets. These include production techniques.

9. A. The Counterfeit Access Device and Computer Fraud and Abuse Act of 1984 prohibits the use of a computer to obtain information contained in a financial institution's records or in a consumer reporting agency's files on consumers.

10. D. The right to privacy is protected under tort law and, to a certain extent, under the Constitution. Congress has enacted several laws relating to the potential abuse of personal information collected by the government and other institutions, and many laws that states have enacted to address computer crime are also concerned to an extent with privacy.

11. C. To obtain a patent, an applicant must satisfy the U.S. Patent and Trademark Office that the invention or design is genuine, novel, useful, and not obvious in light of contemporary technology.

Issue Spotters

1. The developer cannot prevent a competitor from producing another game that is based on gladiators, but the developer can prevent competitors from copying the graphics. An idea is not copyrightable, but the way in which an idea is expressed is.

2. Under the Berne Convention, if an American writes a book, his or her copyright is recognized by every country that has signed the convention. If a citizen of a country that has not signed the convention first publishes a book in a country that has, all other countries that have signed the convention must recognize the author's copyright.

3. Yes. Firms cannot use names in ways that deceives consumers.

4. Northern King can sue Burley for theft of trade secrets.

5. Jennifer can sue Bret for invasion of privacy.

Chapter 16

True-False Questions

1. T

2. F. If the debtor does not or cannot pay, a creditor can go back to court and obtain a writ of execution through which property of the debtor can be seized and sold to satisfy the judgment.

3. F. State and federal statutory exemptions can be applied together.

4. F. This is the most important concept in suretyship: a surety can use any defenses available to the principal, except personal defenses.

5. F. The adequate protection doctrine protects secured creditors from losing the value of their security as a result of the automatic stay.

6. T

Fill-in Questions

1. suretyship; surety; surety; guaranty; guarantor

2. suretyship; guaranty

Multiple-Choice Questions

1. D. A collective bargaining agreement can be rejected if it would aid the successful rehabilitation of the debtor and if a debtor proposes necessary contract modifications to the union and makes a good faith attempt to reach agreement on the modifications, but the union fails to adopt them without good cause.

2. C. Obeying a lawful bankruptcy court order is not grounds for denial of a discharge. Refusing to obey a lawful court order is ground for denying a discharge.

3. C. A surety is primarily liable: the creditor can hold the surety responsible for payment of the debt when the debt is due, without first exhausting all remedies against the debtor.

4. D. The debt is $30,000. The amount of the homestead exemption ($35,000) is subtracted from the sale price of the house ($60,000), and the remainder ($25,000) is applied against the debt. The proceeds from the sale of the nonexempt personal property ($5,000) is also applied against the debt. $25,000 + $5,000 = $30,000.

5. C. If a creditor receives a payment within the ordinary course of business, the payment cannot be recovered.

6. C. A debtor continues in possession of a business under Chapters 11 and 13.

Issue Spotters

1. Sinclair can use prejudgment attachment. Attachment occurs at the time of or immediately after commencement of a suit but before entry of a final judgment. The court issues a writ of attachment, directing the sheriff or other officer to seize property belonging to the debtor. If the creditor prevails at trial, the property can be sold to satisfy the judgment.

2. Oran can use garnishment, a collection remedy directed at a debtor's property or rights held by a third person. A garnishment order can be served on the bank or the employer so that part of Eli's accounts or Eli's paycheck will be paid to Oran.

3. Yes. Bob is a surety. A surety has a right of reimbursement from the debtor for all outlays the surety makes on behalf of the suretyship arrangement.

4. Yes. Under Chapter 13 of federal bankruptcy law, a debtor can submit a plan under which he or she continues in possession of his or her assets, but turns over disposable income for a three-year period, after which most debts are discharged.

5. No. Claims that are not dischargeable include claims for back taxes accruing within three years before bankruptcy, claims based on misuse of funds while acting in a fiduciary capacity, and, unless payment imposes undue hardship, certain student loans.

Chapter 17

True-False Questions

1. T
2. T
3. F. Sole proprietorships and many partnerships are not separate legal entities, but corporations are.
4. F. Failing to follow statutory corporate formalities can result in the corporate veil being pierced and individual shareholders being held personally liable for corporate debts.
5. T
6. T

Fill-in Questions

chain-style; distributorship; chain-style; manufacturing

Multiple-Choice Questions

1. C. A sole proprietor has unlimited liability for all obligations incurred in doing business.
2. C. Like sole proprietors, general partners have unlimited liability for partnership obligations.
3. B. Ordinarily, limited partners have no voice in the business's management.
4. B. The shareholders elect a board of directors, which manages the business and normally employs officers to oversee day-to-day operations.

5. B. Directors must act as a body in carrying out routine corporate business.
6. D. A business trust is similar to a corporation, and, like corporate shareholders, beneficiaries are not personally liable for the organization's debts and obligations.
7. A. This practice would violate federal antitrust laws. A franchisor can suggest retail prices, but it cannot insist on them.
8. A. If no set time for termination is provided, a reasonable time will be implied.

Issue Spotters

1. When a business is relatively small and is not diversified, employs relatively few people, has modest profits, and is not likely to expand significantly or require extensive financing in the immediate future, the most appropriate form for doing business may be a sole proprietorship.
2. When a business is larger than a sole proprietorship with greater capital needs, the most appropriate business form may be a partnership.
3. When a business is expanding, becoming more profitable and diversified, or when a more institutional framework is appropriate, it may be best to do business in a corporate form.
4. Yes. Small businesses that meet certain requirements can qualify as S corporations, created specifically to permit small businesses to avoid double taxation.
5. Probably not. If a franchise is a "written agreement," an oral promise would not be part of a franchise agreement.

Chapter 18

True-False Questions

1. T
2. F. Officers have the same fiduciary duties as directors, but they may not have the same rights—officers' rights are determined by employment contracts.
3. F. The rights of shareholders are established in articles of incorporation and under the state's general incorporation law.
4. T
5. F. Any damages recovered in a shareholder's derivative suit are normally paid to the corporation

on whose behalf the shareholder or shareholders who exercised the derivative right.

6. T

Fill-in Questions

but ownership is not; can; must; recorded ownership in the corporation's books

Multiple-Choice Questions

1. A. Directors are expected to be informed on corporate matters and to understand advice rendered to the board.

2. D. There is no such right.

3. C. This claim states a shareholder's direct claim—that is, the shareholder is pursuing a right or benefit for the shareholder personally. The others are derivative claims.

4. B. A shareholder who receives watered stock and has not paid the difference between its price and its stated value may be liable to unpaid creditors of the corporation.

5. C. Directors have no inherent right to compensation for their services.

6. A. A court will not compel the declaration of a dividend unless abuse of discretion is clearly shown.

Issue Spotters

1. Directors' fiduciary duty requires them to make a full disclosure of any potential conflicts of interest that might arise in any corporate transaction. In addition, if the contract between the corporations is fair and reasonable at the time it is made, and it is approved by a majority of the disinterested directors or shareholders, it will likely be upheld. A director cannot, however, support a business that competes directly with a corporation on the board of which the director sits.

2. The board can assert the business judgment rule—that is, that an honest mistake of judgment on its part does not make it liable to the corporation for resulting damages.

3. Under these circumstances, a minority shareholder can petition a court to appoint and receiver and liquidate the assets of the corporation.

4. Yes. A shareholder can bring a derivative suit on behalf of a corporation, if some wrong is done to the corporation. Normally, any damages recovered go into the corporate treasury.

5. Yes. A single shareholder—or a few shareholders acting together—who owns enough stock to exercise *de facto* control over a corporation owes the corporation and minority shareholders a fiduciary duty when transferring those shares.

Chapter 19

True-False Questions

1. T

2. F. An agency relationship must be based on an affirmative indication that the agent agrees to act for the principal and the principal agrees to have the agent so act.

3. T

4. T

5. F. A principal who authorizes an agent to commit a tort is liable to persons or property injured.

6. T

Fill-in Questions

Performance; notification; loyalty; obedience; accounting

Multiple-Choice Questions

1. D. Ryan is an agent, and O'Neal is a principal.

2. C. In considering whether an agent had implied authority to do a specific act, the test is whether it was reasonable for the agent to believe that he or she had the authority.

3. C. A failure to disclose material information bearing on an agency relationship is a breach of an agent's fiduciary duties, and the agency is voidable at the option of the principal.

4. A. Farrah causes Ormrod reasonably to believe that Gerhard had authority to borrow $6,000, and Ormrod changed position in reliance on Farrah's representations, estopping Farrah from denying that Gerhard had authority.

5. B. Mowing the field was not within Henry's scope of employment.

6. A. An agent who fails to perform his or her duties will generally be liable for breach of contract.

Issue Spotters

1.   Yes.   A principal has a duty to indemnify an agent for liabilities incurred because of authorized and lawful acts and transactions and for losses suffered because of the principal's failure to perform his or her duties.

2.   No.   An agent is prohibited from taking advantage of the agency relationship to obtain property that the principal wants to purchase.

3.   Margaruerite could be held liable on the note if Margaruerite ratifies it on her return.

4.   Probably.   A principal is liable for loss due to an agent's knowing misrepresentation if the representation was made within the scope of the agency and the agent's scope of authority.

5.   Third persons injured by an employee's negligence can sue the employee or the employer, if the tort was committed while the employee was acting within the scope of employment.

Chapter 20

True-False Questions

1.   F.   Secondary boycotts—including hot-cargo agreements—are illegal.

2.   F.   Programs that are designed to correct imbalances in a work force are upheld as long as employers consider factors in addition to race or gender when making decisions.

3.   T

4.   F.   Employment "at will" means that either party may terminate the employment at any time.

5.   F.   Under the Fair Labor Standards Act, persons cannot work in hazardous occupations unless they are no longer minors.

6.   T

Fill-in Questions

either; unless; may; Some; A few states; may not

Multiple-Choice Questions

1.   A.   Drug testing and electronic monitoring of employees are available to employers under other circumstances.

2.   C.   Employers recruiting workers from other countries must complete a certification process with the Department of Labor.

3.   C.   Intentionally inflicted injuries are not covered by workers' compensation.   Many states cover problems arising out of preexisting conditions, but that is not part of the test for coverage.

4.   A.   COBRA is the Consolidated Omnibus Budget Reconciliation Act of 1985.   It prohibits the elimination of most workers' medical, optical, or dental insurance on the termination of employment.

5.   C.   FMLA is the Family and Medical Leave Act of 1993.   Employees are also guaranteed the same, or a comparable, job on returning to work.

6.   C.   Employers recruiting workers from other countries must complete a certification process with the Department of Labor.

Issue Spotters

1.   Some courts have held that an implied employment contract exists between employer and employee under an employer's handbook that states that employees will be dismissed only for good cause.   An employer who fires a worker contrary to this promise may be held liable for breach of contract.

2.   No.   Generally, the right to recover under workers' compensation laws is determined without regard to negligence or fault.

3.   Yes.   Under the Employee Polygraph Protection Act of 1988, employers may use polygraph tests when investigating thefts.   Such tests cannot otherwise be required of private-sector employees, however.

4.   Possibly, yes.   State laws vary, however, and employees may be protected from refusing to participate in a drug test.   Such protection may arise under a state constitution, statute, or private agreement.

5.   The Social Security Act of 1935 provides individuals with retirement insurance.   Under the Employee Retirement Income Security Act of 1974, pension plans and employees' rights to pension contributions receive some protection.   The Federal Unemployment Contribution Act of 1935 created a system that provides unemployment compensation to eligible individuals.

Chapter 21

True-False Questions

1.   F. Programs that are designed to correct imbalances in a work force are upheld as long as employers consider factors in addition to race or gender when making decisions.
2.   F. An employer may be liable even though an employee did the harassing, if the employer knew, or should have known, and failed to take corrective action, or if the employee was in a supervisory position.
3.   T
4.   T
5.   T
6.   F.   The Equal Employment Opportunity Commission (EEOC) can file a suit in federal district court in its own name against alleged civil rights violators. The EEOC can also intervene in a suit filed by a private party.

Fill-in Questions

can; and; may sue if conciliation between the parties does not occur; reinstatement, back pay, and retroactive promotions; also

Multiple-Choice Questions

1.   B. Then, on failing to resolve the dispute with the employer, but before filing a lawsuit, the person must contact a state or federal agency to see whether a claim is justified.
2.   A. Sexual harassment occurs when, in a workplace, an employee must put up with comments and contact that is perceived as sexually offensive. An employer may be liable even though an employee did the harassing, if the employee was in a supervisory position.
3.   C. The other choices would not avoid liability under the Age Discrimination in Employment Act.
4.   D. An employer can demand that an employee possess the actual skills required for a job.
5.   B. An employer cannot exclude arbitrarily a person who, with reasonable accommodation, could do what is required of a job.
6.   D. Title VII also prohibits using physical characteristics that are typical of some races to distinguish applicants or employees and discriminating

against members of a minority with darker skin than other members of the same minority.
7.   D. These were some of the purposes of the civil rights laws. In particular, in the area of employment, the intent of the laws was to create equal employment opportunities.

Issue Spotters

1.   Yes. In a lawsuit, the burden of proof would then shift to the employer to articulate a legitimate reason for its action, and the applicant would have to show that this is a pretext, that discriminatory intent was the motivation.
2.   Yes. Sexual harassment occurs when a request for sexual favors is a condition of employment, and the person making the request was a supervisor or acting with the authority of the employer.
3.   Differently abled persons are those with a physical or mental impairment that substantially limits "one or more major life activities."
4.   The court would probably overturn the statute. Under Title VII, states are prohibited from enacting laws that ban the employment of women in certain occupations or that bar women from working during the night or from working more than a given number of hours per day or per week.
5.   Yes. Numerous cases have distinguished discrimination on the basis of color. Also, the intention of the drafters of Title VII was evident in their inclusion of both race and color in Title VII.

Chapter 22

True-False Questions

1.   T
2.   F. This is the central legal right of a union.
3.   T
4.   F.   Secondary boycotts—including hot-cargo agreements—are illegal.
5.   T
6.   F. The NLRA does not limit its protections to certified unions.

Fill-in Questions

1.   Norris-LaGuardia
2.   National Labor Relations
3.   Relations; allows; proscribes

Multiple-Choice Questions

1.   B. The National Labor Relations Act protects employees who engage in union activity and prohibits employers from refusing to bargain with employees' designated representative.
2.   A. Giving union workers pay for time spent on union activities could be considered undue support for the union.
3.   C. Management is not required to bargain with a union over a decision to close a facility—although it may if it chooses to do so. Economic consequences of the decision must be bargained over, however.
4.   C. Denying nonunion workers access to the plant is illegal.
5.   D. An employer cannot threaten employees with the loss of their jobs if a union wins a scheduled union election.
6.   B. Former strikers must be given preferential rights to new vacancies and must retain their seniority.

Issue Spotters

1.   A closed shop—a firm that requires union membership as a condition of employment—is illegal, but a union shop—a firm that does not require union membership as a condition for employment but requires workers to join the union after a certain time on the job—is not, unless the shop is in a state with a right-to-work law, which makes it illegal to require union membership for continued employment.
2.   These include safety rules, insurance coverage, pension and other employee benefit plans, procedures for employee discipline, and procedures for employee grievances.
3.   In the absence of a clause providing for the arbitration of unresolved disputes, an employer cannot obtain an injunction against a strike under a no-strike clause.
4.   Yes. Factors to be considered in determining whether an action had an unlawful discriminatory motivation include applying rules inconsistently and more strictly against union advocates.
5.   Yes. An action by a single employee is protected concerted activity, if it is taken for the benefit of other employees, if the employee discussed the action with other approving workers, and if the employer is aware that it is concerted activity taken with the assent of other workers.

Chapter 23

True-False Questions

1.   T
2.   T
3.   F. In some real estate transactions, consumers do not have a right to rescind their contracts if all required disclosures are made. Under certain circumstances, however, consumers in non–real estate transactions have a right to rescind their contracts even though all required disclosures are made.
4.   T
5.   T
6.   F. Under the Fair Credit Reporting Act, consumers can correct any misinformation that leads to a denial of credit, employment, or insurance, and they can receive information about the source of the misinformation or about anyone who was given the misinformation.

Fill-in Questions

$50; before; prohibits; from billing; if

Multiple-Choice Questions

1.   C. In corrective advertising, an advertiser admits that prior claims about a product were untrue.
2.   B. This information is required under the Smokeless Tobacco Health Education Act.
3.   A. Marlena had three days within which to rescind the sale, but she did not act until the fourth day.
4.   D. The Real Estate Settlement Procedures Act, which is primarily concerned with disclosures that mortgage lenders must make, requires that a booklet prepared by HUD be sent within three business days to a person who applies for a mortgage. The Interstate Land Sales Disclosure Act primarily concerns HUD's oversight of sales by sellers of one hundred or more lots of unimproved real estate.
5.   C. These are only some of the disclosure requirements.
6.   D. Under the Fair Debt Collection Practices Act, once a debtor has refused to pay a debt, a collection can contact the debtor only to advise him or her of further action to be taken.

7. A. The Consumer Product Safety Commission has sufficiently broad authority to remove from store shelves any product that it believes is imminently hazardous and to require manufacturers to report on products already sold.

Issue Spotters

1. Yes. The Federal Trade Commission has issued rules to govern advertising techniques, including rules designed to prevent bait-and-switch advertising. Under the FTC guidelines, bait-and-switch advertising occurs if the seller refuses to show the advertised item, fails to have in stock a reasonable quantity of the item, fails to promise to deliver the advertised item within a reasonable time, or discourages employees from selling the item.

2. There are a number of federal and state laws that deal specifically with information given on labels and packages. The restrictions are designed to provide accurate information about the product and to warn about possible dangers from its use or misuse.

3. Yes. Under FTC rules, used-car dealers must also include a suggestion that the buyer obtain an inspection of the car and get any promises made by the dealer in writing.

4. Under the Fair Credit Billing Act, once a buyer has made a good faith effort to settle a dispute, he or she can withhold payment for a product that was purchased with a credit card and that is allegedly defective. the credit card issuer then must intervene and attempt to settle the dispute.

5. Under an extensive set of procedures established by the FDA, drugs must be shown to be effective as well as safe before they may be marketed to the public. In general, manufacturers are responsible for ensuring that the drugs that they offer for sale are free of any substances that could be injurious to consumers.

Chapter 24

True-False Questions

1. F. Common law doctrines that were applied against polluters centuries ago may be applicable today.

2. T

3. T

4. F. To penalize those for whom a violation is cost-effective, the EPA can obtain a penalty equal to a violator's economic benefits from noncompliance.

5. F. The applicable law is the Safe Drinking Water Act.

6. T

Fill-in Questions

federal; federal; environmental impact that an action will have; environment; an action might cause to the environment; and.

Multiple-Choice Questions

1. A. Businesses that engage in ultrahazardous activities are strictly liable for any harm—proof of a failure to exercise reasonable care is not required.

2. B. An action that affects the quality of the environment is "major" if it involves a substantial commitment of resources and "federal" if a federal agency has the power to control it.

3. C. Different standards apply to existing sources and major new sources, and to sources in clean areas and sources in polluted areas.

4. C. These limits are based on the technology available for controlling the discharges.

5. D. Under the Resource Conservation and Recovery Act, the EPA monitors and controls the disposal of hazardous waste. Under the Comprehensive Environmental Response, Compensation, and Liability Act, the EPA regulates the clean-up of hazardous waste sites when a release occurs.

6. D. Under the Resource Conservation and Recovery Act, producers of hazardous waste must properly label and package waste to be transported. Under the Comprehensive Environmental Response, Compensation, and Liability Act, the party who generated the waste disposed of at a site can be held liable for clean-up costs.

7. D. A party improperly releasing radioactive materials into the environment may be held liable under any of a number of statutes.

Issue Spotters

1. On grounds that the hardships to be imposed on the polluter and on the community are greater than the hardships suffered by the residents, the court may deny an injunction—if the plant is the core of a

local economy, for instance, the residents may be awarded only damages.

2. Other federal agencies with authority to regulate specific environmental matters include the Departments of the Interior, Defense, and Labor; the Food and Drug Administration; and the Nuclear Regulatory Commission.

3. Under federal law, dumping of chemical warfare agents and high-level radioactive waste into the ocean is prohibited. There are permit programs for other material, with some exceptions.

4. Clound, Speidel, Osakwe, or Uno, jointly and severally.

5. A party creating a radioactive hazard may be held liable under a theory of strict liability.

Chapter 25

True-False Questions

1. F. Gas, water, and other utility services are generally considered personal property.
2. T
3. F. The owner of a life estate has the same rights as a fee simple owner except the value of the property must be kept intact for the future interest holder.
4. F. An easement merely allows a person to use land without taking anything from it, while a profit allows a person to take something from the land.
5. F. This is a tenancy for years. A periodic tenancy does not specify how long it will last.
6. F. Under the Fifth Amendment, private property may not be taken for public use without "just compensation."
7. F. To be entitled to a variance, a landowner must show that a granting of the variance would not substantially alter the essential character of the zoned area.

Fill-in Questions

1. possibility of reverter; original owner
2. reversion; reversion
3. an executory interest; remainder

Multiple-Choice Questions

1. A. Under the Fifth Amendment, the federal government cannot take property for public use without just compensation.

2. D. A general development plan provides information about growth in a community, a specific area plan indicates special requirements, and zoning ordinances relate to particular land uses.

3. C. Subdivision development typically takes shape in a process of give and take between a developer and local authorities.

4. B. The regulation may be held unconstitutional and void unless the county pays for effectively confiscating the land.

5. D. The most important of these criteria is the effect of the variance on the character of the neighborhood.

6. B. This is not a profit or a license but an easement, and it may be created by implication.

Issue Spotters

1. Yes. The interests that exist, how they are transferred, and limitations on their exercise are discussed in this and the next chapter.

2. Yes. When a parcel of land that is benefited by an easement appurtenant is sold, the property carries the easement with it.

3. The lease passes to the tenant's heirs as personal property.

4. The buyer can recover from the seller the purchase price of the property, plus any other damages incurred in being evicted.

5. The authorities may limit issuance of permits to prevent population growth from racing ahead of the community's ability to provide public services.

Chapter 26

True-False Questions

1. T
2. T
3. T
4. T
5. F. No person can be a director in two or more corporations at the same time *if* elimination of competition among the corporation would violate any of the antitrust laws (and either of the corporations has capital, surplus, or undivided profits aggregating more than the statutory limit).
6. F. The remedies that the Department of Justice has asked courts to impose include dissolution.

Fill-in Questions

Restraint of trade; monopoly power; monopolist; monopoly power; Monopoly power; monopoly power

Multiple-Choice Questions

1. C. The Railway Labor Act relates to collective bargaining between railroad employees and management.

2. D. The elements of the offense of monopolization include monopoly power and its willful acquisition. Market domination that results from legitimate competitive behavior—such as foresight, innovation, skill, and good management—will not be condemned.

3. A. Price discrimination occurs when sellers charge different buyers different prices for identical goods. To violate the Clayton Act, the effect of the price discrimination must also be to substantially lessen competition.

4. C. Most lower courts hold that an attempted violation requires a "dangerous" probability of success. Many courts hold that the probability cannot be dangerous unless the alleged offender possesses at least some degree of market power.

5. D. A person wishing to sue under the Sherman Act must prove that an antitrust violation either directly caused or was a substantial factor in causing the injury that was suffered and that the violation affected the party's business activities that were protected by the antitrust laws.

6. B. This activity cannot restrain trade in the United States or injure other U.S. exporters.

Issue Spotters

1. The term monopoly is used to describe a market in which there is a single seller.

2. The court could find that there is a sufficient degree of interchangeability between sugar and other sweeteners and conclude that Dexx did not control a share of the relevant market sufficient to constitute market power.

3. The behavior is illegal only if it substantially tends to lessen competition or create monopoly power.

4. One reason is that successful plaintiffs can recover three times the damages that they suffered, as well as attorneys' fees.

5. A union can lose its exemption if it combines with a nonlabor group rather than acting in its own self-interest.

Chapter 27

True-False Questions

1. F. If an agreement is *not* deemed a *per se* violation of Section 1 of the Sherman Act, a court analyzes its legality under what is referred to as a rule of reason.

2. F. The line between *per se* violations and agreements judged under a rule of reason is seldom clear.

3. F. This is a vertical restraint.

4. T

5. F. This is a horizontal restraint.

6. F. Exclusive dealing contracts are those under which a seller forbids the buyer from purchasing products from the seller's competitors.

7. F. Price discrimination occurs when sellers charge different buyers different prices for identical goods.

Fill-in Questions

1. horizontal; Horizontal; may; or; horizontal

2. vertical; Vertical; vertically; vertically

Multiple-Choice Questions

1. D. Territorial or customer restrictions are judged under a rule of reason. Here, Montezuma's restriction on its dealers reduces intrabrand competition, but promotes interbrand competition.

2. A. A group boycott is treated as a *per se* violation of Section 1 of the Sherman Act if the group possesses market power and the boycott it intended to restrict or exclude a competitor. A rule of reason analysis is applied only if these elements are missing.

3. B. This is a factor in determining the legality of vertical restraints.

4. C. Consideration is given to fluctuation in prices due to changes in market conditions.

5. C. Without a provision for setting prices, this agreement is not a *per se* violation of the Sherman Act.

6. A. Most courts consider the legality of a tying arrangement by considering whether the seller has sufficient market power in both products' markets to coerce the purchase of one product and affect a substantial amount of commerce in the other's market.

7. C. A horizontal market division is an agreement to divide a market up among rival firms.

Issue Spotters

1. These agreements threaten open and free competition. Once all profitable markets are taken, suppliers may begin to limit warranties, for example, prices may rise, and service may diminish.
2. These firms might use the trade association to fix prices, allocate markets, or conduct boycotts, with the objective of lessening competition.
3. Boyd might argue that the condition promotes interbrand competition by achieving an efficiency in the distribution of its bicycles. Boyd might also argue that it could achieve the same result by simply selling through its own, rather than independent, dealers.
4. Perhaps the best argument in these circumstances is that the price was lowered in good faith to meet the equally low price of a competitor.
5. Yes. The court may look at the market conditions after the agreements are instituted and find that competition was foreclosed in a substantial share of the relevant market.

Chapter 28

True-False Questions

1. T
2. T
3. T
4. F. Securities resulting from a corporate reorganization issued for exchange with the issuer's existing security holders are exempt from the SEC registration requirements.
5. F. The Securities Act of 1933 concerns primarily disclosure on the issuance of securities, and the Securities Exchange Act of 1934 concerns primarily the resale of securities.
6. F. Under the Securities Exchange Act of 1934, the SEC regulates the content of these proxy statements, requiring full and accurate disclosure.

Fill-in Questions

prosecution; triple; ten; 1; 2.5

Multiple-Choice Questions

1. A. The executive officer is the traditional inside trader. The attorney and the accountant are a tippee and a remote tippee.
2. A. Because of the low amount of the issue, it qualifies as an exemption—no specific disclosure document is required, and there is no prohibition on solicitation. The chief problem with the other offerings is that the issuers solicited investors—the amounts of the offerings disqualified them from general solicitation. Also, in the second situation, the issuer should have given the information to all investors.
3. A. These are the elements under Section 16(b). Whether the officer used the inside information is irrelevant.
4. C. The point is to supply enough information so that an unsophisticated investor can evaluate the financial risk involved.
5. D. Under the Securities Act of 1933, a security exists when a person invests in a common enterprise with the reasonable expectation of profits derived primarily or substantially from the managerial or entrepreneurial efforts of others.

Issue Spotters

1. These are all responsibilities of the Securities and Exchange Commission.
2. The average investor is not concerned with minor inaccuracies but with facts that if disclosed would tend to deter him or her from buying the securities. This would include facts that have an important bearing on the condition of the issuer and its business—liabilities, loans to officers and directors, customer delinquencies, and so on.
3. No. The Securities Exchange Act of 1934 extends liability to officers and directors in their personal transactions for taking advantage of inside information when they know it is unavailable to the persons with whom they are dealing.
4. Yes. All states have their own corporate securities laws.
5. Before taking a business public—that is, selling shares in the firm to the public—a representative of the company should visit the offices of a qualified securities law attorney.

Notes

Notes

Notes

Notes